ON TARGET

Gun Culture, Storytelling, and the NRA

The National Rifle Association (NRA) is an important actor in the American gun debate. While popular explanations for the group's influence often focus on the NRA's lobbying and campaign donations, it receives lesser attention for the mass mobilization efforts that make these political endeavours possible.

On Target explores why the NRA is so influential and how we can understand the group's impact on firearms policy in the United States. The book looks at how the NRA both draws upon and shapes historical meta-narratives regarding the role of firearms in America's national identity and how this is part of a larger effort to expand the community of gun owners. Noah S. Schwartz demonstrates how the NRA portrays a vision of the past through events such as its annual meeting; communications such as *American Rifleman* magazine and NRATV; and points of contact including the National Firearms Museum.

Based on fieldwork in Indiana and Virginia, including participant observation at NRA events and firearm safety classes, thematic analysis of audio-visual material, and interviews with NRA executives and members, *On Target* sheds light on the ways in which the NRA tells stories to build and mobilize a politically motivated network of gun owners.

NOAH S. SCHWARTZ is an assistant professor of Political Science at the University of the Fraser Valley.

NOAH S. SCHWARTZ

On Target

Gun Culture, Storytelling, and the NRA

UNIVERSITY OF TORONTO PRESS
Toronto Buffalo London

Toronto Buffalo London
utorontopress.com
Printed and bound by CPI Group (UK) Ltd, Croydon, CR0 4YY

ISBN 978-1-4875-4661-8 (cloth)   ISBN 978-1-4875-5195-7 (EPUB)
ISBN 978-1-4875-4844-5 (paper)   ISBN 978-1-4875-5030-1 (PDF)

_____

Library and Archives Canada Cataloguing in Publication

Title: On target : gun culture, storytelling, and the NRA / Noah S. Schwartz.
Names: Schwartz, Noah S., author.
Description: Includes bibliographical references and index.
Identifiers: Canadiana (print) 20220210454 | Canadiana (ebook)
    20220210500 | ISBN 9781487546618 (cloth) | ISBN 9781487548445
    (paper) | ISBN 9781487551957 (EPUB) | ISBN 9781487550301 (PDF)
Subjects: LCSH: National Rifle Association of America – Influence. |
    LCSH: Storytelling – Social aspects – United States. | LCSH: Firearms
    owners – Political activity – United States. | LCSH: Gun control – United States.
Classification: LCC HV7436 .S39 2022 | DDC 363.330973 – dc23

_____

We wish to acknowledge the land on which the University of Toronto Press
operates. This land is the traditional territory of the Wendat, the Anishnaabeg, the
Haudenosaunee, the Métis, and the Mississaugas of the Credit First Nation.

This book has been published with the help of a grant from the Federation for
the Humanities and Social Sciences, through the Awards to Scholarly Publications
Program, using funds provided by the Social Sciences and Humanities Research
Council of Canada.

University of Toronto Press acknowledges the financial support of the Government of
Canada, the Canada Council for the Arts, and the Ontario Arts Council, an agency of
the Government of Ontario, for its publishing activities.

Canada Council   Conseil des Arts
for the Arts   du Canada

ONTARIO ARTS COUNCIL
CONSEIL DES ARTS DE L'ONTARIO
an Ontario government agency
un organisme du gouvernement de l'Ontario

Funded by the   Financé par le
Government   gouvernement
of Canada   du Canada

Canadä

Contents

Acknowledgments

The process of writing a book is never completed by one person. It takes hundreds, many of whom may never realize the important role that they played. I apologize that I cannot thank all those hundreds of people.

I would first like to thank my mentor and former supervisor, Professor Mira Sucharov, for your endless supply of knowledge, support, and encouragement. You always knew when to challenge me, when to help me, and when to let me follow my heart. I would also like to thank Professor Melissa Haussman and Professor John Walsh for bringing your unique expertise into my project, and for the guidance that you have given me along the way. You have truly shaped the way I see the world.

I want to thank Professor Kevin Avruch and Dr. Jay Moon from the George Mason University School for Conflict Analysis and Resolution for their guidance and support while in the field.

A big thank you to the various funding agencies that made this project possible. First and foremost, the Social Sciences and Humanities Research Council, for your generous graduate and publication funding. The Mitacs Globalink program, for helping to fund my field research. The Institute for Humane Studies, for providing funding for my trip to Lynchburg. Finally, Carleton University, for investing so much in your graduate students.

To my editor, Daniel Quinlan, thank you for taking a chance on a first-time author with big dreams.

I want to thank my colleagues, family members, and friends, without whom I would never have been able to complete this project. My father, Ian Schwartz, for teaching me the meaning of hard work, dedication, and the power of networking. My mother, Professor Karen Schwartz, for always believing in me when others did not and for blazing a trail that I hope to follow. My sister Shira, for keeping me humble. My brother Shane, for understanding. My grandmother, Betty, for your love and encouragement. My best friend Nathan, for sticking with me through thick and thin. My colleagues Rob Currie-Wood, Will Little, Mary Coulas, Amanda Roberts, Mark Ashford, Lucas Jerusalimiec, Elsa Piersig, and countless others, for making my work time so enjoyable. And of course, Marie, the love of my life, without whom none of this would have any meaning.

I dedicate this work to my participants. It takes a tremendous amount of courage to trust someone with your story. Thank you for sharing your thoughts, your dreams, and your passion with me. I only hope that I have done them justice.

Acronyms

MAGA	Make America Great Again
NAAGA	National African American Gun Association
NPF	Narrative Policy Framework
NRA	National Rifle Association
NRAAM	NRA Annual Meeting
NRA-ILA/ILA	Institute for Legislative Action
NSSF	National Shooting Sports Foundation
SASS	Single Action Shooting Society

ON TARGET

1 The Great Gun Debate

When asked about statistics released by the American Medical Association on the potential danger of guns in the home, Lt. Jeff Cooper responds:

> I will not accept that; A. In the first place I don't believe it's true. I believe my statistics are better than those. But in the second place I don't think it really matters, because we are not talking about numbers here, we are talking about individual dignity. It's more important what happens to you than what happens in two out of three cases.[1]

On a foggy morning in May, I found myself driving along a backroad highway. The speed limit was 50 mph, but the road twisted and turned so often I never got above 40. My GPS was going haywire, alternating between welcoming me to Virginia and West Virginia as the road snaked along the state line, leading me towards the gun club. For me, the state line was an arbitrary boundary. For many who choose to carry concealed firearms, it could be the difference between a Sunday drive and a legal headache depending on the laws of the state into which they crossed. This is the nature of the many-colored patchwork that is American firearms policy.

The sky had cleared by the time I arrived at the National Rifle Association (NRA) firearms safety class. It was being held in a gun club in a rural area. The clubhouse was itself a former dwelling, a two-story home with a beige exterior and brown roof, and the class was to take place in what must have once been the living room. I walked in through a set of double glass doors and shook hands with the instructor. We had spoken a few times over the phone, and I had explained my project to him. He handed me an unloaded Glock 19 handgun and a black plastic holster.

"Put this on."

For the instructor, it was as casual as handing a student a pen. Unloaded, the polymer-framed Glock 19 weighs a little over one pound and a quarter. It weighed much more heavily on my consciousness. Every few minutes my hand would slide down, making sure it was still in place, as if the gun might suddenly move of its own volition.

The other students eyed me with suspicion. I could feel the heat from their glances. Who was this bespectacled stranger in their midst, whose very demeanor oozed urban academia? A few weeks earlier, I had been back in Canada, in the four-person office I share with some of my fellow graduate students. My day had consisted of reading, writing, and teaching; a consistent and comfortable rhythm, punctuated by the occasional latte at the campus café. We debated Kant and Locke, not Colt and Glock. Now I was at the center of one of the most heated debates of the twenty-first century. What had I gotten myself into?

It is widely acknowledged that the NRA is a powerful advocacy group in American politics. What is less clear is where that power comes from. Early scholarly attention paid to the NRA focused principally on its congressional and state-level lobbying efforts,[2] positioning the organization's success as a result of its Institute for Legal Action (ILA), the organization's lobbying wing. This view is further perpetuated by popular media discourse surrounding the NRA, which frames the organization as a shadowy special interest group funneling money to congressmen to keep them in line. Yet, closer examination shows that the key to the organization's success is its ability to mobilize its supporters towards collective action. For example, in Florida, where gun control legislation was defeated in the state legislature even in the aftermath of the Parkland shooting, not a single legislator had received campaign money from the NRA.[3] Further, examining the NRA's tax returns demonstrates that the organization actually spends much more on their teaching and communications programs, useful tools for cultivating a political community of gun owners, than on the lobbying for which they are famous.[4,5]

How has the NRA become such an influential advocacy group? How can we understand the NRA's impact on firearms policy in the United States? More specifically, what role do narrative and memory play in understanding this influence? These are the questions this book aims to address.

While it is undeniable that the ILA has won important victories for the NRA, there is a missing piece of the puzzle. Until recently, scholars have largely ignored the organization's extensive function as a service group and the influence of its communications program on American gun culture. The NRA's service branch is a major contributor to gun culture in the United States. This large wing of the organization runs educational programs across the country, such as the Eddie the Eagle gun safety program in US elementary schools, and provides firearm-related training to over one million Americans every year.[6] But the reach of the organization runs far deeper than the classroom. The NRA also operates three museums that combined attract about 350,000 visitors every year.[7] The organization's flagship magazine, the *American Rifleman*, regularly reaches over two million people.[8] Until the summer of 2019, the NRA even had its own online television platform, accessible through the group's homepage or various streaming services like Apple TV.

The terms narrative and memory have popular meanings that differ from their use in scholarly literature, so it is important to clarify what I mean before I continue. It is common in today's political conversation to hear someone use the word "narrative" to imply that something is untrue. This is not how academics use the term. Narrative refers to storytelling, a fundamental part of human communication. We all communicate using stories, in our everyday lives and in politics. Narratives can be either true or false, often a bit of both, and the use of the term narrative is simply meant to highlight the form that the communication takes, not the quality of its content.

Memory is another term that has a specific meaning within academic discussions. We often think of memories as things that we own; my memories, her memories, our memories. More recently, however, scholars have drawn attention to the fact that memory is also an action, remembering or commemoration, and that sometimes the act of commemoration has political motives.

This book examines how the NRA has attempted to influence the perceptions of the American public not just towards their present, but their past. It argues that the organization both draws upon and shapes historical meta-narratives regarding the role of firearms in America's and Americans' pasts as part of its larger effort to expand and mobilize the community of gun owners. It does this because this political community provides the organization with the base of its support and is the source of its influence on American firearms policy. Speaking on behalf of this large and highly motivated community gives the NRA the clout it needs to achieve its policy goals. These narratives are intended to reinforce the idea that firearms have played an integral part in American history, more so than in other countries, and that the United States has a historical tradition of gun ownership not just for sporting and hunting purposes, but for civilian self-defense. I demonstrate how the NRA portrays this vision of the past through events like its annual meeting; communications like *American Rifleman* magazine and NRATV; and points of contact like the National Firearms Museum.

The stories that the NRA tells have three intended audiences. The first is existing NRA members who the organization aims to galvanize and motivate towards further political action, whether that be contributing funds to the group's coffers, writing letters to their elected representatives, or coming out to vote for the NRA's preferred candidate. The second group are gun owners who are not currently deeply engaged in gun culture. They may own a single firearm for self-defense purposes but do not participate regularly in the shooting sports or gun collecting, which are powerful predictors of political behavior.[9] The final group targeted by the NRA are the "gun curious."[10] These people may be open to the idea of gun ownership but have not been introduced to guns or gun culture yet. Recruiting them is a major focus for the NRA.

While the NRA draws on numerous historical narratives in their communications material, there are a few core macro-narratives that are often repeated in NRA material. These narratives are malleable, and often shaped to fit a variety of historical contexts. The first is that of the "Good Guy with a Gun." This narrative involves a heroic individual using firearms to defend themselves as well as their wider community. This story is tied to the image of the lone hero, which is quite powerful in American culture, and is often reproduced in literature, film, and television. It is a key pillar of support for policies like the expansion of concealed carry laws.

The second meta-narrative that the NRA employs is linking gun ownership, and the right to gun ownership, with the cause of freedom. This narrative is often linked to American history and events such as the American Revolution and the Second World War. It serves as a kind of template the NRA uses to talk about foreign conflicts and has been a strategy the organization uses to reach a wider, more diverse background, emphasizing the role that firearms played in the abolition movement and in the struggles of Indigenous peoples against colonial rule. This narrative helps to buttress the argument that the Second Amendment is a key protection against tyrannical government.

The third macro-narrative that the NRA often disseminates is that firearms are an essential piece of American culture. It does this by linking firearms to personal and public memories and to key ideas like the quintessential American childhood; the American family; American ingenuity and scientific prowess; and American exceptionalism. These narratives are important for establishing that Americans have a special relationship with firearms, one that does not exist in other countries. They establish firearms as American heritage, something in urgent need of protection.

The proliferation of mass shootings in the United States, and advocacy by the growing pro-control movement, have created a shift in the way that large institutions grapple with guns. As a growing number of industries and cultural institutions, from Hollywood to history museums, have declared war on gun culture,[11] the NRA realizes that they are fighting a battle over the meaning of guns in America, a battle in which identity, memory, and history are important weapons.

Though the focus of this book is on understanding and explaining the role that the NRA's historical and cultural work plays in their political strategy, it is important to note at the outset that the NRA's historical narratives are not uncontested. A growing movement of scholars have emerged to challenge the NRA's vision of American history and the individual rights interpretation of the Second Amendment. Historians like Atlas,[12] Charles,[13] Haag,[14] and others have attacked this interpretation of American history, just as scholars like Halbrook,[15] Landsford,[16] and Malcolm[17] have buttressed it.

The Great Gun Debate

Anyone who has paid even cursory attention to American politics in the last few decades is at least peripherally aware of the Great Gun Debate.[18,19] The debate centers around the role that firearms should play in American society. While sometimes latent, it often surges into the headlines after a major focusing event, like a mass shooting. The Great Gun Debate is popularly characterized as a fight over specific policies, with flashpoints in America coalescing around issues like Stand Your Ground laws, concealed carry, and "assault weapons."[20]

Like most policy issues, the Great Gun Debate is not only about facts. This becomes apparent as soon as one seriously attempts to study it. That is not to say that facts do not enter the debate; both sides readily lob data at one another. It is to say, however, that in this debate there are things that matter more than facts. There is culture and the meanings that cultures generate for their practitioners. There are feelings, emotions, and affect; whether that be fear of guns or fear of losing them. The debate is not about guns, but about the meanings that both sides attach, or do not attach to them, and the role that culture plays in generating those meanings.

While gun control laws, and debates over those laws, have existed in America since colonial times, the contemporary period of this debate intensified in the 1960s, when the assassinations of prominent figures like John F. Kennedy and Dr. Martin Luther King Jr. raised public concern about gun control.[21] In this book, therefore, I focus on the debate from that time up to the present day. Within this debate, several key advocacy groups, foremost among them the NRA, the Second Amendment

Foundation, the Brady Campaign, Everytown for Gun Safety, March for Our Lives, and Moms Demand Action have worked hard to influence the decisions of policymakers by fighting for the hearts and minds of the public.

Firearms policies are created at multiple levels of government in the United States. Given the unique institutional structure of the American federal system, no single level of government has a monopoly on regulating firearms. Thus, the United States has a patchwork of gun laws. While some laws do exist federally, such as the National Firearms Act (1934) or the Brady Handgun Violence Prevention Act (1994), most firearms policymaking takes place at the state and local level.

This book, however, is less about observing the influence of the NRA on specific policies and more about "ideas." I lay this out more clearly in chapter 2 but it is important to specify here why ideas are important in the gun debate. At the level of ideas, the Great Gun Debate generally takes place within the media, academic journals, social media, and reports and communications by advocacy groups. Groups win at the level of ideas by convincing members of the public of the truth of their perspective. The battleground of ideas forms the context within which policymakers make decisions.

In the past, academics have largely tackled the Great Gun Debate through an empirical lens, focusing on measuring the effectiveness of various gun control laws on criminal behavior rather than understanding how people think and feel about gun control laws. These studies have addressed various iterations of the question, "do more guns make society less safe or more?" This makes sense, as most people who work on this issue want to see a reduction in violent crime, especially gun crime. Further, generating empirical data that claims to offer policymakers solutions to this complex policy problem is a lot easier to sell to a funding agency than unraveling the complexity and, perhaps, the intractability of the problem. In general, however, these efforts have failed to provide a broad consensus on the solution to gun violence in America,[22] even amongst expert groups.[23]

The problem with this sort of thinking is that people, and policymakers, do not form opinions based on the neutral assessment of evidence. Evidence is always interpreted through the lens of a person's worldview, which is in turn shaped by culture, personal experience, and emotion.[24] It is difficult for the social sciences to have an impact on the gun debate if we ignore the symbolic function and meaning of firearms for Americans. This is because "how an individual feels about gun control will depend a lot on the social meanings that she thinks guns and gun control express, not just on the consequences she believes they impose." Rather than focusing exclusively on evaluations of various gun control policies, "academics and others who want to help resolve the gun controversy should dedicate themselves to identifying with as much precision as possible the cultural visions that animate this dispute, and to formulating appropriate strategies for enabling those visions to be expressively reconciled by law."[25]

The Great Gun Debate is animated by culture. Cultures are created and practiced by communities. The community I focus on in this book is the gun-owning community, sometimes called the Second Amendment community, Pro-Second Amendment Community or 2A Community.[26] This is an imagined community composed of a diverse group of people united around a set of ideas, symbols, practices, and serious leisure activities. The gun culture is practiced in both physical and digital spaces, through shared activities like hunting and sports shooting, as well as through online communities. Better understanding this culture can help us to understand the *meanings* that gun owners attach to their firearms, and thus help us to better explain why this community has been so effective in its advocacy efforts.

Meaning, one might say, is a nebulous term, so I will be more specific. Gun owners attach deep emotional and personal significance to guns. That is, firearms mean something to them, they have a significance that goes beyond their practical utility as objects. The bolt-action .308 that a hunter takes into the woods every fall is not just a tool for harvesting game. It means something to its owner. Maybe it was inherited from her father, who took her out hunting for the first time. Perhaps the firearm has a particular lineage. Many deer are taken with military surplus rifles from the Second World War, that were sold onto the civilian market, like the Lee Enfield carried by British and Canadian troops. Maybe it was her first gun that she spent hours researching in gun magazines and online forums before settling on a model that she liked. She might even see the gun as a political statement, a way of enacting or performing her values. Regardless of the reason, the firearm has been transformed from a simple mechanical combination of wood and metal into an object of meaning.[27]

The meanings that gun owners attach to their guns are also shaped by aspects of an individual's identity. To the African American gun owners that I met and read about, guns were a potential remedy to the systemic disempowerment they felt, and the heightened risk that their identity or ZIP code placed them in. Many of the women I met saw guns as a tool to ensure their safety in a world of systemic gender violence. Even for white, male gun owners, guns are a form of empowerment. Whether this is empowerment to defend oneself against crime[28] or a remedy to the feelings of disempowerment felt by much of rural and middle America in an age of outsourcing and the increasingly widening income gaps brought on by policies that have weakened the middle class.[29]

Culture also shapes ordinary Americans' views of guns because it influences how people perceive risk. Social psychologists know that cultural and moral attitudes towards certain activities shape how risky individuals think they are.[30] This is because humans face so many risks in our everyday lives, it is difficult to process each one. If we perceive an activity as normative within our socio-cultural world view, we are likely to downplay the potential risks in our assessment of that activity. If we perceive an activity as deviant, we are likely to overestimate the risks involved. The risks that we take communicate our values. Since societies, governments, and political movements are "sites of competing norms," there will always be public differences over risk assessment. Firearms policy involves weighing risks and benefits, the potential benefits that firearms provide with regards to self-defense or recreation, versus the potential risks they pose to society. Culture thus has a profound influence on the politics of guns.[31]

Looking at gun control through the theoretical prism of the perception of risk helps to understand the lack of connection between crime rates and concerns surrounding gun control. "In fact, numerous studies have found that neither actual crime rates, perceived crime rates, prior victimization, nor fear of victimization strongly correlates with public opinion towards gun control." This also helps to explain why dramatic and highly publicized shootings do not generally result in shifts in public opinion on gun control. People interpret evidence through the prism of culture. "Confronted with competing factual claims and supporting empirical data that they are not in a position to verify for themselves, ordinary citizens naturally look to those whom they trust to tell them what to believe about the consequences of gun control laws." Most often, this means those who share their cultural outlook.[32]

Yamane,[33] writing from the field of sociology, notes that the overwhelming majority of the literature on firearms across the social sciences tends to focus on negative outcomes with firearms. Within academia, it is not a stretch to say that the study of guns is synonymous with studies in support of gun control. Yamane notes that "Entering the field, I was struck by how hard it is to find scholarship on the lawful use of firearms by legal gun owners ... The study of guns is dominated by the criminology and epidemiology of gun violence, which is a very small part of the social reality of guns, in American society at least."[34] The focus on criminal violence with firearms, which makes up a minute portion of the everyday use of firearms in America, impedes scholars from properly understanding gun culture in the United States and its political impacts. The overwhelming majority of gun owners will never use their firearm in the commission of a crime. Rather, guns form a part of their everyday lives, whether through carrying a concealed firearm to work, heading out to hunt ruffed grouse, or spending a sunny Sunday afternoon at the gun range. Looking at this reality allows us to understand why so many people in the United States are so deeply attached to firearms, and thus willing to fight so hard to keep them.

With this book, I aim to chart a middle way through treacherous waters. This will not please everyone, and both opponents and proponents of gun control will likely find much they agree with and much they disagree with in the pages to follow. I do not attempt to pretend to be neutral on this topic, but an important precondition of this study was that it would set aside prescriptive questions on gun control in the United States. It is my hope that this attempt can help chart the path towards a meaningful compromise on firearms policy, or that it can at least shift the conversation beyond the realm of extremist rhetoric and harmful stereotypes in which it so often dwells.

This represents something of a paradox. To understand the politics of firearms, we must move beyond scholarship that focuses exclusively on the most political elements of firearms use and ownership. I seek to bridge this cultural divide, engaging with gun culture on its own terms and providing an opportunity for academics and the public to better understand its construction. This book examines the ways in which the NRA has worked to influence the opinions of its members, the wider American public, and policy makers on issues of gun rights. I have chosen to focus on the NRA for several reasons. First, it represents the largest and most powerful organization within the broader gun rights movement. Second, it is one of the oldest and best-established collective actors in the United States, having been founded in the aftermath of the American Civil War. Finally, the NRA is also amongst the most notorious collective actors in the United States and is often the focus of media attention in the aftermath of mass shootings.

The National Rifle Association (NRA)

It is no exaggeration to say that the National Rifle Association (NRA) is the most infamous collective actor in the history of American politics. Well known around the world, the NRA is the key figurehead of the American gun rights movement and has heavily influenced the gun debate. The NRA was founded in 1871 with the mission of improving marksmanship following the American Civil War. Military leaders had noticed that most ordinary Americans were not skilled with a rifle and sought to change this.[35] The war also led to a boom in the development of new firearms technologies, as repeating rifles and revolvers became more and more commonplace in North America.[36] The twentieth century, however, would see the organization shift from a sportsman's club to a political juggernaut.

In 1975, the NRA established the ILA, which to this day remains the most visible face of the organization.[37] Harlon B. Carter, the former NRA president, was chosen as the leader of the new ILA. Carter increased the organization's reach through the use of computers, began the tradition of embroiling the organization in electoral politics, and took a much harder stance on dealing with pro-gun control politicians.[38]

This stance created an internal schism between those who felt the NRA should remain a sportsmen's organization focused on firearms training (labelled "the Old Guard"), and those hard-liners who felt the NRA should expand its political role.[39]

On May 20, 1977, at the NRA's Annual Convention in Cincinnati, Ohio, Carter orchestrated the Cincinnati Revolt with the help of a loyal group of supporters.[40] Carter and his associates used their deep knowledge of NRA meeting rules and procedures to remove from the board anyone they perceived as an obstacle to their new vision of the NRA, replacing them with their own supporters. This eventually led to Carter's election as NRA President[41] and cemented the change in direction. The NRA subsequently hired almost 50 new lobbyists and researchers tasked with creating a "gun-rights intellectual renaissance."[42] Riding the wave of social conservatism that swept America in the 1980s, the NRA's membership swelled as did its funding. In 1964, the NRA had an annual income of $4.5 million. By 1986, this had increased to $80 million. In 2001, the figure rose to $200 million.[43]

There is some controversy in accounts of the NRA's history over whether this represented a real departure from the NRA's past political efforts, or a continuation. Authors like Melzer,[44] Spitzer,[45] and Carlson[46] trace the beginning of the NRA's major advocacy efforts to this revolt. Others, like Charles,[47] however, note that the NRA was politically active in the nascent gun debate all the way back to 1932. While the NRA was certainly a political entity before the shift in leadership, these political efforts tended to be less partisan. It was after this shift that the NRA firmly entrenched itself within the Republican camp, as the modern battle lines of the gun debate began to be drawn.[48] The timing of this shift generally coincides with a larger movement in American politics, which saw the formation of a number of conservative groups, largely in response to the mass mobilization of the Civil Rights movement a decade earlier.[49]

Since the Revolt at Cincinnati, the NRA has won several political victories. The NRA was a large player in the movement towards shall issue firearms permits in the 1970s and 1980s,[50] that require that the state grant a permit to carry a concealed weapon to citizens who meet the basic requirements, like a clean criminal record.[51] As a result, 21 states now have Shall issue concealed carry laws, with an additional 21 states not requiring a permit to carry a concealed firearm at all. Only eight states and the District of Columbia still heavily restrict the practice of carrying handguns in public,[52] though the ease of acquiring a permit can vary from county to county, and city to city.[53]

No single cause can explain the NRA's success in these efforts over time. It is undoubtedly true that the organization has been successful because of its campaign donations, "access to key decision makers" and the efforts of the ILA and the NRA's Political Action Committee. But this top-down view of the NRA misses out on the source of the organization's power, a power that makes these direct political interventions possible. It is common wisdom that the NRA is effective because they spend money donating to political campaigns. In fact, this idea is "mostly unsupported by analysis."[54] Instead, "The key to the NRA's effectiveness that distinguishes it from other interest groups lies in its highly motivated mass membership and the organization's ability to bring pressure from that membership to bear at key moments and places."[55] In short: "it's people, not money."[56]

It is this mass membership, and the NRA's relationship with other key actors within the gun culture, that make the lobbying and campaign donations possible. This often-overlooked element of the organization's success, its ability to mobilize a large segment of the American populace, is the focus of this book.

Though the NRA has often seemed an invincible force in US politics, recent scandals and legal battles have rocked the organization. In 2019, the NRA cut ties with their advertising firm Ackerman McQueen, which accused the organization of overcharging them. Wayne Lapierre, who has been the executive vice president of the NRA since 1991, has faced a series of personal expense scandals that almost saw him lose his position to an internal coup by then-President Oliver North.[57] More recently, the Attorney General of New York has sued the organization and is seeking to dissolve the NRA completely.[58]

While the fate of the NRA is uncertain at time of writing, understanding why the NRA was so powerful for so long is still useful. It may also add a necessary dose of reality to those who think defeating the NRA would clear the path for large scale policy shifts on gun control in the US. As we will see, the NRA is powerful given its large number of highly motivated supporters, a reliable contingent that does not appear to be diminishing. Any gap left by the NRA will soon be filled by other gun rights groups less institutionalized, and thus less conducive to compromise, than the NRA.[59]

An Ethnography of the NRA

Narrative analysis helps us understand the stories that political actors, like advocacy groups, tell to achieve their policy goals, though it poses some distinct challenges. Narratives are forms of communications that are deeply based in culture. Those reading narratives from outside of the culture face the risk of misunderstanding elements of the narrative.

To overcome this problem, I used a mixed-methods approach to better understand the NRA's service and communications programs, and their impact on the political debate. This includes combining a content analysis of NRA material, like the *American Rifleman* magazine and NRATV, with ethnographic participant observation at NRA events, museums analysis, and interviews with NRA members and executives.

Ethnography is a useful tool to overcome this cultural barrier, and several authors have used ethnography to study elements of gun culture and the NRA.[60] To glean meaning from the stories the NRA tells, and the transformative political power they contain, we must endeavor to understand the people who tell them and the people who listen. As a bespectacled, city-dwelling, Jewish academic, descending from a lineage of progressives, neither hunting nor sports shooting were a part of my upbringing. If I was to understand the NRA and its members, I needed to walk a mile in their shoes. To not attempt this was to risk reproducing the tired cliché of a well-dressed, wealthy reporter going "undercover" to show the alleged depravity of American gun owners.[61]

Ethnographic research seemed the most appropriate venue through which to do this. It allowed me not only to understand the people I spoke with and the world they came from, but to also experience them firsthand.

Though originally the purview of anthropologists, an increasing number of political scientists are turning to ethnography to shed light on political problems. Having accepted that "ideas matter" in political science,[62] it is only natural to want to study how these ideas impact the political thoughts and behavior of individuals. Understanding the way that people make sense of the world helps us to understand how that worldview influences their decision-making.

Political scientists have noted several advantages that ethnographic methods can offer the field of political science. First and foremost, because ethnography involves getting close to research subjects and attempting to gain an insider's view into their lives (known as the emic perspective), it allows scholars to gain a richer and more detailed understanding of the lifeworlds'[63] of their subjects.[64] This can help political scientists to ground theoretical assumptions, explain anomalies, and gain insight into a group's self-understanding. It is particularly useful for studying group politics, given the role that personal meanings play in motivating advocacy.[65] The immense levels of polarization in the gun debate further necessitate the use of methods that involve generating deeper understanding. While statistics and surveys can offer powerful snapshots into the gun debate, they cannot capture the complex thoughts, feelings, and meanings that drive political behavior. For example, statistical accounts that focus on gun ownership amongst white, rural, middle-class men paint over the growing minority of liberal gun owners.[66]

The next chapter provides the theoretical framework for the book, explaining the Narrative Policy Framework in more detail, as well as incorporating relevant insights from the field of memory studies. Chapter 3 marks the beginning of my analysis. I begin by looking at the NRA's written and audio-visual material, studying the *American Rifleman Magazine*, and the now-defunct NRATV, since it is through these modalities that most of its supporters likely connect with the NRA.

It was also important to go beyond these forms of communication and to experience these narratives in the settings in which they are told. I, therefore, undertook three months of fieldwork in the United States. In chapters 4 and 5, I outline the results of my participant observation at the NRA Annual Meeting, demonstrating that this meeting serves as a venue for the NRA to build the community of gun owners, and tell stories to their membership. Chapters 6 and 7 then present the results of my participation observation in five NRA firearm safety courses, shooting with participants, attending gun shows and my interviews with members and employees, as well as my analysis of the NRA's Firearm's History Museum. Chapter 8 traces the implications of the data on our understanding of narratives in politics and the gun debate, and identifies future areas for research.

The politics of the Second Amendment are contentious. Opinions about guns are heavily influenced by culture, and cultures are built on the stories that members tell. As we have seen in this chapter, culture is important in shaping our worldview because it influences how people make sense of the social world and the objects within it, and shapes how we understand risk in our lives. The NRA is an important actor shaping the gun culture. It shares narratives, especially narratives about America's and Americans' pasts, so that it can build and mobilize this community of supporters that are essential to providing the people power and financial support to run its lobbying and advocacy efforts.

2   Narrative and Memory

Remembering the past is crucial for our sense of identity ... to know what we were confirms that we are.

– Lowenthal, 1985

I came of age in the early 2000s. As such, the memory of the Columbine High School massacre weighed heavily on my mind even as an elementary school student. The story and footage of the massacre, which claimed the lives of 15 people, injuring dozens more, was widely circulated in the media, and provoked a global conversation on guns. Though too young at the time to really understand what was going on, the fear and urgency of the stories and images I saw on the nightly news, or heard my parents discuss, had a profound influence on my early views of guns and the gun debate. The story of Columbine became a rallying cry for the pro-control movement, repeated by advocates, politicians, and perhaps most famously by documentarian Michael Moore in his influential film *Bowling for Columbine*.

Though Canada has stricter gun laws than most US states, our school boards were so moved by the event that they introduced lockdown drills, which saw us hide under desks or cluster together for safety away from the windows. The memory of Columbine was etched into the social practices of a generation of schoolchildren, for whom stories of school shootings would become tragically common as a new template of mass violence was popularized and reproduced. Stories have tremendous power to shape political opinion and public policy, especially when these stories are tied to highly emotional events.

The NRA understands this. Just as pro-control advocates draw on the stories of mass shootings to influence public policy in favor of gun control, the NRA has its own set of narratives to draw on and disseminate. To understand how the NRA uses narrative and memory to influence the gun debate, we first need to unpack these concepts.

In the chapters that follow, I use two central theoretical concepts to unpack the NRA's ideational influence: narrative and memory. As we will see, narrative refers to how political actors use storytelling to influence the way that people see the political and social world. Memory, and the act of past presencing, refers to how we interact with the past, or how the past is brought into the present, and to what end. Both memory and narrative are intrinsically social practices; both have instrumental uses and lend themselves to political stratagems.

This book belongs within two distinct literatures and attempts to build a bridge between them. The first is the literature on the theories of the policy process. This body of scholarship aims to better understand the way that policy is made, rather than evaluating or analyzing specific policies.[1] The second is the literature on memory studies and the politics of memory. Scholars of memory look beyond the narrow focus of traditional history, which attempted to reconstruct or discover the past, to instead try and better understand how people interact with the past, and bring it into the present.

In this chapter I outline my approach to understanding the influence of the NRA on the formation of firearms policy in the United States. I identify the gaps in popular explanations of the organization's influence on policy, which tend to focus on the NRA's lobbying and campaign contributions while ignoring other important tools that the organization has at its disposal. Instead, I argue that the power of the NRA is rooted in its ability to grow, shape, and mobilize the gun-owning community to support the organization financially, to vote for pro-Second Amendment candidates or initiatives, or to volunteer their time and effort to engage politically.

I then lay out my theoretical approach to studying the NRA, the Narrative Policy Framework (NPF). The NPF was selected because it allows scholars to account for the power of ideas at three separate levels: policy solutions, problem definition, and background ideas, and because it provides a precise operationalization of narrative. I then connect these theories to the literature on the politics of memory. This includes unpacking the concept of past presencing,[2] and examining how history, memory, and heritage can serve as political tools.

The Limits of Money and Power

The NRA is a large organization with many branches. Despite this, most of the coverage in the media, and the rhetoric of many politicians, focuses on the NRA's influence as related to its direct lobbying and campaign spending. From this perspective, the NRA is often presented as the sole barrier to substantive changes to American firearm policy, one that subverts the democratic process by lining the pockets of friendly politicians. The reality of the situation is more complex.

First, for much of its history the NRA has enjoyed a substantial amount of popular support. It is estimated that the organization has about four to five million paying members. In addition to this, polling research done by Pew Polls shows that about 20 per cent of America's 60–70 million gun owners claim to be NRA members. While the discrepancy in numbers shows that many respondents to the poll are not being completely honest about paying their annual dues, it does demonstrate that they identify with the goals of the organization.[3] Why has the organization enjoyed so much support? Is the group's lobbying success enough to explain this?

Taking a closer look at the numbers presents an interesting puzzle and complicates the popular money and power explanation. Though the NRA is not the official lobby group of the Small Arms & Ammunition industry in the United States,[4] they do receive material support from the industry in the form of sponsorships and advertising revenue. That being said, this is far from the largest source of the NRA's funding; in fact, 90 per cent of NRA donations are less than $200 per year, with their average donation in 2014 being $35.[5]

Despite this, the popular perception of the American gun debate is that the industry dominates through big money politics. The problem with this explanation is that the Small Arms & Ammunition industry simply is not that big, especially when compared to other industries with large lobbies. In 2019, the value added to the US economy by the Small Arms and Ammunition industry was about $8.14 billion USD. For comparison, the insurance industry contributed $1,320 billion in the same time frame, while the pharmaceutical industry contributed $1,300 billion. Oil and Gas was worth $193 billion, and big tobacco $48 billion. Even the legal cannabis market in the US was larger at $13.6 billion (see Figure 2.1).[6]

Other industries consistently out-spend the NRA on lobbying. In 2020, for example, the NRA spent about $1.23 million on lobbying. In the same year, pharmaceutical companies spent $306.23 million, Oil and Gas spent $110.69 million, and health professionals spent $87.62 million (see Figure 2.2).[7]

The NRA's tax returns (see Figure 2.3) cast further doubt upon the centrality of lobbying to the NRA's success.[8] Here we see that the NRA consistently spends more money on their other programs than the ILA,

Figure 2.1. Value added to US economy (US billions)

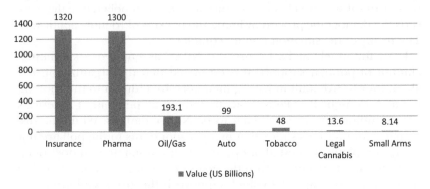

Insurance: 1320
Pharma: 1300
Oil/Gas: 193.1
Auto: 99
Tobacco: 48
Legal Cannabis: 13.6
Small Arms: 8.14

■ Value (US Billions)

Figure 2.2. Spending on lobbying in million USD

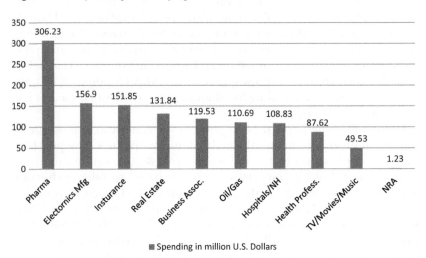

Pharma: 306.23
Electornics Mfg: 156.9
Insturance: 151.85
Real Estate: 131.84
Business Assoc.: 119.53
Oil/Gas: 110.69
Hospitals/NH: 108.83
Health Profess.: 87.62
TV/Movies/Music: 49.53
NRA: 1.23

■ Spending in million U.S. Dollars

the lobbying wing of the organization. These programs include their communications material, their annual meeting, and their education and museum initiatives. This includes certifying its large network of NRA-accredited instructors. Even in 2016, a high-stakes Presidential election year, the NRA spent more on these programs than on the ILA, if only by a small amount.

If the NRA's material contributions through campaign spending are the most important factor explaining its political victories and thus its

Figure 2.3.   NRA spending 2013–17 (in million USD)

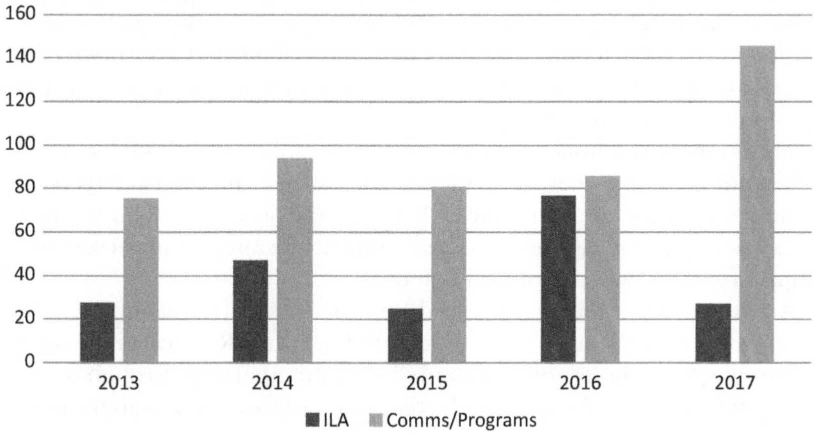

ILA   Comms/Programs

success, why does the organization spend almost twice as much in a normal year on its other programs?

Further, big spending is no guarantee of legislative success. The existing literature on campaign spending demonstrates that political donations can have mixed results.[9] While groups like the American Medical Association or the National Association of Realtors spend the most money donating to candidates, they are often the "biggest losers on Capitol Hill."[10] As the data on the NRA's spending shows, more work is needed to provide a three-dimensional picture of the group's influence. The perspective that I take in this book locates the central locus of the NRA's power in its relationship with the gun-owning community. This is not to say that lobbying is not important. Rather, what makes these formal political efforts possible is the sustained support of a highly motivated political community. It is the NRA's ability to speak on behalf of this segment of voters that gives it power. More attention is needed, therefore, to explain how the NRA manages this relationship.

Recent scholarship on firearms policy in the United States has noted that gun ownership, the gun culture, and gun owner social identity play a powerful role in motivating gun owners to participate politically. Evidence of this impact can be seen in the "gun gap" in voting behavior between gun owners and non-gun owners.[11] As we saw in the previous chapter, not only were gun owners more likely to vote for Donald Trump in the 2016 election, the more guns a person owned the more likely they were to vote Republican. Those who owned four or more guns were 45 per cent more likely to vote for Trump than non-gun owners.[12] This shows that not only does gun ownership influence political behavior, but the greater an individual's involvement in the gun culture, the more their behavior changes.[13] Further, this gun gap is not unique to men. Women who reported owning guns were more likely to have voted, contacted an elected representative, or given money to a gun rights advocacy group than non-gun owning women.[14]

More recently, scholars have examined the ability of the NRA to cultivate a unique gun owner social identity, mobilize its followers, and create connections with the Republican Party, as the source of its influence. This social identity can be measured empirically and has an observable impact on gun owner's political behavior.[15]

Academics have made great strides in theorizing this element of the group's influence. Charles's historical study of the NRA locates the organization's power in its ability to mobilize its membership through magazine publications and columns like the *Armed Citizen*,[16] letters to its membership, its network of gun clubs, and its ability to foster strong group cohesion.[17]

Carlson[18] also argues that while many authors have studied gun culture in the US, too little attention has been paid to "the critical role that the NRA has played in shaping this culture – not just through ideological rhetoric but also through the everyday practices and meanings attached to guns."[19] She looks at how the NRA shapes this culture through its concealed carry classes.

While Spitzer, Carlson, and Charles begin to investigate the relationship between the NRA's power and its relationship with the gun culture, none of them fully theorize this relationship. Alternatively, Lacombe[20] draws on Social Identity Theory to argue that "the NRA has assiduously and strategically cultivated a distinct, politicized gun-owner social identity over the course of many years, which enables it to influence politics by mobilizing its supporters into frequent and intense political action on its behalf."[21] Noting that pro-gun supporters tend to be more "politically engaged" than their opponents, Lacombe explains this by arguing that the NRA draws on ideational power to mobilize its membership to action. It does this through "alteration of the preferences and behavior of members of the mass public, whose political behavior … then affects policy outcomes." Gun owners are politically engaged as a result of their "politicized gun-owner social identity" and the NRA "has played a crucial role in creating this identity, disseminating it, and connecting it to politics."[22]

The NRA can bring to bear the power of its followers in several ways. First, through direct participation like contacting elected representatives, or mobilizing voters, but also through cultivating a relationship with the Republican Party. In this symbiotic relationship, the party benefits from the NRA's ability to mobilize supporters, and rewards the group by forwarding their political agenda. Put simply, the source of the NRA's political influence is "its people, not its money."[23]

Lacombe's work is very useful for empirically demonstrating the influence that the NRA has on the gun culture, and how it is able to translate that work into concrete political results. He makes an important contribution in theorizing the ideational power of the NRA but his analysis focuses mainly on the NRA's written material, its magazines, and on its overt political messaging.[24] In this book, I expand on this paradigm for understanding the NRA using ethnographic evidence and work with several of the NRA's communications mediums to broaden our understanding of this relationship. Further, I look beyond the group's overt political messaging towards the background ideas that make these arguments intelligible to their audience.

It is important, when looking at the NRA's influence, to look not only at its overtly political messaging, but to tune into the transmission of background ideas that make these foreground political appeals intelligible to their intended audience. To understand the ideational power of the NRA, we must look at the relationship between the NRA and the gun culture, that is the system of thoughts, ideas, understandings, and meanings shared between gun owners and enthusiasts. The NRA emerged from the gun culture in its early development but has since exerted a tremendous amount of influence on that culture, using its various publications and direct points of contact with its membership. The NRA is far from the sole actor shaping this culture, though they are a powerful actor within it.

Much of the NRA's power comes from their ability to manage their relationship with the community of gun owners. Thus, we can see the organization going to great lengths to shape the gun culture and grow the community, which it can draw on for political support. This is because individuals within a group will act to defend it against perceived external threats. These individuals are easier to motivate towards collective action given that the threat posed by their opponents could have a profound impact on their everyday lives. It is logical for people to be supportive of legislation that leads to the confiscation of property they do not own, or the restriction of liberties they do not use, to attain a public good. Yet few people would vote to have their property taken by the state, or voluntarily surrender liberties that they enjoy. Belonging to the gun-owning community and participating in the gun culture provides a powerful incentive for people to become politically active. Going to the gun range, watching pro-gun content on YouTube or through NRATV, attending a gun show or convention; all of these serve as constant reminders to Second Amendment supporters to remain politically active.

While this community of gun owners may be primed toward activism, a central actor is needed to mobilize and focus the group's efforts towards achieving concrete policy goals. After all, though all group members benefit from pro-gun advocacy, theorists of group politics have long noted that it is natural for individuals to free-ride off of the advocacy of others.[25] Thus, the NRA plays an important role in galvanizing the group towards collective action.

Here it is important to distinguish communities and cultures from networks. The term "issue network" describes groups of experts and concerned individuals that work together to influence policy. Issue networks are made up of individuals who have an interest in, or who identify with, a particular political cause. They can be made up of ordinary people who participate in the political system, as well as experts and intellectuals who policy makers draw on for expert advice. It is a "shared-knowledge group having to do with some aspect (or, as defined by the network, some problem) of public policy." These groups are difficult to measure as they can remain latent, only to activate later in response to an important event.[26] Outside of issue networks lies the attentive public, waiting to be brought into the discussion.

The idea of the gun-owning community is slightly different in that it involves a group of people centered around the gun culture rather than an area of expertise. This leisure-based community is not intrinsically political but can be activated by interest groups or politicians in response to threats to their leisure pursuit. The central locus of the gun-owning community is not in politics, but in practicing gun culture. Members of this community engage with one another through internet chat rooms, social media, events like gun shows, reading firearm-related material, meetings on the gun range, and/or organized shooting sports activities.

The NRA has an interest in developing the gun culture and growing the community. First, they understand that there is strength in numbers. The more Americans that own guns, the more leverage they have to argue for the rights of gun owners. The more people become involved, the more likely they are to support the gun rights movement. It is important to acknowledge that many of those working within the NRA work towards the creation and maintenance of the gun culture for non-instrumental purposes. Many of them are lifelong gun owners who simply want to see the activities and sports that they love grow.

Acknowledging that the NRA is a major player in the social construction of the gun culture, we must ask *how* they do this. Here, I believe, policy process theories offer some insights when put into conversation with the literature on the politics of memory. To better understand this, we must unpack two important concepts: narrative and memory.

Narrative and Public Policy

Storytelling is a fundamental part of what it means to be human. Stories are highly impactful forms of communication as they impart not only information but emotion. They transport the listener or reader, allowing them to identify with characters or imagine themselves within the action of the story. The field of public policy has recently added the study of narrative to its theoretical toolkit, following what is known as the ideational turn.

Those who study the policy process increasingly argue that ideas matter in shaping public policy. What is more difficult is establishing how "ideas go from thought to word to deed" or how they are "conveyed, adopted, and adapted."[27] Scholars of ideas in public policy note that ideas impact policy at three analytical levels – policy solutions, problem definitions, and public philosophies.[28] The most basic level is that of policy solutions. These are the remedies that politicians, activists, or civil servants put forward to the problems we face as a society. Background checks, assault-weapons bans, or stand your ground laws are all policy solutions supported by different sides of the gun debate. At this level of ideas, the policy problem and objectives are considered to have already been identified and defined, and the ideas represent the solutions proposed to address them. Work in this vein attempts to look at why certain policy solutions are adopted and others are not.[29]

Scholarship that studies the second level of ideas focuses on examining the role of ideas in shaping problem definitions. Rather than seeing ideas simply as solutions to policy problems, they look at how political actors work to shape the very contours of the problems they are trying to solve. Scholars adopting this approach focus on unpacking the process of contestation by which policy problems are defined.[30] How a policy problem is defined is important for shaping the choices of solutions that policymakers have, as well as for deciding whether that issue makes it onto the political agenda. If the problem is understood as widespread gun ownership, then background checks and assault-weapons bans make sense. Rather, if the problem is understood as the disarmament of good people, then stand your ground laws are the logical solution.

The third and final level where ideas influence policy is as public philosophies and policy paradigms.[31] Public philosophies, in this case, refers to "a view, often voiced by political parties, about the appropriate role

of government given certain assumptions about the market and society." The concept of public philosophies is similar to that of ideology
but without the negative baggage associated with the term. These "background ideas" or "philosophical ideas," "generally sit in the background
as underlying assumptions that are rarely contested except in times of
crisis."[32] They work to impact the makeup of legislatures and the behavior of those within the legislatures.[33] To continue our example, gun bans,
background checks, and stand your ground laws are premised on different understandings of how the world works – background ideas.

The NPF was created by scholars of public policy to trace the influence of ideas at all three of the levels mentioned above. The NPF focuses
on how political actors use narratives to win supporters and influence
policy.[34] The purpose of the NPF is to uncover and clarify the ways that
political actors use ideas instrumentally and theorize the relationship
between the different levels of ideas.

The strength of the NPF is its ability to take a vague concept – narrative – and provide a precise empirical operationalization.[35] Theorists
in this perspective focus on narratives as they are infused within policy
debates whether they are told on the floor of the house of representatives or in Twitter discussions, and because narratives can impact a policy
at all three levels of the policy making process. This approach attempts
to build a bridge between positivist and post-positivist understandings
of narratives, arguing that "narratives both socially construct reality and
can be measured empirically."[36] This is done through the NPF's precise
operationalization of a policy narrative. Policy narratives are made up
of several elements: a setting, characters, a plot, and, most importantly
a politically relevant moral. Narratives contain different combinations
of these elements, though the minimum standard for something to be
considered a narrative is that it must have at least one character and a
reference to a policy solution.[37]

Authors who adopt this framework accept that stories are a meaningful form of political communication used to create and shape the social
meanings through which policy is understood. In the context of the
policy world, the storytellers are stakeholders, including interest groups,
who tell stories to citizens and other important actors to shape the contours of the policy problem, sway public opinion, and move the status
quo in their intended direction.[38]

Narratives are made up of three parts. The first, narrative elements.
Narrative elements refer to the characters (heroes, villains, victims, and
allies); the setting; the plot; and the policy prescription or moral of the
story. The second, belief systems, are deeply rooted ideas that are shared
by allied groups or the wider society. Finally, narrative strategies are the

methods that actors use to persuade the public, like strategically expanding or contracting the scope of a policy conflict.[39]

A key narrative strategy is framing.[40] The conceptualization of a policy frame was taken from Framing Theory, which is often employed in the social movement literature to trace the influence of ideas on public opinion or support for an issue. Popularized by Goffman[41] and imported into the social movement literature by Giltin[42] and Snow and Benford,[43] the study of framing theory is now a popular approach within the literature on group politics. Frames allow actors to highlight a social injustice that they wish to tackle (called the punctuating function of the frame), identify a culprit or assign blame for the problem, and propose a resolution, the diagnostic and prognostic element of the frame.[44] These frames serve to section off reality, drawing attention to certain ideas and events while bracketing off others.[45] Frames are an important part of the second level of ideas, problem formation, as they "help interpret problems to define problems for action and suggest pathways to remedy the problem."[46]

In his analysis of the NRA, for example, Melzer focuses on the organization's use of framing in its communications to mobilize members against a perceived threat to their right to bear arms. He notes that part of their strategy in doing this is to appeal to a type of frontier masculinity popular with their key demographic. This frontier masculinity stresses the importance of conservative values like self-reliance while perpetuating the view that firearms were an essential element of America's past and, thus, American culture. For Melzer, this frontier masculinity predates the NRA, and he is agnostic about whether its origins are real or constructed.[47]

These frames, however, cannot exist independently of their cultural context. Culture forms the background ideas that make these frames intelligible. The use of framing in the debate over women's reproductive rights is a good example of this at work. The phrase "A woman's body is her own" is used to frame abortion as a medical issue or issue of bodily autonomy. This frame is only intelligible "in a cultural discourse that highlights the notions of individual autonomy and equality of citizenship rights."[48]

By incorporating framing into its analysis of narratives, the NPF allows us to understand how these frames fit into larger narrative strategies of organizations. This is important because "policy narratives contain both narrative elements and strategies that are not included in what constitutes an issue frame."[49] This allows us to expand beyond the second level of ideas, how ideas shape the contours of policy problems, and look at how these frames fit together with the third level of ideas, the public philosophies or background ideas of different cultures.

In the NPF, narratives help to explain how ideas translate to action. Politicians, advocacy groups, ordinary people, and members of the media use narratives to attempt to sway others and win over allies. This approach is useful because it allows us to look at the specific techniques that actors use to mobilize the power of ideas. To systematically study narratives, the NPF separates them into three separate analytical levels: micro, meso, and macro, which map onto Schmidt's three levels of ideas: policy solutions, policy problems, and public philosophies.[50] Studies of micro-level narratives focus on how narratives impact individuals. These studies are generally more experimental and examine things like how narrator trust impacts whether or not people will accept certain narratives.[51]

Meso-level NPF studies take the policy subsystem as their unit of analysis and examine how actors within it use narratives to try to achieve their policy outcomes. For example, McBeth et al.[52] look at how environmental interest groups mobilize narratives to shape how ordinary citizens saw the issue of wild bison conservation near Yellowstone National Park.

Two theorists have already applied the NPF to study the NRA, both focusing on the meso-level of analysis. Merry[53] examined almost 10,000 tweets from the NRA and the Brady Campaign to Prevent Gun violence to demonstrate how both organizations use social media to spread their narratives about mass shootings. Similarly, Smith-Walter et al.[54] completed a content analysis of *American Rifleman*, as well as the Brady Campaigns Legal Action newsletter to examine the role that evidence played in narrative construction.

Finally, and most importantly for the purposes of this book, macro-level narratives are grand narratives shared by broader communities. "These grand policy narratives create socially constructed realities that manifest as institutions, society, and cultural norms."[55] These are the background ideas that Schmidt describes. This conceptualization of grand narratives or meta-narratives was imported into the NPF from the wider social sciences, where they are sometimes called macro-narratives or Sacred Stories.[56]

Given that micro and meso-level studies lend themselves better to empirical research designs, most research within the NPF has focused on these levels. A few macro-level studies do exist, however. Danforth draws on the NPF to look at how shifting meta-narratives in educational policy have impacted students with disabilities in the era of the No Child Left Behind policy. Danforth labels meta-narratives as broad narratives, defining them as "communal, historical narratives that are expansive enough to explain a variety of human events across time and place."[57] He goes on to say that: "These large-scale cultural tales infuse situational specific activity sequences with social meaning while supplying useful theories of individual identity, moral action, and community life."[58] Similarly, in their aforementioned study, McBeth et al. examined how groups like the Buffalo Field Campaign draw upon symbols to help their narratives resonate with "underlying cultural elements characteristic of targeted publics."[59]

Yet, Peterson and Jones[60] note that the macro-level of NPF research is currently under-theorized. Many important questions remain unanswered. How do collective actors draw on these macro-narratives to influence public opinion and rally support? Do collective actors simply draw on a given culture's Sacred Stories, or do they actively influence and shape them? This is the gap my book fills by examining how the NRA not only draws upon but actively shapes historical macro-narratives surrounding America's past to construct the gun culture, attract and mobilize supporters, and ultimately shape American firearms policy.

It also adds methodological diversity to the NPF's research program. NPF studies tend to use experimental research[61] or content analysis[62] of collective actor's communications in order to examine the influence of narratives on group members and ordinary citizens. Ethnographic research has the potential to make an exciting contribution to this research program.

Given the under-theorization of the macro-level in the NPF and the importance of macro-level narratives surrounding America's, and Americans' pasts to the gun debate, it is important to reach across disciplinary boundaries to supplement this paucity. It is here that I think the literature from the field of memory studies has much to offer.

The Politics of Memory

Narratives are useful tools that political actors use to influence how people see a particular policy issue, and thus what pressure they put on their political leaders. But macro-narratives about the past are particularly powerful given the centrality of memory to how people navigate the world. It is thus important to unpack what I mean by memory, and how the practice of past presencing is used by political actors to influence policy.

To understand why the past is political, we must first accept a basic fact: that there is no pure and authentic past. The past is gone; irretrievable; forever beyond our grasp. What survives are snippets that we piece together to try to better understand what came before now. These snippets, assembled and carried into the present by human hands, bear the fingerprints of the assembler upon them.[63] Thus, those who study the politics of the past do not concern themselves with trying to piece together the past as it was. Instead, we focus on the past as it is remembered and brought into the present.

The remembered past is important because our understanding of that past heavily informs our understanding of the present. Human beings evaluate current events, construct our identity as individuals and as groups, make choices, and understand the world based on this understanding.[64] Cultures, like individuals, must have a remembered past if they are to have an intelligible present. Yet, unlike with the individual, the remembered past for cultures is constructed by a group of individuals and exists in a constant process of contestation, reinvention, and renewal. While the potential for the reinvention of the past is not unlimited, it is open to reinterpretation.

Ways of Knowing the Past

Throughout the twentieth century, historians grappled with questions surrounding the nature and uses of the past. This conversation began as an introspection into how history as a discipline explores the past. During this time, authors like Foucault,[65] Anderson,[66] Lowenthal,[67] Collingwood,[68] and Carr[69] questioned the traditional positivist view of history as a collection of objective facts about the past discerned using the scientific method. These authors instead argued that history is made up of narratives, or stories about the past, and that these stories are often mobilized by the state to achieve its goals. Further, they expanded the conversation to include previously ignored or devalued epistemologies such as memory and heritage. These authors acknowledged that knowledge of the past does not exist in and of itself but is brought to light to serve a purpose. Thus, the stories that get told often reflect existing power structures in society.

In the late 1970s and early 1980s, the field of memory studies emerged, adding new insights to the conversation.[70] Largely based on a rediscovery of the works of Maurice Halbwachs, a sociologist and student of Emile Durkheim,[71] this field looks at the social construction of the past on many levels, from the individual to larger organizations like the nation-state. The field reimagined memory, turning it from a noun to a verb. Rather than something we possess, remembering is something that we do. Further, it emphasized the role of narrative in shaping people's view of history and memory. There is no single history, but multiple competing histories, whose success depends on the power of their proponents. A key insight from the field of memory studies is that there are several epistemologies, or ways of knowing, the past. It is important to briefly review them before moving on to our discussion of the NRA's communications program.

The first way of knowing the past is through history. The field of history enjoys a tremendous amount of respect and attention in the wider society. It is often seen as the most authentic account of past events and impacts multiple facets of public life; trusted in court cases to help determine and interpret the laws of the land; referenced by politicians in debates and important for every scholarly discipline, whether they choose to acknowledge it or not. History is often referenced in the Great Gun Debate, especially the history surrounding America's revolutionary founding.

The second epistemology of the past is memory. While memory is often thought of as an individual activity, there are both individual and social elements to remembering. As such, scholars have noted that memory can be both individual or collective.[72] Memory makes public events private. When we think about a major event that occurred during our lives, we think of our own experience of it, of how we and those around us felt at the time it was happening (consider how I began this chapter with my memory of the shooting at Columbine High School). Remembering is a social process, as other peoples' memories serve to confirm and reinforce our own.[73] Most importantly, memory is always tied to identity. While individual memories allow us to develop our own sense of identity, of who we are, collective memories do the same for groups. Within groups, competing narratives related to memory vie for supremacy, for what is at stake is the very heart and soul of the group.[74] As we will see, the NRA often mobilizes the collective and personal memories of its members as part of its communications programs.

The relationship, or perhaps the distinction, between history and memory is complex.[75] Developing a sharp distinction between history and collective memory is not necessary for this book. For the purposes of my analysis, I will defer to indigenous meanings when making the distinction. If information is presented as a "history," I use that term. Developing a strict operationalization of the difference is less important than acknowledging that both the production of history and memory are actions.

The third way of knowing the past is heritage. Heritage is simultaneously a way of knowing the past and a way of laying claim to it. Heritage is the past that is owned. It is our heritage. Or your heritage. Or my heritage. Heritage "turns the past into something visitable" and lays claims of ownership for one group over another.[76]

Like history and memory, heritage appears to be apolitical; the simple celebration, ownership, and continuity of a group's historical traditions. However, heritage is deeply political, as it serves to validate political ideologies and identities.[77] Debates over heritage, including controversies like the fight over the meaning of the Confederate Battle flag, or the dispute over removing statues from public places, highlight the political nature of claims to heritage. Heritage establishes ownership or claim of something, and is by nature "exclusive and exclusionary,"[78] thus tying into core political debates. If politics is about "who gets what, when, how,"[79] recognition becomes the "what."

Heritage can be tangible as well as intangible. The term "intangible heritage" was created by historians seeking to preserve dying traditions, to expand the way we think about heritage to "include not only the master-pieces, but also the masters." This term was useful for those seeking to preserve cultural traditions because it was difficult to use existing copyright law to protect traditions that, by their very nature, belong to groups of people rather than individuals.[80] UNESCO defines intangible heritage as:

> traditions or living expressions inherited from our ancestors and passed on to our descendants, such as oral traditions, performing arts, social practices, rituals, festive events, knowledge, and practices concerning nature and the universe or the knowledge and skills to produce traditional crafts[81]

The concept of heritage, especially intangible heritage, is important to my analysis of the NRA's communications material for several reasons. The NRA works hard to present the traditions associated with firearms' ownership and the Second Amendment as a heritage that must be protected and passed on to the next generation. This includes both tangible objects, like firearms, as well as cultural practices, like shooting competitions.

Each of these three epistemologies of the past are important for our understanding of the NRA's political communication program. Though the boundaries between the three can be fuzzy, the most important point to focus on is that, for the past to become political, it must be actively brought into the present. Scholars within the field of memory studies have examined how narratives about the past are produced and communicated through different mediums, in different locations, and within the context of different social groups, what MacDonald[82] calls past presencing. "Past presencing is concerned with the ways in which people variously draw on, experience, negotiate, reconstruct, and perform the past in their ongoing lives." This term was created to avoid the problematic distinctions between different epistemologies of the past.[83]

The Instrumental Past: Opportunities and Limitations

Having acknowledged that history, memory, and heritage are better seen as actions, or ways of knowing, than as objects, we can understand that past presencing becomes political when the past is retold or reimagined to work towards a political goal. But how can the past be used as a political tool? What are the limitations of the instrumentality of the past?

The remembered past has five primary utility functions for individuals and groups.[84] The first is that these ways of knowing allow us to make sense of the present. Were it not for the remembered past, we would not be able to function as we would not recognize the objects, places, and people in our environment, or be able to perform the simplest tasks. These do not have to be things we have directly experienced, but can be what are called "prosthetic memories"[85] that we gain through media like television or film.

The past is used to reaffirm or validate certain practices or beliefs by referring to historical precedent or tradition. This can work in two ways. The first is preservation, or justifying current practices based on their survival through time. The second is restoration, which is looking back in time to bring something back that is perceived to have been lost or trying to right a historical wrong.[86] This is what Trump evoked when he asked his supporters to help him "Make America Great Again." On the other hand, the past can also be used to aggrandize the present, reminding people that their lives are better now than they were "back then," or as a form of escape from the present when the past is used to entertain.[87]

Both for the individual and group, the past is used to create a sense of identity. On an individual level, our pasts make up our individual stories. Our memories are tied to our sense of worth. People seek links to history to affirm their value or importance. This is why we treasure things like family heirlooms that link our personal story to something grander. The same is true for groups, where this past takes the form of communal or national stories and traditions.[88]

All of the functions of the past can be used to build and maintain political movements, identities, and institutions. If the past helps groups make sense of the present, then controlling the most popular narrative about the past can be tremendously important for shaping the conditions of political possibility. If the past helps us to affirm and validate practices through preservation or restoration, it can be a tool for preserving institutions and power structures or rallying movements to oppose them. If the past helps us to form group identity, it is essential for the creation of any political movement, which must not only have its own story but link itself somehow to the story of the broader polity.

What about historical truth? Is our understanding of the past purely instrumental? What about narratives of the past that stand the test of time? While philosophical debates about the nature of a pure historical truth lie beyond the scope of this book, looking at the instrumental past does mean we have to acknowledge that actors like the NRA are not without limits in their ability to shape historical narratives and memories to suit their own purposes. After all, there are "enduring memories" that societies hold, those elements of our understanding of the past that remain largely stable over time. Actors are not free to rewrite history. After all, memories are only credible if they "conform to an existing structure of assumptions about the past."[89]

Three factors constrain political actors in their effort to reconstruct the past. The first is the "structure of available pasts," which refers to the way that the existing historical record limits the ways that individuals can manipulate the past. While they can always interpret events differently, it is very difficult to invent events entirely, at least in democratic countries with a free press and vibrant academic community. Further, historical events, once popularized, are difficult for people to ignore. Once an infrastructure of commemoration is created – for example, statues and museums are built – it can be difficult to dismantle them, and doing so is controversial. This infrastructure can also be social rather than physical as, for example, when a classic work of literature becomes part of an established "canon."[90]

"The Structure of Individual Choice" refers to the way that the past shapes us psychologically, whether we like it or not. This includes past traumas, like the way that Germans must deal with the Holocaust whether or not it is comfortable for them to do so. It includes "channels" or "precedents," which refer to established ways of doing things within organizations that shape the way that things are done in the future, similar to how political scientists see institutions. It also includes "commitments," that is, how people become invested in certain elements of the past and are reluctant to give up their preestablished views.[91]

Finally, groups are limited in their ability to dominate the popular understanding of the past by other groups within society working towards their own goal.[92] These three factors can help us understand why certain narratives about the past are resistant to reinterpretation as they possess "self-sustaining inertia."[93] Narratives about the past are especially resistant to change when they are protected by powerful institutions. These institutions, like the state or the church, supervise the past through the creation of commemorations, archives, and traditions.[94]

In sum, while powerful actors work to shape how people understand the past, their efforts are constrained by existing infrastructures of commemoration and by conflicts with rival groups. This is important for our discussion of macro-level narratives. By their very nature, the sacred stories of a group are highly resistant to change and reinterpretation. They are deeply institutionalized, with a vast infrastructure of commemoration dedicated to their maintenance. This does not mean, however, that actors cannot draw on different elements of these narratives to suit their purposes.

How Do We Experience the Past?

History and memory are conveyed through narratives, but they are also experienced. Understanding how the past is experienced is crucial for understanding the strategies that make narratives about the past useful tools for political movements. The past is experienced by people in several ways: through connection to family, through materiality, through place, and through media.

A key insight from the field of memory studies is the important role that family plays in how we experience the past. Researchers were concerned that people seemed less interested in traditional scholarly history. What they found, however, was that people often interacted with the past "in ways molded by their own personalities, experiences, and traditions and that their engagements were often quite different from what producers of these texts had hoped for."[95]

Family is central to how we understand the past as people feel closest to the past when gathering with family members. This includes things like looking at old pictures, sharing stories at family gatherings, telling family stories, or reminiscing about old times. People often trust their grandparents more than their teachers when it comes to sources of authority on the past. When people do engage with national history, it is often connected to their personal or family story. When discussing major events, people are most interested in exploring these events through the prism of their own family story.[96] Family is a consistent theme within NRA communications material. The centrality of family to the act of remembering cannot be understated and helps us to explain why this is such a frequent and impactful strategy deployed by the NRA.

Another way human beings experience the past is through material objects.[97] People attach meaning to objects, and this meaning can be both personal and shared by broader groups. Objects imbued with meaning are called "affective objects" and they take many forms. One such form is relics; objects that serve as evidence of the past. Relics help to bolster the knowledge we gain through memory and history, though they are only useful to us when placed in the context of our existing knowledge about that period.[98] To someone who knows nothing about the history or popular representations of the American West, for example, a Colt Peacemaker, the gun carried by most cowboys in western movies, would be meaningless. To those raised on stories of heroic cowboys and lawmen fighting outlaws, it becomes a symbol of chivalry, courage, and masculinity.

The materiality of an artifact is what often gives it its power. They are a bridge between the past and the present, giving the past a sense of presence.[99] How an individual feels about guns plays a large part in their position on the gun debate, since facts are interpreted selectively based on a person's background, much of which is shaped by culture.[100]

Place is also important for understanding how people experience the past, and how the past can be brought into the present. Much like affective objects are objects that are assigned meaning, place refers to physical spaces imbued with personal or social meaning, feeling, or emotion. It is a physical space that is transcribed with meaning through the process and practices of memory.[101] A good example of place is the concept of home. The idea of home is an elastic term that expands depending on the scale in which it is employed, from one's dwelling to one's homeland.[102] Place is important for how we experience the past because of the emotions and authority assigned to particular spaces. This becomes especially relevant when I explore the NRA's National Firearms Museum.

We experience the past through material and place, but also through the media. Movies, books, television shows, video games, and online videos are important media through which people engage with history, heritage, and collective memory.[103] Historical material is often dealt with in popular culture and then interpreted by the audience. Audiences must then "negotiate" between the versions of history presented to them and their particular group in society.[104] The portrayals of the past contained in mass media are powerful vectors of memory and "possess the potential to generate and mold images of the past which will be retained by whole generations."[105] The popular memory of the Wild West, for example, has been heavily shaped and transformed by popular western novels, television shows, and Hollywood films.

Looking at the role that media plays in our understanding of the past is important for our discussion of guns in media portrayals of American history. Hollywood producers likely do not intend for their portrayals of gun-wielding heroes and villains to serve as a repertoire of cultural imagery for gun rights organizations to draw on, yet this is exactly what happens.

It should be clear, then, that material explanations for the NRA's influence are insufficient for properly understanding the organization's effectiveness. We must conceptualize the NRA's influence as stemming from the group's relationship with the gun culture, and their ability to grow and shape this culture through the use of narratives.

When organizations like the NRA disseminate large, macro-level policy narratives about America's past, they are engaged in the process of past presencing; that is, they are bringing the past into the present for political purposes. These macro-level narratives draw on material from America's history and public memory, from the private memories of Americans, and American symbols and heritage. These narratives are not infinitely mutable. To be successful, narratives about the past must conform to existing infrastructures of commemoration. They cannot rewrite the past, but they can tell their side of it.

The NPF is a powerful tool to trace the influence of narratives in political discourse. It provides us with a conceptualization and an operationalization of narratives, and an opportunity to account theoretically for the intersections between broad, societal "sacred stories" and everyday policy narratives that are regularly told by policymakers.

Bringing the policy literature into discussion with the literature on memory studies and the politics of the past is a way to theoretically develop the macro-level of the NPF. The NRA both contributes to and draws from macro-level policy narratives through the processes of past presencing, drawing on history, public and personal memory, and heritage to build a political community of gun owners and sway the public debate on gun control.

3   On Paper and Online:
The *American Rifleman* and NRATV

Guns evoke powerful, emotive imagery that often stands in the way of intelligent debate. To the pro-control point of view, the gun is symbolic of much that is wrong with American culture. It symbolizes violence, aggression, and male dominance, and its use is seen as an acting out of your most regressive and infantile fantasies. To the gun culture's way of thinking, the same gun symbolizes much that is right in the culture. It symbolizes manliness, self-sufficiency, and independence, and its use is an affirmation of man's relationship to nature and to history.

– James D. Wright, "Ten Essential
Observations on Guns in America"

The NRA understands that guns have meaning beyond their immediate function. Much of the print and online content the organization produces is devoted to tapping into these meanings and translating them into political support. This chapter draws on the NPF and important concepts from the field of memory studies to evaluate how the NRA use narratives about America's (and Americans') pasts to build a political community of gun owners. These narratives are disseminated through the organization's network of instructors, their communications materials, and through points of contact with the membership. The organization uses these modalities to attract new members and new gun owners and motivate existing members to deepen their involvement with the organization. These members, in turn, provide the organization with the resources it needs to advance its desired policy agenda. The resources members provide are not just financial. The NRA's large group of dedicated followers provides them with an important voting block to mobilize, as well as a group of highly energized advocates willing to write letters, volunteer, and take political action on gun issues.

In this chapter, I will focus on unpacking two key NRA communications mediums; both means through which the organization engages in storytelling bout America's and Americans' pasts. As we have explored, these macro-level narratives are "sacred stories," important and foundational background ideas that shape the way members of a given society think about the world. I want to understand how the NRA both draws upon and shapes macro-level narratives about the nation and its citizens' pasts.

The first medium I consider is the *American Rifleman* magazine, the NRA's flagship publication. It was selected because it is the oldest NRA publication, and has the greatest reach. The second medium is NRATV. I analyze samples drawn from two very different NRATV programs: *Curator's Corner* and *Armed & Fabulous*. The NRA does not publish statistics on viewership, and therefore I could not select the most popular NRATV shows. Rather, these shows were selected due to their subject matter. Given its focus on historical content, I selected *Curator's Corner*. *Armed & Fabulous* was chosen given that it is one of the NRA's explicitly gendered programs, aimed at attracting women to the gun culture and organization.

The NRA disseminates narratives regarding the role of firearms in America's (and Americans') pasts as part of its larger effort to expand and mobilize the gun-owning community, from which it draws political support, to influence the debate on firearms and thus firearms policy. These narratives are intended to support the underlying argument that guns have played an integral part in American history, more so than in other countries, and that the United States has a historical tradition of gun ownership not just for sporting and hunting purposes, but for civilian self-defense and resistance to tyranny at home and abroad. It does this by focusing on key macro-narratives regarding America's history and culture, and by tying firearms to America's (and Americans') pasts.

What I present here is based on a thematic analysis of a sample of 100 articles from the NRA's *American Rifleman* magazine as well as 35 episodes of NRATV. Conducting a thematic content analysis of NRA written and online material is important for understanding the messages that the organization is trying to send to its members. In later chapters I focus on how these messages are received and incorporated into the lifeworlds of those members.

The American Rifleman

The *American Rifleman* magazine is the organization's central communication mechanism, delivered directly to the mailbox of NRA members on a monthly basis. Since its founding in 1885, it has been continually published and was acquired by the NRA in 1916.[1] According to the Alliance of Audited Media, as of June of 2020, the American Rifleman's regular circulation was 1.7 million subscribers.[2] This is the largest in the world of firearms magazines, and comparable to many large-scale mainstream magazines in the United States.

The *American Rifleman* magazine is a mix of political articles, product reviews, and historical pieces aimed at gun owners. Each issue follows a familiar structure. The first third of the magazine contains direct and overt political messages. These include editorials from senior NRA officials, as well as the *Armed Citizen* column, which publishes stories of ordinary Americans defending their lives and their property with firearms. The rest of the magazine contains product reviews and historical pieces, as well as regular smaller columns like "I Have This Old Gun" or "Favorite Firearms."

The magazine is provided for free with the purchase of an NRA membership, which as of the time of writing costs about $45 USD per year, or $1,500 for a life membership. When purchasing their membership, the buyer has the choice between subscribing to the *American Rifleman* or one of the organization's newer magazines, like the *American Hunter* (873,444 avg. subscribers) which caters to the hunting community, *America's 1st Freedom* (595,522 avg. subscribers) which focuses more on political issues, and *Shooting Illustrated* (582,260 avg. subscribers) which is targeted at the sports shooting community.[3] Members can also opt-out of the magazine subscription if they so choose or receive subscriptions to more than one magazine for a small additional fee. The magazines also make their most recent articles publicly available through their websites and their free mobile applications. The NRA does not release data on online viewership or app downloads.

The Rise and Fall of NRATV

The NRA launched its first foray into online news in 2004 in an effort to give itself a broader role in shaping the discourse on firearms policy. The first show on the network was called *Cam & Co.*, and like much of the content that would follow, took the form of a talk show.[4] In 2016, the group expanded its online offerings, launching NRATV with the help of its advertising firm Ackerman McQueen.[5] They quickly expanded to offer 39 different programs that, until the summer of 2019, were available online through their website, as well as through several streaming services like Roku, Amazon Fire, and Apple TV.[6] Hiring more racially and gender-diverse spokespeople, like conservative commentator Dana Loesch and lawyer and entrepreneur Colion Noir, their programming seemingly reached out to groups that the organization had failed to court in the past while providing plenty of material for its base.

In 2019, as I was in the middle of conducting my fieldwork, scandal forced the NRA to abruptly cancel NRATV. Concerns by some board members surrounding the cost-benefit analysis of NRATV, which was allegedly suffering from poor viewership, and a dispute between the NRA and their marketing firm, Ackerman McQueen, over alleged overbilling,[7] caused Wayne Lapierre to pull the plug on NRATV in June.[8]

NRATV garnered a lot of media attention in the three years of its existence. From an episode of the progressive political comedy show *Last Week Tonight* with John Oliver[9] to critical commentaries from newspapers and magazines like the *Atlantic*,[10] or *GQ*,[11] the programming generally elicited either mockery or ire from the mainstream media. Despite this, only a few academics have drawn on this treasure trove of digital content for their analyses of the organization. Those that have, like Gilpin,[12] tend to focus on the explicitly political content, ignoring the deeper social meanings beneath the surface. I began to correct this with my gender analysis of NRA's content aimed explicitly at women.[13] This chapter continues that work through a thematic analysis of NRA-written and online material.

Data

Before starting my fieldwork, I became an NRA member. You do not need to live in the United States to become a member, nor do you need to provide proof of citizenship, though I am an American citizen. Becoming a member allowed me to attend the NRA Annual Meeting and gain access to a subscription to the *American Rifleman*. My sample of *American Rifleman* articles is drawn from issues I received with my own NRA membership between 2016 and 2020. Other academics studying the NRA have used the *American Rifleman* magazine as a data source focusing mainly on the political editorials from the magazine[14] or on advertisements within it.[15]

Thematic analysis involves: "identifying and describing both implicit and explicit ideas within the data, that is, themes."[16] The researcher attempts to identify and analyze the patterns that emerge in the dataset.[17] Here, I employ a theoretical thematic analysis,[18] given that the identification of the themes was driven by my theoretical perspective, which focuses on examining the use of narrative, specifically narratives focused on the past.

In order to qualify for inclusion into my dataset, articles had to contain at least one narrative related to history, memory, or heritage. I used the

NPF's inclusion criteria for the selection of a narrative: that it contains at least one character and a policy relevant moral.[19]

These articles generally comprise half of the content of *American Rifleman* and yet are completely ignored in the academic discussion of the magazine, which focus on more overtly political messaging. I selected a sample of 100 articles. Each issue of the magazine contains at least one article labeled "Historical," which covers the use of a particular firearm in a famous conflict, often by Americans or American allies. Other recurring segments included "I Have This Old Gun," "Favorite Firearms," and "In Memoriam." Sometimes, product reviews were chosen for selection when the product they were reviewing was a historical firearm.

The selected articles were then scanned and imported into NVIVO 12 for coding and analysis. An initial scan of 20 articles allowed me to develop a coding scheme based on reoccurring themes in the data. Three central codes were informed by my theoretical framework: history, memory, heritage. The history theme covered narratives within the magazine that were presented as part of the nation's past. These included articles about World Wars, the American Revolution, or the Old West. The major theme of memory was used for narratives related to individual America's pasts. Finally, heritage related to the embodied past, or history that is owned. I was then able to develop sub-codes based on my initial scan, such as American identity, family memory, personal memory (see Table 3.1).

A key indicator of the importance of a theme is prevalence: how often a particular theme shows up in a data set. Prevalence can be calculated in one of two ways, either by looking at how often each theme shows up in a single text or how often they show up in the entire data set.[20] I decided to focus on the prevalence of themes within the data set (see Table 3.2). While a theme could show up multiple times in a single issue or episode, it is much more likely to make an impression on the reader if it is repeated across time. Further, I did not want to cut off these two communications mediums from their political context. The themes I chose were important because they were presented in other NRA material that I came across during my research, either at the NRA Annual Meeting, during classes, or at the NRA museum.

Given that magazines and digital content are visual mediums, I was careful to pay close attention to the meanings that are created or embellished by the combination of text, dialogue, and imagery. The themes contained within these texts are not only expressed in words but images, just as the National Firearms Museum combines text and artifact to create meaning.

Table 3.1. Themes and codes

Major Themes	History	Memory	Heritage
Codes	American Revolution Civil War Wild West World Wars Recent History (Post-War to Present) Invention and Innovation	Famous Firearms First Time Shooting Collecting Hunting In Memoriam Sports Shooting Self-Defense Sports Shooting Tinkering	American Heritage American Guns

Table 3.2. Theme prevalence (across total dataset)

Major Theme	Code	Prevalence[21]
Memory		
	Collecting	51
	Family Memory	39
	Hunting	35
	Sports Shooting	22
	Famous Firearms	21
	First Time Shooting	14
	In Memoriam	8
	Tinkering	4
History		
	Invention and Innovation	42
	World Wars	41
	Wild West	29
	Recent History (Post-War to Present)	27
	American Revolution	9
	Civil War	8
Heritage		
	American Guns	56
	American Heritage	25

The selection of NRATV data was more complicated. Once again, I focused my case selection on NRATV programs aimed particularly at historical content. This led me to begin my analysis of *Curator's Corner*. Filmed in the NRA Museum, *Curator's Corner* features museum employees telling the stories of important or curious objects from the museum's collection. In order to be able to speak more to the gendered elements of the NRA communications material I included the program *Armed & Fabulous*. This show was found under the *NRA Women* section of NRATV and is quite unambiguously aimed at women. The show profiles important women in the world of shooting, from professional sports shooters to business owners to NRA board members.

Mid-way through my research, both shows were abruptly removed from the organization's website due to the collapse of NRATV. Despite this, I was able to analyze 15 episodes of *Curator's Corner* and 20 episodes of *Armed & Fabulous*. The process of analyzing these shows was similar to that of the *American Rifleman* articles. While watching the selected shows, I took careful notes, focusing on the use of narrative and past presencing, and once again using NVIVO 12 to record them. These notes were then coded using the same coding scheme as the magazine articles and analyzed to draw out major themes.

Drawing on both print and online material allowed me to gain a better understanding of the breadth of the communications tools that the NRA has at its disposal to speak directly with members and the public. Analyzing both of these mediums also helps to ensure that I was drawing from NRA material that would have been consumed by the widest possible demographic of NRA members, given that older members would be more likely to read the magazine, and younger members to access the web-based content.

Politics Is Personal: The Importance of Family and Memory

A key theme that emerged from the data was the importance placed on family memories. This is unsurprising given that the NRA goes to great lengths to present itself as an organization with strong family values. Further, appealing to emotions tied to family is an impactful form of past presencing. People interact with the past most often with and in relation to their families. This included everything from looking at photo albums to telling stories and even learning history.[22] Being able to connect firearms to the concept of the American family is an important way that the organization reinforces the link between American identity and guns, once of its central meta-narratives.

This appeal to themes of domesticity and family are strengthened by the way that NRA members consume this material. It is likely that both the magazines and online television content will be consumed in the home. Many of the videos, especially those aimed at women, are also designed to be shared with family members and friends. These communications materials are not just *about* family, they are made to be watched and shared *by* and *with* families.

Family memories showed up 39 times within my dataset. Of the 100 *American Rifleman* articles I analyzed, 17 per cent contained narratives that took the form of family memories. These narratives showed up the most in the regular series "Favorite Firearms." In this series, readers are invited to write in and tell a story about their favorite firearm. These stories are then curated and edited by the magazine's editorial team.

Memories from childhood were a recurring theme, often involving a family member who is now gone. One reader wrote in to tell the story of his first firearm, a military surplus German Luger pistol, which he had purchased as a teenager by selling his comic book collection. His mother had gone with him to buy it and took him to the range to shoot it for the first time. "I shot the Luger a couple of times and could not hit anything with it. Then my mom insisted on shooting it, so I loaded three cartridges into the Luger for her." The author describes how his mother resoundingly trounced him, hitting their target, a can, three times. The author ends the story with this: "Mom is gone now, but I still have what I call 'Mom's Luger' – my favorite firearm."[23]

Another reader wrote about a double-barreled shotgun that had been given to him as a gift by his father-in-law, Jack, shortly after his marriage in 1991. The firearm was a family heirloom, a 1916 Ithaca shotgun that had been passed down from Jack's father, Bud. The reader took it on several successful hunts, and it quickly became his favorite firearm, not just because of his success with it but because of its connection to its lineage. "Being able to carry a little bit of Jack and Bud with me afield makes the firearm that much more special. I hope my future grandchild or son-in-law might cherish it someday, the way we have." The title of this article – "Side-By-Side" – refers to both the firearm the author describes and his relationship with his father in-law. Double-barred shotguns like Bud's Ithaca come in two forms, side-by-sides and over & unders, depending on whether the barrels are arranged horizontally or vertically.[24]

The past serves many functions: it helps us navigate the world, validate certain practices and beliefs, create and affirm individual and group identity, and as a form of escape or entertainment.[25] The family memories shared in the *Favorite Firearm* column, though particular to the individuals sharing their stories, are universally accessible. They invite the reader to identify with them, conjuring their own family memories. They validate the cultural practices of gun ownership, hunting, and sports shooting by anchoring them in the past of not just America the nation, but individual Americans. They cement gun owners' connections to the NRA through the collective practice of remembering.

Further, these stories draw on the material power of family heirlooms as objects of memory. Objects gain meaning through memory, and firearms, as durable goods, have a lot of time to gather memory about them. The process of ageing is part of what makes relics important objects of memory.[26] It is difficult to imagine another piece of sporting equipment that could be used more than 100 years after its making.

The NRATV content, especially the show *Armed & Fabulous*, drew extensively on family memories to form the central narratives of the episodes. The purpose of the show was to feature famous women in the world of shooting to encourage other women to take up the shooting sports and hunting. As a result, it walked a delicate tightrope between emphasizing the femininity of the women involved and subverting it by showing their participation in the shooting sports, as if to say: "you can be a girly girl, and a tough shooter as well." This is a big part of the NRA's efforts to expand the gun culture to include women by overcoming deeply entrenched gender norms that discourage women's participation in the gun culture.[27]

Several of the episodes that I analyzed featured personal and family memories surrounding hunting, self-defense, and the shooting sports. Many of these were memories from childhood. In an episode profiling her achievements, Olympic trap and skeet shooter Kim Rhode notes: "Shooting was just something that was a way of life. It was passed down generationally in my family." She talks about her grandfather's use of guns as a houndsman, which he passed down to her father. The episode shows us black and white images of her grandfather and father shooting, hunting, and fishing. Her father says it was natural when she was born that she would learn to hunt and fish. Images of a young Kim holding a shotgun on her father's lap are shown as is a picture of her with a series of harvested rabbits holding a shotgun. "Everything we did we did as a family, so we just took Kim with us."[28]

Gaye Kelsey talks about how shooting was a big part of her relationship with her father. "My dad just put a gun in my hand when I was 17." She describes how her father entered her into a "Pigeon shoot." "Once you get a taste like that … you're hooked." Gaye is described by the narrator as a "Proud Texas gal, born and raised." She is shown, shotgun in hand, walking around her family ranch, the "site of ultimate retreat." Footage is displayed of competitors taking part in a clay pigeon shooting competition, which was described as a new sport. She describes her father's prowess at trap shooting, citing it as the reason for her own success in the shooting sports.[29]

Featuring these personal family memories does three things at once. The main purpose of *Armed & Fabulous* is to get women involved in the gun culture. By presenting these women as role models, both traditionally feminine yet at ease in the world of guns, the show hopes to attract other women to the sport and present participation in the gun culture as empowering. The sharing of these family memories also serves to legitimate the social practices of the gun culture. The NRA realizes that its image as a male-dominated organization is hurting it. It is a testament to the success of the feminist movement, and the increasing diversity of American society, that even deeply conservative organizations must now seek the social legitimacy that diversity provides. By drawing on family memories, the organization hopes to present the gun culture as inclusive, family-friendly, and thus legitimate. Finally, the stories of these women reinforce the connection between firearms, family, and American identity.

While most of the show's content focuses on warm, family memories, *Armed & Fabulous* also draws on darker, more traumatic personal memories to warn viewers of the dangers of failing to arm themselves. This is a commonly used tactic by the organization. For example, the *Armed Citizen* column mentioned earlier is present in every issue of *American Rifleman*. It recounts stories of ordinary Americans fighting off criminals with firearms. The episodes of *Armed & Fabulous* that feature this narrative take a similar structure. Each of the victims was unarmed at the time that they were victimized. In each of the cases, the incident is presented as a wakeup call to the women, who took steps to arm themselves to defend against future predation.

The very first episode of *Armed & Fabulous* features this narrative. Sandy Froman, the NRA's first female president, was at the time living in Hollywood and working as a lawyer. She describes a man attempting to break into her home, emphasizing that the police did not show up until after he had given up on the lock and fled the scene. She talks about her fear of what would have happened if he had got in. The next day she bought a Colt M1911. "In no time she went from being afraid to being prepared." Guns are presented as a way for women to ensure their safety in an uncertain world. The episode concludes that: "Every woman is entitled to such security."[30]

These incidents are intended to remind the viewer of what the NRA believes are the potential consequences of failing to arm oneself. Firearms are presented as a tool for women's safety and empowerment. Looked at through the lens of gender, this represents a departure from more traditional American narratives, which often focus on the male protector role. Here, women are presented as capable of defending themselves and their partners if given the proper tools. We can observe the NRA pushing back against masculinist American cultural norms that relegate women to the role of protected. The narrative of the good guy with a gun is thus expanded to include the "good gal."

This is driven home particularly by the story of Hilary, the victim of a violent home invasion. As the narrator describes the incident, ominous music plays in the background and a black and white city is depicted. The show first turns to Ben, Hilary's boyfriend, who describes the experience. Ben was stabbed eight times during the encounter, had his Nintendo gaming system stolen as well as Hilary's phone. Ben says the event changed his life and that "a part of me died that night." "Nobody ever thinks this kind of thing could happen to them. I didn't have a gun in the house at the time, and the fact of the matter is nobody can guarantee my safety but me." Images of dark downtown streets are shown. Sirens blare in the background as the camera zeroes in on an ambulance with open doors, as if to show the viewer the fate that awaits them should they fail to heed the narrator's warning.

The camera then turns to Hillary: "I'm proof that it can happen, and the message is: find a way to protect yourself." Rather than focusing on Ben arming himself, it is Hilary who is presented as the hero of the story. Hilary is shown walking her German shepherd, who she describes as a fully trained police dog. Following her father's advice, she moved out of the city to a ranch. Her and Ben now have two dogs, alarm systems, motion detectors, and Hilary got her concealed carry license. The narrator notes that she now sleeps with a loaded shotgun and a pistol, which she is fully trained to operate. "I don't know how having firearms would have changed anything at the time. But I know having one now sure makes me feel a lot safer," Ben adds.[31]

The cautionary tale is a consistent narrative strategy across NRA material. It complements the narrative of the good guy with a gun by demonstrating what happens when good people are prevented from, or fail to avail themselves of that protection. By drawing on the personal memories of victims of violent crime, the organization emphasizes the urgency of its message. Viewers are told to learn from the protagonists' pasts and take steps to protect themselves. Personal memories, whether quaint family memories or traumatic ones, are powerful vectors for NRA messaging. Though the viewer is aware they are being shown material by the NRA, the subjects of these shows bear witness to the organization's message in a way that makes it seem like it is coming from a neutral source. The viewer is being shown, not told. Given that these communications materials are likely being consumed in the home, the urgency of the message is reinforced. Further, the major themes emphasized in these memories are universal: family, parent-child relationships, romance, and fear of violence. This means that a wide swathe of viewers can empathize and connect with them.

Each of these narrative structures fit the NPF's operationalization of a narrative as having characters, a plot, and a policy-relevant moral. The stories contain heroes, everyday gun owners like the eagle-eyed mother and her Luger, alongside the celebrities of the gun world, like Olympic shooter Kim Rhode. They contain villains, both the explicit villains like the shady, masked criminals who assaulted Hillary and Ben, and implicit villains that hide in the background of the narrative: politicians who threaten gun ownership. The moral of the touching family stories is that firearms are an essential part of the American family and the American way of life, while the moral of the cautionary tales is that firearms are a key tool for the physical protection of your family. These morals are both particular, in the sense that they will appeal most to those who share the belief system of those within gun culture, and universal, as they touch on transcendent themes like family and fear of violence. Either way, these stories send a message to supporters, gun owners, the gun curious, and policy makers: an attack on guns is an attack on the safety and sanctity of the American family.

Grand Historical Meta-Narratives

The most common themes that showed up in the NRA written and online material were references to grand historical meta-narratives. These are macro-level narratives that touch on major events in American and world history. The two World Wars were favorite historical themes in my dataset, showing up 41 times. Articles that included these themes focused primarily on American troops in the Second World War. Narratives surrounding the Wild West were also prevalent, showing up 29 times, and more recent historical events (the Vietnam War, the Israeli-Palestinian conflict, etc.) appearing 27 times. Given the centrality of the Colonial Period and American Revolution in other forms of NRA communications, I was surprised that these themes were not more prevalent in my dataset. They were referenced only nine times.

Regardless of the period or conflict they covered, each of these articles were focused around either a specific firearm, a specific conflict, or both. Their titles generally went like "On Guard for America: Wartime Winchesters," "The Arab Revolt and the Guns of Lawrence of Arabia," or "An American Rifleman in the Battle for Germany." No matter the characters and setting, the central narrative of each article worked to emphasize the importance of a given firearm in the hands of individuals and groups, mostly Americans, who have fought and bled for the global cause of freedom.

For example, one article tells the story of Private Marsh, an American soldier during the Second World War in Germany who was issued the M1 Garand. Though the story is centered around Marsh's experiences, the M1 is the true protagonist of the story, while Marsh slides neatly into the archetype of the American hero. The article recounts Marsh's various adventures with the M1 Garand, from violent encounters such as his attacking a German machine gun to allow his troops to move forward, to moments of mercy, where he shared his food rations with two captured German deserters.[32]

The *American Rifleman* does not limit the scope of its historical articles to pieces on Americans, but often covers other historical periods, events, and people that it considers to be part of the broader global struggle for freedom. An article on "The Guns of Lawrence of Arabia" focuses on telling the story of T.E. Lawrence's exploits during the Arab Revolt. While the first half is focused on Lawrence, the second half shifts to telling the story of the firearms he used to achieve his exploits and his influence on the innovative use of technology in warfare. "The equipment used by T.E. Lawrence and his colleagues against the Turks was innovative, as was his untraditional approach to the employment of intelligence, aerial reconnaissance, and mobile gun platforms. His methodologies were game-changers."[33]

Yet another article tells the story of German Mauser rifles in the conflict that Israelis call the War of Independence (*Milhemet ha-Atzma'ut*), which lasted from either November of 1947 or May of 1948, depending on the starting date one uses, and lasted until early 1949.[34] The article begins by recounting the Israeli narrative of the state's foundation, and the crisis that Israel faced following its establishment. The author argues that the newly formed Israeli army did not have enough weapons to arm their soldiers since the Israelis relied on "older independence groups" like the Haganah to fight and that these soldiers were "poorly outfitted" underdogs fighting against "well-equipped armies from Egypt, Iraq and Jordan." According to the author: "It was a fight for survival and a fight against a second Holocaust."[35,36]

This article goes on to explain that two of the few nations friendly to Israel at the time were Czechoslovakia and Belgium, both countries with well-established firearms industries that had been left with large quantities of surplus German rifles from the war. "The Israeli War of Independence was, ironically, fought with large quantities of arms manufactured by Nazi Germany." So great was the need for weapons that the Israelis did not even remove the markings on the firearms. Soldiers, especially foreign volunteer fighters, "were issued wartime German flight suits and asked to fight in German planes. Signs of Nazi Germany were present on much of the equipment."[37] The Israelis eventually adopted the FN K98 Mauser Rifles as their main battle rifle. They bought thousands of them through Czechoslovakia. The author highlights that the Mauser continued to be used beyond the Six-Day War in 1967, but is now a collector's item. The article concludes: "Seventy years ago, after the atrocities of the Holocaust, men and women from all over the world took the initiative to go to Palestine and fight for an independent Jewish state. Their bravery and determination live on in the tools they used: those Mausers we now cherish as collectibles."[38]

These narratives contain several commonalities. On their own, they seem like rather innocuous pieces of writing, full of historical minutia to satisfy the curiosity of gun enthusiasts and amateur historians. Yet, considered together, patterns emerge. Each of the stories emphasizes the role that firearms played in the hands of individuals fighting for the global cause of freedom. Most often, these individuals are courageous American troops, or American allies. Despite their differences, they each contain the same policy moral: that firearms in the hands of individuals are an important part of the fight for liberty.

These articles further add to the mystique of the guns, imbuing these objects with deep meanings. Through the stories of these heroes and the firearms they used, these objects are tied to the meanings of these conflicts, in a way that motivates passionate gun owners to collect and shoot these gun decades later. These articles thus form an important part of NRA messaging that works to tie firearms to core American values like individual liberty through the use of historical narratives. By choosing macro-level narratives surrounding key points in American and global history, the NRA harnesses the deep meanings already attached to these events, tying firearms to the existing infrastructure of commemoration. The NRA does not need to rewrite these macro-narratives to do this. They simply need to emphasize the role that guns played in a part of that story.

The Israeli Mauser article is particularly noteworthy because it furthers the NRA's oft-repeated messaging that it is not the firearm itself that is evil, but the people using it. In this story, the Mauser Kar98k rifle, marked with the swastika, is symbolically redeemed by saving the nascent nation of Israel. Further, these same rifles are now available to collect, allowing the gun owner to join their own story to the history of this firearm.

The episodes of NRATV's *Curator's Corner* featured more personal stories of firearms in the hands of individuals in American history, though the sample of historical periods the show drew on was more varied than the pieces in the *American Rifleman.*

While the strategy of tying firearms to grand narratives is often used to connect guns to values, it can also be used to connect them emotionally. Understanding this involves touching on the thin line between history and memory. Oftentimes, our knowledge of historical periods is mediated by popular culture. Few time periods exemplify this as much as the so-called Wild West, the period of American expansion onto the western frontier. Our understanding of this period has been heavily distorted by Western novels and Hollywood blockbusters. Yet, while not entirely accurate, these pieces of popular culture have profoundly shaped how most Americans understand their history. They have introduced important archetypes into the popular imagination: the lone hero, the good sheriff, the robber, or the strong frontierswoman. They have also established the key plot tropes of the time: the gunfight, the train robbery, the bank robbery, the hanging, the Native American attack, and others. The popular understanding of this period, and the feelings and values that it elicits, are an important part of the frontier mentality that permeates American politics and provides a rich symbolism for politicians and movements to draw on.[39]

The NRA loves to tell these stories, emphasizing the importance of firearms as tools of survival and self-reliance in this period. A prime example of this is an episode of *Curator's Corner*, which profiles a silver Colt .45 six-shooter, the quintessential cowboy gun. The Colt is placed on a stand at the center of the table, while the two hosts discuss its design, features, and story. The barrel and receiver of the gun are richly engraved. The revolver's ivory handle has a bull's head carved into it. Behind the hosts, another table with the skull of what appears to be a bull rests atop an animal fur. Further back we see an American flag partially hidden by the displays of firearms: guns behind glass cases surrounded by dark wooden frames. The viewer gets the impression of being in a museum or a hunting lodge.

John, the host, opens the episode with a joke, noting that "It almost looks like if I called the props department and said 'give me something right out of a western,' they would produce a firearm like this, but this … this is not a prop." Jim, the other host, laughs at the joke, noting that the gun in front of them, like others in the museum, were "actually used by the lawmen and outlaws of the old west."

They explain that this particular firearm belonged to an outlaw, Black Jack Ketchum. The audience is shown a black and white photo of Black Jack. He is wearing a suit and bowtie, glaring at the camera, his meticulously groomed handlebar mustache perched atop a frown. "He not only was a bad man, but he was also very bad at being a bad man." It turns out he was, "one of the most bad luck train robbers you'll ever run into." The camera shows bounty posters for Black Jack. Jim also explains that he "ran with the Hole in the Wall Gang," an infamous gang of outlaws made famous by Butch Cassidy. Jim tells the story of Black Jack's falling out with his brother, who was killed following a botched train robbery. Black Jack tried to rob the same train a month later. The conductor, having been robbed twice before, was armed with a shotgun and shot Black Jack in the arm during the robbery. Black Jack was found by the law the next day and was hung.[40]

The NRA works to connect the excitement and nostalgia of popular depictions of historical periods towards the guns of that time. Thus, tying guns to grand historical narratives is done not only to draw on the values of the time but on the emotion that this period evokes, due to the exposure of gun owners to popular depictions of guns in movies and television series. Popular representations of history are yet another aspect of the infrastructure of commemoration that the NRA works to turn into support for its cause.

The macro-narrative that I labelled innovation and invention is a powerful theme in American culture. The idea of constant progress through science and technology emerged during the industrial revolution and has been a fixture of the American psyche ever since. It has led Americans to seek technological solutions to every problem imaginable. The history of great discoveries, and the famous women and men who invented them, has made the names of Americans like the Wright Brothers, Henry Ford, Bill Gates, and countless other household names. The NRA taps into this macro-narrative often in its communications, touting the intelligence and ingenuity of the American inventors of the gun world like Benjamin-Tyler Henry, Oliver Winchester, Samuel Colt, John Moses Browning, Eugene Stoner, and Eliphalet Remington. Tying firearms to the narrative of technological progress is important for linking these objects with American identity. Firearms are presented as uniquely American innovations and a symbol of American scientific prowess. This narrative is present in both the NRA's written and online communications material.

This narrative was one of the most common and showed up in 37 out of the 100 *American Rifleman* articles. Though it was usually conveyed through language, it is often done through imagery as well. For example, the centerfold of the February 2019 issue features a two page-sized image of a Winchester Repeating Arms cartridge board from the late nineteenth century.[41] The magazine explains that these cartridge boards were used to advertise firearms in a time before catalogs were sent to houses, or people could browse guns on the internet. This is interesting for several reasons. First, it attempts to build the reader's affective ties with Winchester Repeating Arms through nostalgia. The ad, and the context given to it by the editors, evoke a yearning for a simpler time in American life. Further, they emphasize the longevity and American pedigree of the Winchester company. Winchester's guns and ammunition are positioned as important American artifacts, telling the story of the development of modern American capitalism.

Though firearms that are perceived to be associated with hunting tend to be less controversial in the Great Gun Debate, the *American Rifleman* also works to tie more contentious firearms to the story of American innovation as well. The February 2019 edition featured a full-page photograph of an American soldier test-firing an AR-15 during the firearms trials with the Air Force. When the military holds a competition to select the firearms that it will issue to soldiers, the guns are put through a series of rigorous tests. The design of the semi-automatic AR-15 would ultimately be chosen by the Air Force, and then the army, and adapted into the fully automatic M16 and M4 carbine. A small paragraph gives the reader the context for the image, concluding that "The results of the tests, which were conducted to determine the rifle's competency in replacing the old M1, is now well-recorded in history."[42] Given the symbolism of the AR-15 in the gun debate since the Sandy Hook massacre, this seemingly innocuous black and white photo conveys quite a bit of meaning. Devotees know what comes next, but like a comic book fan reading the origin story of their favorite superhero, tracing the foundations is exciting. Further, showing this piece of the origin story of the semi-automatic carbines helps to weave it into the story of American innovation and development.

Firearms and the Second Amendment as Heritage

Heritage is the past that is owned. It is a way of claiming ownership over certain elements of the past and is often intimately linked to political identity and political claims.[43] Heritage can be something tangible, like historic sites, sites of natural beauty or objects and buildings; things that can be touched, felt, experienced, tasted, seen, and heard. Considering certain traditions, crafts, social practices, and sports, it is clear heritage can be intangible as well.[44] Given that heritage is owned, it must, therefore, be cared for and protected. Being able to claim something as heritage or tradition is a powerful tool to justify the preservation of that object, site, or practice. The NRA understands the value of claiming the Second Amendment, private gun ownership, hunting, and the shooting sports as American heritage. It is a technique that they employ often in their written and online material.

Themes related to American Heritage emerged 25 times across the dataset. For example, 10 per cent of the *American Rifleman* articles that I analyzed contained references to the Second Amendment, firearms, hunting, or the shooting sports as American heritage. A further 56 items attempted to tie guns to American heritage (coded as American Guns). Articles focusing on firearms as tangible heritage generally presented the objects as important pieces of Americana, emphasizing that they represented history that you could take home with you, collect, and possess. These articles focused on touting the mechanical innovation of these objects, as well as emphasizing their links to key moments or themes in American history, such as sacrifice.

For example, an article on the last Colt M1911 pistols ever issued to the military focuses heavily on this theme. The piece notes the long service record of the M1911, having served as America's principal sidearm in both the First and Second World Wars and into Vietnam. It concludes that the current trend of equipping soldiers with Austrian-made Glock's will soon see the M1911 retired from service "thus ending a long and historic run for the M1911 and its .45 ACP cartridge." The article emphasizes, however, that the firearm will live on in the hands of American collectors. "The pistols are exceptional purely as shooters and scarce and significant for several military and historic reasons. We are fortunate that they found their way onto the public market."[45]

The NRA also works hard to present the cultural practices associated with gun ownership as intangible cultural heritage. Two examples stand out in this regard. The first is an article on traditional rifle making at Colonial Williamsburg. The article is an overview of the gunsmithing program that operates in Colonial Williamsburg. This program aims to preserve the traditional craft of making the American Longrifle, a muzzle-loading, single-shot rifle used extensively during the revolutionary period and the initial westward expansion of the US. The article provides a brief history of the firearm but focuses mostly on the process of making them. The article notes that the design of these rifles was "adapted to the requirements of surviving on the American frontier," and that they have been described as the first uniquely North American technological innovation. The process of making these rifles is presented as a key part of American heritage: "With every stroke of the hammer, every pass of the file, the gunsmiths of Colonial Williamsburg are perpetuating the art of handmaking the American rifle." The article also highlights the musket firing program at Colonial Williamsburg, which allows visitors to experience shooting a musket. The experience is described as "immersing yourself in a historical context that you not only see but also feel, smell and taste." It was designed to "put history into people's hands." The participant is said to gain a deeper understanding of history through this practice, acquiring "A fundamental understanding of the historic battlefield down to its most basic technology" and learning "lessons that can't be learned from reading a book or looking at objects behind glass." The article concludes by describing the men whose hands are said to be keeping the tradition alive. "At Colonial Williamsburg, those hands belong to men standing right behind the counter, preserving the history and heritage of gunmaking in America by living it each day, and in the process, reminding us that a rifle can still be built one piece at a time."[46] Here we see both the firearm and the process of making it claimed as American heritage.

True to its name, the *American Rifleman* also presents rifle shooting as an important and unique part of American heritage. In the article *Three Traditions of the Rifle,* this is made explicit from the very beginning. The article opens with the claim that even the word rifleman is uniquely American. "Many cultures embrace hunting, and quite a few have rifles commonly accessible for defense, but none as populous as ours has such a large and vital following dedicated to real skill at arms with the long gun." The current practice of rifle shooting is connected to the long history of riflemen in America. "From early colonists with their matchlocks to the present, a continuous thread of cultural association with the rifle and the importance of marksmanship runs through our history." The article goes on to present three different disciplines of modern rifle shooting: precision shooting, classic shooting, and defensive shooting. While the cover page for this article features a vintage, sepia image of a man firing a wooden-stocked, M1 Garand rifle, the images that accompany the explanations of each discipline are much more modern, as are the sporting rifles these images feature. Besides the page devoted to precision rifle shooting, an image features a man in khaki pants and a sports polo kneeling on a set of rocks. The rocks have been spray-painted with the number three, clearly the third station in the competition. The man's rifle is a bolt action but could easily be mistaken for an AR-15 by someone less familiar with firearms, given its black metal construction and use of modern accessories, like a barrel shroud.[47] It is adorned with a scope and a silencer. The image next to the section on classic rifle shooting features an Olympic shooter. Wearing a team USA jersey and standing on a laminate gymnasium floor, her rifle is an Olympic-style precision rifle. Next to the section on defensive shooting, we see yet another man, also in a dynamic pose. The man is wearing a sports polo with the logo of his team and sponsors, khaki pants, dark-tinted eye protection, and a backward baseball cap. Rather than center the shot on his face, the center of the image is occupied by his rifle. The rifle is an AR platform rifle, with a low-powered scope mounted on top.[48]

The combination of the opening text, descriptions, and images make a series of political claims. First, the article opens by declaring the tradition of rifle shooting, not pistol shooting, to be a unique part of American heritage. This is further supported by the sepia image of the man firing the M1 Garand, the main battle rifle of American soldiers fighting the Second World War. As the article transitions into the modern rifle sports, it connects these sports and the contentious "modern sporting rifles" like the AR-15 to this American heritage of rifle shooting. Positioning modern shooting sports and semi-automatic carbines next to Olympic athletes also serves to de-politicize these tools.

While the strategy of presenting firearms and the Second Amendment as heritage was common in the *American Rifleman*, it was most pronounced in the NRA's online television content, especially in *Armed & Fabulous*. Virtually all the episodes directly referred to heritage or used terms that referred to heritage such as preservation, legacy, and conservation. For example, one episode features the Hill family and their large farm. Julie Hill, the protagonist of the episode, describes having been inspired by attending the NRA meeting with her husband. "I want to be able to protect myself, and I fear that those rights are going to be taken away, and I really wanted to help." She recounts meeting NRA Chief Executive Wayne Lapierre at the meeting, a longtime friend of her fathers. She talked to Wayne about wanting to help the NRA like her father had, carrying on her family legacy. She asked Lapierre how she could help, but he told her that it was "up to her to choose." She says this gave her an epiphany, as she realized "What the Second Amendment meant to me." She is shown touching her heart for emphasis when giving this line. "A person who doesn't hunt ... doesn't really hunt, but believes yes I want to protect myself and I want to protect my family." This led her to the Women's Leadership Forum, a sub-organization within the NRA that runs much of the NRA programs targeting women. With the help of Lapierre, she created the "Women's Leadership Forum Endowment," insisting, "It's time. It's time for the women to stand up. All women. Ones that work. Ones that are moms. Moms that having nothing to do with guns at all. Ones that believe in their Second Amendment rights."

Julie goes on, noting that her friends were surprised that women were involved in the NRA, and scoffing at the fact that the organization is portrayed as an "old boys' club." Julie's daughter Margo is then shown, and talks about how happy she is that her mom is carrying on her family legacy, having donated her massive family farm, complete with a working private railroad, as a hunting ground for the NRA. She describes the farm and the train as part of her grandpa John's legacy, and how the NRA is connected to this legacy. Julie says: "I really feel this is how I could stand up and fight, by starting this endowment and paying that forward for my children." Her children Margo and Aidan talk about wanting to join this legacy and protect the Second Amendment. Her husband gets the last word: "We're gonna carry on the family tradition big time."

Here the Second Amendment is clearly presented as heritage, an imperiled tradition in need of protection by the NRA, with the help of "ordinary" families. The concepts of family and the NRA are interwoven into this narrative as well, for maximum emotional impact. Just as the Hill family contributes to the protection of American heritage through the generous donation of their family farm, so too is the NRA positioned as a key defender of this heritage.[49]

Olympic shotgun shooter Kim Rhode, who I had the opportunity to meet in person at the NRA convention, refers to heritage several times in her own NRATV episode. She emphasizes the way that the NRA helps women and youth and raises awareness of the shotgun sports. She says the NRA is "on the forefront fighting for our rights and also for our children's rights." She feels that it is important to pass on the heritage of shooting sports to her children, and feels the NRA is a big part of that.[50] In all three of these examples, we see the NRA positioned as an ally to families, and individual women, seeking to preserve their tradition of firearms ownership, hunting, and sports shooting. The language of heritage is directly employed, and it is suggested, though never said allowed, that these traditions are in danger.

The practice of hunting is most consistently presented throughout the series using the language of heritage. Sometimes this is done literally, such as Gaye Kelsey, who describes her fashion sense, a mix of traditional hunting gear with more feminine accents, paying tribute to the heritage of wildlife and hunting.[51] Others evoke the language of heritage to describe hunting, like Melanie Pepper who says that hunting is in her flesh and blood.[52]

Given that gender is omnipresent in the *Armed & Fabulous* series, several of these episodes also make sure to reference the special place that women hold in preserving the Second Amendment and the traditions of the outdoors. Sandra, one of the women interviewed, sums this up nicely in her episode: "A woman doesn't have to hunt, but if they know the truth about hunting and conservation they can pass that on to their children and encourage them to support it in any way they can."[53]

The conclusion of Hilary's episode features an especially emotional appeal from her father that follows this theme. While video footage of Hilary and her father on various old hunting trips is shown, his voice plays over the screen: "You know I never thought that a daughter would be able to take the place of a son in the world of adventure ... She has entered a field which was previously male-dominated and has excelled and been a role model for other girls and women." Hilary interjects: "My voice is powerful. It can be used for something valuable. That's what I'm here for. That is my purpose." Her father talks about Hilary being his legacy, and how she is carrying on his ideas into the next generation. "The greatest gift I give to the NRA is my daughter, who can continue the fight and the mission for decades to come, long after I'm gone." The video ends with pictures of Hilary and her father.[54] This emotional sequence packs a lot into a short space. Once again, the organization is drawing on the raw emotion of the family bond, a bond that most of us can relate to, and tying it in to the fight to preserve gun rights. Here gun rights are once transformed into heritage, Hilary's father's legacy, that supporters are called to defend. Further, defending that heritage is positioned as an act of empowerment for women who, after years of exclusion from the gun culture, are now being called upon to embrace and defend it.

By claiming ownership over the past, heritage is a powerful tool for motivating supporters. We see many examples of this in the NRA's written and digital material. The organization very effectively ties the Second Amendment, the shooting sports, hunting, and private gun ownership into a unique American heritage that its supporters must protect.

Close to Home

Examining this set of articles from *American Rifleman* and episodes from NRATV episodes gives us a better understanding of how the organization tells stories about America's and Americans' pasts in order to build a political community of gun owners. As we have seen, the organization draws on three forms of the past: memory, history, and heritage. This past presencing is used to connect firearms to American history and identity. Through memory, firearms are personalized. They are transformed from an ordinary object to a family heirloom and family protector. Through history, these objects are tied to the nation's past, and to the broader cause of freedom considered so central to its dominant narrative. Through heritage, firearms, hunting, the shooting sports, and the Second Amendment are claimed as uniquely American, things that must be protected by the NRA and the wider community of gun owners.

4 Building Culture at the NRA Annual Meeting

But culturally, guns aren't just a reaction to anxieties. In a way gun control advocates rarely consider, but gun owners may find obvious, they're a meaningful social asset for their owners. In a fragmented society, guns connect people at a time when making connections is ever more difficult.

– Austin Sarat & Jonathan Obert[1]

On April 26, 2019, the NRA took over Indianapolis. It was a windy day, and I got up early to attend the first day of the NRA convention. After a few days on the road from Ottawa, this would be my first face-to-face contact with the organization. The wind buffeted my SUV from side to side as I pulled onto the highway. I was still groggy as I had not bothered to grab a cup of weak hotel coffee on my way out in the morning. Driving along the I-70 expressway toward downtown Indianapolis, I passed trailer parks, suburban homes, and then apartment buildings as I made my way to the city's compact downtown core. Suddenly my eyes locked onto a large blue billboard that read "Indy Welcomes the NRA." A lightning bolt of exhilaration broke through the clouds of my decaffeinated brain. I had arrived.

When asked to describe the NRA Annual Meeting (NRAAM) by friends, colleagues, and journalists, I find the best metaphor is that of a comic book convention. Perhaps the fact that this resonates with my audience is a testament to my social circle, but I find the comparison conveys the pure frenetic energy of over 80,000 people gathering in a large convention center to engage with something that they are passionate about. At the convention, Second Amendment supporters come together to meet their peers as well as their idols, from right-wing political leaders to YouTube celebrities, Olympic shooters, and Hollywood icons. They come to learn more about their serious leisure pursuit, to shop, and to hear and tell stories.

Understanding the role that points of contact between the NRA and its active and potential membership play in the organization's larger political strategy is important for tracing the organization's influence. These points of contact include the Annual Meeting, firearms safety classes, gun shows, and the NRA museum. The next two chapters will focus on my participant observation at the 2019 NRAAM in Indianapolis, Indiana. Several authors have used participant observation to study the NRA,[2] and I am not the first to attend the Annual Meeting as part of my ethnography.[3] Given that the meeting is the largest gathering of NRA members in the United States, it provided an ideal first field site for participant observation.

In this chapter, I argue that the NRA uses points of contact, like the Annual Meeting, to work towards the social construction of the gun culture in America, which provides it with a foundation of political support. As we have already discussed, there is ample evidence that individuals who are deeply involved in the gun culture are more likely to take political action, and that this is true regardless of gender identity.[4] Providing an opportunity for the community of gun owners to gather and deepen their ties with the organization; in other words, engaging in community building, is a political strategy for the NRA. The annual meeting provides an opportunity for them to reach out to the three core groups it aims to attract. First, it allows the organization to deepen its relationship with its existing members, encouraging them to become more involved through purchasing membership upgrades, participating in programs, buying merchandise, and becoming more politically active. For the gun-curious, and members of the gun-owning community who have not yet joined the organization, it uses the lure of a gun show to bring them in, compel them to become members, and encourage them to get active.

Showtime

I pulled off the freeway into downtown Indianapolis, where my phone's GPS led me to the parking lot I had researched online. Normally reserved for NFL football games, the parking lot had been taken over by the convention. I was more than an hour early for the opening of the event and the lot was already almost full. I walked past the hulking brick façade of Lucas Oil stadium to make my way toward the convention center. Though it was not set to begin until 11 a.m., hardcore supporters were already lined up to get in to see the ILA Leadership Forum, which would feature a speech by President Trump.[5] Airport-style security stations were set up by the entrance to the stadium, staffed by heavily armed and armored secret service agents. A recording of a woman's voice played over the loudspeaker: "Lucas Oil Stadium is under the control of the United States Secret Services. The following items are prohibited."[6] Given security concerns surrounding the VIPs in attendance, the stadium was the only place in the convention where carrying a concealed firearm was not permitted.

Walking past the stadium, I entered Indianapolis Convention Center from a side door, passed the press registration, and emerged into the main thoroughfare, which was already filled with people. I walked up to the visitor registration area, where NRA volunteers standing in front of touch screens checked membership cards and handed out convention passes. I waited in a short line behind a greying man, dressed in business casual clothes and holding a bag and a lunch box. In front of him stood a couple in their 40s or 50s. The man wore a leather biker vest with a section of the Second Amendment stitched onto the back. When I finally reached the front of the line, I was greeted by a volunteer, a kindly woman in her 60s with brown hair and glasses.

"Do you have a membership card, dear?" she asked, smiling nervously.

Unlike the volunteers helping other guests, she did not try to up-sell my membership. She seemed a bit frazzled by the computer system and her supervisor, a young man with brown hair wearing a grey suit, was losing patience with her.

Thanking the volunteer, I slipped the lanyard with my convention pass over my head, and crossed the lobby to yet another line: breakfast. While waiting, I struck up a conversation with a large man with a long, forked salt and pepper beard behind me. Like many people there, he was wearing a t-shirt with pro-gun messaging, and was quite chatty.

"Quite the crowd, eh?" I said. I would have to get better at concealing my Canadian idiosyncrasies.

"It's going to be a busy day," he replied. "Where are you from?"

The experience of being at a convention has interesting impacts on people's social behavior. Knowing that others around you share a common interest makes convention-goers more comfortable striking up conversations with strangers. Though I had come to the convention alone, I never wanted for conversational partners.

Coffee and muffin in hand, I walked to a nearby table and settled in to watch the crowd. The exhibition hall doors were not yet open, and the lobby was filling with people milling about and registering. Everywhere I looked I saw camo, cowboy boots, denim, and leather. There were businessmen, friend groups, and families. The average age of most people there was probably in the upper 40s. The crowd was overwhelmingly white and male, yet I was surprised by the number of women and people of color in attendance. Though there were a few groups of women who had come alone, most were accompanied by a husband or boyfriend, whereas there were many groups of male friends that had come together. Families were in attendance, parents pushing strollers or with young children walking in tow. As I scanned the crowd, the most popular items of dress I noticed were camo baseball caps, but a few people also wore cowboy hats and red "Make America Great Again" (MAGA) hats as well, indicating their support for then-President Trump. Many people sported NRA or firearm related t-shirts or wore polos or tactical clothing like cargo pants and polyester shirts. This is a testament to the recent success of clothing brands like 5.11 Tactical, which cater to gun owners and especially concealed carriers. Clothing items like these are designed to make it easier for the wearer to carry a concealed firearm or other items in what the community refers to as their "everyday carry" (EDC).[7] These companies also cater to those with an appetite for "tactical"[8] wear, which is becoming increasingly popular within the gun-owning community.[9]

The families and groups waiting in the lobby did not want for entertainment as they waited for the show to begin. The NRA shop had opened an hour before the convention. As a result, it was filled to the brim with people killing time. The shop sold a panoply of NRA paraphernalia, like t-shirts, sweaters, and accessories. Customers left with NRA-branded wallets, keychains, or bumper stickers; gun gear like cleaning equipment and range bags, and objects related to personal security, like a portable door jammer that can be used to secure a room that could not otherwise be locked, presumably in the event of an armed attack. Selling NRA-branded swag allows the organization to market itself and gives members an opportunity to showcase their political beliefs on their person, their car, or their house, an increasingly popular trend in American society.

Leaving the crowded shop, I wandered through the convention center lobby, where companies like Remington were already handing out raffle tickets and promotions to try to drive visitors to their booths. One raffle had already begun. The "Wall of Guns" was placed at the intersection of two of the convention center's main arteries. This large, double-sided glass case was filled with an array of rifles, shotguns, and pistols. There were a few bolt-action or lever-action guns alongside semi-automatic carbines and handguns. A speaker system was set up next to the display and the MC was channeling his inner auctioneer trying to convince people to buy tickets: "A 1-in-100 chance, ladies and gentlemen! Get your ticket here."

Passing the wall of guns, I entered the air gun[10] range, which occupied one of the seminar rooms adjoining the main lobby. Since the Indianapolis Convention Center obviously could not accommodate a live gun range, they had set up the next best thing, sponsored by a major air gun company, to accommodate the itchy trigger fingers of attendees. I got in line and quickly moved up, past a woman in a red volunteer vest handing out safety glasses.

"It seems busy," I said, "How many people have come through here so far?"

"Oh, quite a few," the volunteer replied. She took a quick look at her hand-held clicker counter. "We've only been open half an hour and we've already had about 100 people."

When a bench opened up, the volunteer directed me towards the range safety officer, a stout middle-aged man wearing a bright yellow safety jacket and NRA baseball cap. He explained how to use the air rifle and helped me load my first shot; a conical lead pellet. The wall had been set up to resemble a shooting stand from a carnival. There were swinging metal air rifle targets, whiffle balls on strings, and even a model train set. I pulled the trigger and hit the target. Using a scoped air rifle at such a short distance made me feel like cowboy icon John Wayne. It was hard to miss.

As the convention opening drew closer, I heard a commotion and joined the throng gathering by the main convention center doors, where Oliver North, on the eve of his exit from his position as President, was giving the convention's opening address. There was such a crowd around the retired lieutenant colonel and former Fox News commentator that I could hardly see him and only barely caught the end of his speech.

Following North's address, the national anthem was sung. Everyone removed their hats and sang along, and my voice joined the chorus of bowed heads and solemn faces. I have been to a few sporting events in my life where attendees sing the national anthem at the beginning of the game. Never before had I felt an atmosphere of intensity like the one that I experienced that morning. Given the conservative political values I presumed that most of the crowd held, this was not surprising. The NRA attracts many veterans, who wish to continue shooting as a sport or hobby following their retirement from the military. Some people in the room with me had lost loved ones, friends, or sacrificed personally for their country. Some bore their scars on their person or were missing limbs. Others wished to make a visible show of support and enact or express their political values in some concrete way. This is referred to in the social sciences as "performativity,"[11] and sometimes derided in the public sphere as "virtue signaling" by those on both sides of the political trenches. Yet, just as people in my department perform their political values through the use of language, calling their spouse a "partner" rather than the vernacular "husband" or "wife," and through ritual, such as beginning a lecture or conference with a reference to Indigenous land claims, NRA members perform their political values through paying respect to political traditions and the nation state. Including rituals like singing the national anthem allows people at the convention, and the organization itself, to perform their political values. It is also another way that the NRA actively works to tie the organization to American identity.

The use of the term "performativity" is not meant to suggest that these displays were any less genuine. Standing next to me in the dense crowd there was a family; a blond mother in her late 30s held her infant son in her arms, singing the lyrics of the anthem in his ear. She kissed him on the cheek as the final notes of the anthem rang out and the crowd erupted in applause. The emotional impact of this civic ritual, and this moment of intimacy connected to it, is difficult to convey in writing. Suffice it to say that it makes you feel a part of something larger.

As the final notes died down, North declared the convention open, and the mass of people surged forward towards the bright light at the other end of the showroom doors. I was at the rear of the crowd, and it took me almost five minutes of awkward shuffling to get in. It soon became clear that I was not the only one shocked by the size of the crowd. Entering the exhibition hall, I saw a retailer look up from his clipboard and notice that a queue had already formed in front of his booth. "Holy shit," he exclaimed.

The NRAAM has many moving pieces. The original purpose of the meeting was just that: a meeting of members. This Annual Meeting of Members still occurs, taking the form of a formal board meeting where members raise motions and concerns with the board, and give attendees a chance to hear senior executives "share a vision of the NRA going forward."[12] It was at a meeting like this that the revolt in Cincinnati happened, and the NRA old guard was replaced with newer, more militant members, led by Harlan Carter. Some authors have argued that this event fundamentally changed the nature of the organization from that of a service group to a political lobby group.[13] This is not why people flock to the NRAAM, though. They come for the show.

Serious Leisure

How do we make sense of gun ownership, the gun culture, and the community of gun owners? I argue that gun ownership can be understood as a form of what sociologists call "serious leisure."[14] This concept was first coined by Stebbins[15] and reflects the fact that in post-industrial societies, some leisure activities have moved away from simply being a "happy, carefree refuge from our earnest pursuit of money and social standing"[16] and become "a way of finding personal fulfillment, identity enhancement, self-expression" and other benefits.[17] Serious leisure is increasingly important in shaping "the meanings people give their lives" and has expanded the focus of the social science on more traditional indicators of identity formation like "work, family and religion."[18] Serious leisure is a separate analytical category from casual leisure. Unlike serious leisure, casual leisure is "immediately intrinsically rewarding, relatively short-lived pleasurable activity requiring little or no special training to enjoy." For example, playing a game, relaxing, watching television, having sex, etc.[19]

Serious leisure involves things like volunteer work, amateurism, and hobbyist pursuits, and is separated from casual leisure by six key characteristics: benefit, effort, perseverance, careers, ethos, and identity. The benefits that serious leisure provides can be internal, like self-actualization or feelings of accomplishment and fulfilment, or external, like a sense of community. Because serious leisure provides people with these benefits, participants expend tremendous effort to gain skills, knowledge, and training in their given activity. This involves persevering through difficult conditions like injuries or embarrassments. Participants in serious leisure often have secondary careers within their leisure activities. Finally, serious leisure activities often develop their own unique ethos, or shared "beliefs, values, moral principles, norms and performance standards." Thus, serious leisure activities become a part of participants' identity; their sense of who they are.[20]

Participation in the gun culture is a form of serious leisure.[21] Hunters, collectors, target shooters, and self-defense shooters often invest a significant amount of effort, personal capital, time, and labor into practicing their given activity.

For example, a survey of over 5,000 American target shooters showed that respondents demonstrated a deep level of engagement in the activity. A total of 78.8 per cent of respondents had been engaged in the sport for longer than 15 years. Only 10 per cent had been involved for less than 5 years.[22] More than 57 per cent of respondents reloaded their own ammunition, a laborious and time-consuming process that takes a significant amount of upfront investment and training, yet ultimately provides high volume shooters with a cost-effective means of producing their own personalized ammunition.[23]

More importantly, firearms owners within the gun culture share an ethos and sense of identity and belonging. They attach significant meanings to the tools that they use and are reluctant to surrender them. This ethos and identity did not develop in a vacuum, however. They have been shaped by powerful actors within the community of gun owners, foremost among them the NRA.

Serious leisure differs most from casual leisure in the benefits it offers participants. Since Stebbins first coined the term, there has been an explosion in studies of serious leisure. Stebbins's original piece changed the way social scientists studied leisure and launched an entire subfield of sociology devoted to studying leisure.[24] Researchers have studied numerous serious leisure activities like dog sports,[25] gardening,[26] dancing,[27] off-road driving,[28] and participation in the gun culture.[29] Research in this domain has demonstrated that participation in serious leisure activities is correlated with things like "personal growth and happiness,"[30] "overall life satisfaction,"[31] and the development of their personal and collective identity.[32] Serious leisure participants often reported more satisfaction from these activities than casual leisure participants.[33]

Looking at participation in the gun culture as serious leisure helps us to understand the intense attachment that gun owners have to their guns, sports, and hobbies. It also helps us to understand the political success of the NRA, and why the organization includes a gun show as part of its annual meeting.

Serious leisure participants are primed towards collective action when their leisure activity is challenged. While traditional collective action was seen to revolve around an individual's class identity, and later their sexual, religious, or political identity, more recent scholarship demonstrates that serious leisure may also provide a motivation for collective action. In essence, when individuals "ground a sense of self and community in their leisure activities" they will be more likely to "take action to protect the foundation of their identity narratives when opposing forces threaten these foundations."[34]

The Exhibition Hall

The exhibition hall at the Indianapolis convention was 15 acres large, bigger than 11 football fields, and contained over 800 exhibitors. It was so big that the NRA released a convention app to help attendees navigate the massive space. It was not until the third day of the convention that I was fully able to get around the showroom without getting lost.

There are a few reasons that the NRA includes a gun show as part of their annual gathering. The first is that it brings people in. A post-convention survey conducted by the NRA shows that 78 per cent of attendees came for the sole reason of attending the gun show.[35] The prospect of being able to join in on one of the largest gun shows in the world draws firearm enthusiasts from around the US to the convention in order to explore new guns, accessories, and other products and services.[36] The spectacle of the exhibition hall is also a big part of the draw. People come to see new products being announced and released, to meet celebrities who have become associated with Second Amendment rights, and to be part of the zeitgeist. There is something exciting about being where the action is happening, surrounded by people who share the same passion as you. The largest gun show in the world, Shot Show in Las Vegas, is only open to those who work in the firearms and ammunition industry. Many gun owners get only a glimpse of it through reading magazine articles or watching videos online. Given that it is open to anyone with $45 to buy a membership, the NRAAM gives attendees the feeling of having a peek into an exclusive world, and a sense of belonging within their leisure community.

When talking to participants, a common refrain was their feelings of social exclusion or stigma in everyday life. This was true for gun owners that I met in rural, "red" areas like Lynchburg as well as those living in "blue" zones like DC or northern Virginia. Gun owners often expressed feeling the need to hide their serious leisure pursuit from coworkers, family members, or friends, for fear of judgement. Others spoke of feelings of stigma engendered from the broader cultural and political industries. The experience of being surrounded by people who you know share your opinions on firearm policy and your enthusiasm for firearms, which are often central or deeply held pieces of a gun owners' identity, is intensely enjoyable. This is a central reason why conventions exist in the first place, and another parallel between geek culture and the gun culture.

Another major motivation for the NRA to include a gun show as part of the annual meeting is to help fund the meeting, both through driving increased attendance and through fees collected from exhibitors and advertisers. The National Shooting Sports Foundation (NSSF), the trade association for the firearms and ammunition industry, estimates that the industry is responsible for employing over 330,000 Americans, and has an annual economic impact of over US $60 billion.[37] Vendors coming to the NRAAM know that they will have access to consumers. The NRA actively promotes the event to vendors by providing statistics on attendees, noting, for example, that the average visitor spent over $100 at the show.[38] Vendors, in turn, fund the show through renting space at the convention or through sponsorships and advertisements.

The gun show entices visitors and people in the industry, creating a point of contact between the community of gun owners and the NRA. The organization can then use this point of contact to attract new members and bring existing members more fully into the organization. Certain elements of this are quite material. For example, attending the NRAAM is free, but you must be an NRA member. As a result, the organization sells memberships at the door. This was done using an array of machines

set up at the various entrances to the convention hall, staffed by volunteers helping visitors use the machines. New members were signed
up, and existing members were able to upgrade their memberships at
a discounted rate. For example, an NRA life membership usually costs
$1,200 dollars whereas, at the convention, one could be purchased for
only $600.

The exhibition hall offered an excellent window into the material culture of the gun-owning community. Gun culture is centered around this
material culture. After all, this culture is based around a material object,
a gun, though that material object takes on a variety of symbolisms and
meanings. Exploring the exhibition hall gave me a different vantage
point through which to explore gun culture. No longer was I peering
at it behind a laptop screen, or through a YouTube video. It was right in
front of me.

Throughout the weekend I often felt dwarfed by the sheer scale of
the showroom. It was an intensely overwhelming experience. The hundreds of booths were filled with firearms, knives, clothing, gear, accessories, and everything related, no matter how vaguely, to the gun world.
Though the convention hall was large, it still managed to feel crowded,
and the main arteries were often clogged with people wandering from
booth to booth. Navigating the fracas reminded me of my past travels
to the crowded markets of Bangkok and Beijing as I jostled through the
crowd, trying not to bump into people gazing excitedly at the spectacle
surrounding us.

Some of the larger companies in the small arms and ammunition
industry, like Smith & Wesson, Beretta, Sig Sauer, and Glock occupied the
bigger booths on the showroom floor. Some were so large they had their
own stages which were used for raffles, contests, and product demonstrations or releases. The Glock booth, for example, was framed by a massive
back wall, three times taller than a person, dividing off their booth and
covered with photos of law enforcement, military, and civilians standing
at the ready with their Glock handguns. These dividers helped to direct
the flow of traffic to their booth and advertise their products.

It is no accident that gun companies like Glock have become the giants
of the industry, as they have been the best at capitalizing on recent shifts
in the gun culture by providing guns to cater to the rising demand for
self-defense equipment. For most of America's modern history, firearms
remained largely a tool of hunters and sports shooters, a group labelled
"Gun Culture 1.0" by sociologist David Yamane.[39] Starting in the 1980s
and accelerating into the 1990s and early 2000s however, the "center
of gravity" of the gun culture shifted towards self-defense and "armed
citizenship."[40] For example, between 1999 and 2013, the number of

people claiming that self-defense was a primary motivation for firearms ownership rose from 26 per cent to 48 per cent. This number was even higher, 63 per cent in the 2015 National Firearms Survey. Another way that this shift has been measured is in firearms advertising. The proportion of ads in the *American Rifleman* magazine that feature Gun Culture 1.0 themes (hunting or sports shooting) versus those that look at Gun Culture 2.0 themes (self-defense and concealed carry) has shifted drastically. While the proportion of ads featuring hunting and sports shooting has declined, the number of ads targeting self-defense and concealed carry have risen sharply.[41]

There were also a variety of smaller companies that specialized in firearms parts and accessories. These were often divided into different sections of the convention. Some companies were so specialized their entire business consisted of making triggers for a particular model of firearm. Since the trigger of a firearm can vary greatly in terms of sensitivity, which can then greatly impact shooting performance, many high volume or competition shooters prefer to install custom triggers in their rifles. One of the reasons the AR platform[42] is so popular is because the gun was designed to be very customizable, and because aftermarket parts are so widely available for it. It is comparable to buying a Toyota or Honda, rather than importing an uncommon sports car from Europe; you know you will be able to find affordable parts to upgrade it or fix it when it breaks[43]

Given that this was my first gun show, I was surprised to learn that booth visitors were free to pick up the unloaded firearms at each booth, most of which were attached to the booth using a metal wire, like a laptop displayed at an electronics store. At first, I was shy to do this, relegating myself to looking. But as it became clear through observation that the logic of appropriateness dictated that one could in fact pick up a firearm to test the sights, cycle the action or even pull the trigger, I joined in. While taking my Canadian Firearms Safety Course and gaining experience with firearms in Canada, muzzle control[44] had been so strictly trained into me that the thought of pointing even a disabled and clearly unloaded firearm in an unsafe direction made me uneasy. At a convention like this, such control was impractical, and I was at first shocked and unnerved to see muzzles pointing every which way.

The nearly 15,000 firearms on the showroom floor had been disabled as each bore a yellow NRA tag indicating this. I did not immediately appreciate the scale of this undertaking until I ran into a show volunteer who explained that he and a small army of volunteers had spent most of their night removing the firing pins from every single firearm that would be present on the showroom floor. The firing pin on a gun is what ignites the primer of the ammunition once the trigger is pulled. When removed it renders the gun inoperable, even if someone smuggled live ammunition into the show.

As the convention progressed, I got used to the constant clicking of triggers in the background and started to notice the firearms training ingrained in people. Most still instinctively pointed their firearms up or down while handling them, looking down the sights, testing the actions and trying out the triggers. I never saw anyone intentionally point a firearm at another person.

Having a little over a year of shooting under my belt, I was able to appreciate the differences in sight picture[45] the firearms offered and was beginning to be able to distinguish a good trigger from a bad one.[46]

Other features of the convention floor included the hunting booths, where hunting trips both foreign and domestic were advertised at ornately decorated stalls. Some of the more exotic stalls contained trophies that had been stuffed and mounted, the bounty of successful hunts with their outfit. Highlights included a snarling wolf and a large elk head wearing a red MAGA hat.

Hunting is a serious leisure activity that forms a significant part of the gun culture. Pew research shows that around 34 per cent of American gun owners hunt.[47] The division between hunters and sports shooters is a major fault-line in the community. Hunting enjoys much larger social acceptability than certain forms of sports shooting or self-defense preparedness, given that the firearms traditionally used by hunters, like bolt and lever-action rifles or semi-automatics with wooden stocks, are perceived as less threatening by the public. As a result, hunters can be more difficult to mobilize in the defense of pro-gun causes, as they may perceive that their guns are "safe" from gun control efforts. This helps to show that leisure communities are not intrinsically political but can be motivated towards political action when their interests are threatened. The gun show is an important way for the NRA to reach out to groups like hunters, who may be more reticent to take up the cause.

As I wandered around the displays, company representatives eagerly gave me tours around their wares. Though the larger booths, like Remington and Sig Sauer, were generally too busy to do this, I struck up many a conversation with the smaller merchants, and even some of the nonprofit groups in attendance, including a charity which takes the children of fallen service members and law enforcement officers on hunting and fishing trips. People were surprised and bemused to hear that I was a researcher, and that I had come all the way from Canada to be at the convention.

Many of these smaller booths sold specialized accessories for firearms. Like in other retail industries, accessories and merchandising make up a large amount of the firearms industry's sales every year. Experts in the industry have even gone so far as to say that: "There's no money in guns. It's all in the accessories."[48] This is because, to keep a gun running, even the most frugal gun owner needs certain supplies. The most basic of these is ammunition, without which a firearm is simply a metal tube attached to wood or plastic. In 2018, it is estimated that 8.7 billion rounds of ammunition were produced to be sold in the American market alone.[49] But guns also need to be cleaned, stored, transported, and maintained. Shooters need eye protection and ear protection to shoot safely. This can be as simple as a pair of disposable earplugs and some safety glasses, though most serious shooters often opt for electronic hearing protection which amplifies softer noises, like talking, while blocking out louder noises, like gunfire. These can range from a cheap $50 pair of electronic earmuffs to a $2,500 custom-molded set.

Entire booths were dedicated to accessories like gun cleaning supplies, with slogans like: "Don't risk your life using a dirty gun!" Guns become dirty for a few reasons. The first is the powders used to propel the bullet from the gun's barrel. As the powder ignites, it leaves behind residue in the action and barrel of the gun. The second is the bullet itself. Lead or copper from the bullet can leave behind deposits in the barrel. In theory, dirty firearms can cause a malfunction which in extreme circumstances could result in injury or death, though these accidents are very rare. Regardless, the slogan was catchy and memorable.

Other accessories helped the customer safely store their firearms collection. For example, there were several booths that sold gun safes and storage tools like trigger locks. A good safe with decent theft and fire protection can cost upwards of $1,000, depending on the size of one's collection.[50] One booth even had a giant yellow gun safe, twice the height of most of the women and men who stood to get their photo taken in front of it. For $20,000 they would ship the safe right to you.

Then there are the optional accessories. Optics, things like rifle scopes or electronic red dot sights for the firearm, can often cost as much or more than the firearm itself. In fact, serious hunters and sports shooters often spend more on a quality scope than they do on their gun given the impact these accessories have on their performance.

Those more involved in the gun world often opt to accessorize and upgrade other elements of their firearm with ergonomic stocks and grips, performance gun-barrels and much more. To give you an example of just how expensive the gun world can be, consider that a single, mid-range AR-15 with an entry level red dot sight and the equipment needed to safely store it and spend one day at the gun range costs US $1,544.21,[51] about 5 per cent of the median US income at time of writing. A motivated gun owner can easily spend a small fortune.

In addition to accessories related to the firearms themselves, there are also lifestyle accessories tied to the gun-owning community through marketing. This includes clothing lines like the popular 5.11 Tactical. Though focused mostly on the military and law enforcement community, these companies are finding success selling to the growing number of sports shooters and concealed carriers. Much as yoga clothing brands like Lululemon have made money by providing performance products associated with a particular lifestyle, so too have tactical clothing companies. More than just brands, the clothing becomes yet another way for members of the gun-owning community to showcase their passion, and their politics to the world. Just as my students plaster their laptops or backpacks with stickers and buttons proudly showcasing progressive slogans, wearing a pro-Second Amendment shirt, or a pair of pants from your favorite tactical clothing company is a political statement as much as a fashion statement.

The rise of the material gun culture has also led to a small market in accessories like body armor. I noticed several stalls selling body armor, which is increasingly being marketed as a home defense tool. Most of the body armor is intended to be worn over your clothing and is obviously not meant for everyday use. Rather, these companies cater to doomsday preppers, people attracted to the tactical aesthetic, as well as law enforcement, members of the military, and private contractors.

Body armor is a source of controversy even within the community. Some shooters choose to go to the gun range wearing body armor. They are sometimes derided by those within the community as "tactards" and are a source of embarrassment for many sports shooters and older gun owners who see them as giving the community a bad image. For others, however, owning body armor gives them a sense of preparedness, and dressing up in military garb is a sort of costume play, sometimes abbreviated as "cosplay." More recently, this sort of tactical wear has been on display at Second Amendment rallies, the storming of the US Capitol,[52] and by armed business owners guarding their properties during the protests over police violence that took place throughout the summer and fall of 2020.

Other booths sold armored plates designed to slide into the laptop pouch on a backpack, a grim reminder of the reality of post-Columbine America, and the importance of the politics of the everyday. These items may seem purely commercial but are deeply political. They give us a snapshot of the differences of opinion on solutions to mass shootings between the NRA and the pro-control camp. While pro-control advocates see gun control legislation as a mechanism to reduce gun deaths, the solution proposed by NRA members is free market based and individualistic. For the NRA and many of its members, it is the responsibility of individuals to protect themselves from threats, not the government.

Even coming in with an open mind, it was easy to become cynical when looking at the crass consumerism on display in the exhibition hall. At the same time, looking beyond the commercial veneer often revealed deeper meanings. One booth, tucked away in the corner of the convention center, sold tactical-style electric wheelchairs, complete with tank treads instead of wheels, and camo seats. The devices looked like a Panzer tank and a Rascal Scooter had collided and been fused together. My first instinct was to scoff at the idea of a tactical wheelchair, but I decided to take a closer look. The booth attendant was busy talking to an older man sitting in a motorized wheelchair, so I watched the flat screen television next to him where a video advertising the chair was playing on a loop. The video showed clips of people of different abilities enjoying being outside, and I noticed that these chairs serve a purpose beyond simply looking "tacticool"; they give people with disabilities access to the outdoors, the ability to hike or hunt that they would not be able to do with a standard motorized or manually operated wheelchair. It was an informative moment for me, further illustration of the need to look beyond the facile stereotypes of the gun culture and see things through the eyes of my participants.

In fact, people with disabilities seemed to be the most highly represented visible minority group at the convention, and to its credit the NRA appeared to do a great job of accommodating them. Motorized wheelchairs were available at prominently marked booths. The convention floor was fully accessible to people with disabilities. The NRA even runs their "Adaptive Shooting Program," which finds ways for people with disabilities to participate in the shooting sports. People within the community often discussed the fact that hunting and shooting are lifetime activities that people can enjoy well into their golden years.

Continuing my walk around the convention center, I passed a booth specializing in selling suppressors. Suppressors, more commonly known as "silencers," are legal to purchase in some states, but are tightly regulated by the National Firearms Act (1934). Those wishing to purchase a suppressor must pay $200[53] and submit a series of forms to the Bureau of Alcohol, Tobacco, Firearms and Explosives (ATF). There is also a lengthy waiting period involved. Despite this, suppressors have become increasingly common on the firearms market, given their ability to reduce the noise pollution associated with firearms use. A shot from a rifle like an

AR-15 produces roughly the same sound level as a jet engine taking off. With a suppressor, that noise level can be reduced to the sound level of a jack hammer.[54] Suppressors are commonly owned in New Zealand, the UK, and some European countries,[55] where it is considered a courtesy for hunters to use them.

At the booth, several consoles had been set up to facilitate the purchase of suppressors. Rather than muddle through the paperwork themselves, the machines helped would-be purchasers through the process. The booths looked very high-tech, with electronic pads to record the user's fingerprints, a requirement of purchase. Like much of the convention, the booths illustrated the subtle dance being played out between regulators, the industry, and consumers.

The deeper I delved into the exhibition hall, the more niche the firearms "accessories" and lifestyle associations became. The "Affinity Section" of the convention contained several groups in the larger conservative political advocacy network looking to advertise their programs. Some companies with a conservative twist also occupied this section, including a cellphone provider that advertised itself as America's only conservative cellphone service, highlighting the tensions between big tech and the gun culture.

As I moved from booth to booth, I noticed that most of the people there were doing serious business. There were special convention prices on many items, including firearms and accessories. The companies could not hand out firearms at the convention but would arrange to ship them to the purchaser's local Federal Firearms Licensed (FFL) dealer.[56]

To Live the Past and to Sell It

It is a common refrain amongst pro-control advocates that when the Second Amendment was written, the founders were referring to muskets. These activists would likely not be consoled to know that companies at the NRAAM were selling these as well. Several booths in the Exhibition Hall specialized in offering historical firearms. People get into guns for many reasons. For some that I spoke to, working in the military first introduced them to shooting, and they simply kept it going after transitioning to civilian life. For others, it was the hunting or sporting aspect of it. But many gun owners are also lovers of the past. In her ethnography of gun owners in California, Kohn[57] noted that many of her participants discussed their interest in American history, especially as it relates to firearms and mainly the colonial and Wild West periods. Kohn writes: "history and its implications are an important way that shooters conceptualize their interest in guns now. Guns are rarely understood as objects outside of historical, cultural and social contexts."[58] Gun companies have noticed this too, and a small but significant portion of the industry focuses on selling to these groups.

Some of these companies focus on selling historically accurate replicas of firearms from famous periods in American history; from flintlock muskets that would look at home slung across the back of Davey Crockett, to the lever and wheel guns of the Wild West. Though newly manufactured, these objects act as relics. Though they have been rendered mechanically obsolete by fast shooting polymer semi-auto pistols, their value comes from their ability to conjure the past in the minds of consumers and users. Relics are powerful objects of memory because of ageing, embellishment, and anachronism. While these recreations of old firearms do not look aged or weathered, they fulfill the last two criteria. Embellishments work to "memorialize or call attention to some aspect of the past ...," while anachronism draws attention to the way that these objects "exhibit or echo outdated forms or styles."[59] Seeing these recreated firearms as artifacts is important for our understanding of the emotion that firearms conjure for gun owners. As we have discussed, emotions and feelings, tied to culture, are more important in the gun debate than facts, as these are what make up the minds of the belligerents in the debate.[60] Artifacts conjure powerful emotions as they are a bridge between past and present. They make the past concrete, something you can hold, touch, load, and shoot.

These historical replica guns vary in terms of their historical accuracy. Those who are heavily committed will try to shoot the same calibers that the guns originally came with, while others will be made to shoot more modern cartridges.[61] These guns sell well, especially among those who take part in the historical shooting sports, like Cowboy Action Shooters. Other manufacturers will keep the aesthetics of a historical firearm, and the pedigree, but change the internal components considerably. One such company is Henry Repeating Arms, which specializes in making modernized recreations of the Henry Rifle, the first lever-action rifle, which was created and introduced during the American Civil War and used by some Union Soldiers. The Henry was first sold by the New Haven Arms Company that would later become Winchester. With Winchester and Marlin dominating the lever-gun market for much of the late nineteenth and early twentieth centuries, the Henry rifle had gone out of vogue. But Anthony Imperato, a savvy Brooklyn businessman, designed a modernized version of the famous rifle in the late 1990s. Basing his company in New York, his product was inspired by the original Henry Rifle, though it functioned quite differently, and shot the popular .22LR cartridge.[62]

A large part of the company's success has been its ability to connect its product to American history and nationalism. The company's
motto, "Made in America or Not Made at All," clearly demonstrates
that nationalism is a large part of its marketing campaign. But the
company's ability to tie its brand to an icon of American gun history,
Benjamin Tyler Henry, as well as a key period in the nation's story, the
Civil War and Wild West, gives its products a tremendous amount of
emotional appeal and has made the company successful. The lever-
action rifle, a type of firearm where the action is operated by moving
a small lever below the trigger, has acquired something close to iconic
status. These were some of the first repeating rifles in history and saw
wide use on the American frontier. They have been a mainstay of popular depictions of western history, and you would be hard-pressed to
find a western movie that does not feature at least one lever action
rifle. These rifles were also a largely American innovation, invented in
the United States. They did not see widespread use in Europe given
that most militaries preferred bolt action rifles, which were developed
around the same period.[63]

Connecting their product line to the history of the Henry Rifle has
been a large part of the Henry Repeating Arms success, demonstrating
the way that entrepreneurs recognize the power of identity, history, and
memory when marketing their products. The company is a major spon-
sor of the NRA, and often buys advertising space in the *American Rifleman*
and at NRA events.

After exploring the Henry booth, I moved on to another purveyor of
historical firearms, Cimarron firearms. Based in Texas, this company specializes in importing Italian-made replica western firearms. It may seem
odd to see Italian companies specializing in producing the guns of the
American west, but their history is tied to that of the Spaghetti Western
genre of films. The Cimarron booth was set up to look like a shop in the
Wild West, with gun cases made of dark wood and glass decoratively displaying their firearms. I chatted with one of the young stall attendants,
who was dressed in full cowboy attire.

"This gun here, is a replica of the Colt 1851 Navy," the attendant told
me, handing me a black and bronze revolver with a metal snake embedded into the wood handle. "It's a replica of the gun that Clint Eastwood
used in *The Good, The Bad and The Ugly*. Shoot this and you will feel like
a cowboy, for sure."

As we chatted, the booth attendant noted my interest in historical firearms. We discussed many of the working replica pistols and rifles that
they sold, made to feel and function just like the original antiques, but
for a fraction of the price.

"This one here is a .45 Colt revolver. You can see the silver snake inlayed on the handle. It's a reproduction of the gun that Clint Eastwood used in the movies. This shorter model over here with the bird's head grip is just like the one that Doc Holliday had at the O.K. Corral!"

Television and film are important modalities through which ordinary people engage with the past. For example, in Rozensweig and Thelen's famous study of how Americans engage with the past, 81 per cent of their respondents reported that they had consumed a movie or TV program about the past within the last year.[64] Popular representations of the past are so crucial in shaping public memory of their nation's past, that often the two can be difficult for ordinary people to disentangle.

The attendant finished showing me around the booth, and took my picture holding a replica Winchester 1873, a mainstay of the western movie genre. It turned out he was right. Working the lever action, you cannot help but feel like a cowboy.

"You know, if you really like cowboy guns, you should go around the corner and talk to the people from SASS," the attendant said. I recognized the name instantly from my research and headed out.

SASS, the Single Action Shooting Society, is the governing body for the sport of Cowboy Action Shooting. They have over 600 chapters located all over the world, almost 100,000 members, and produce the official rule book for the sport, including regulating which firearms and ammunition can be used, and even operating an online registry of cowboy aliases to ensure that each player has a unique nickname. The SASS also engages in some advocacy work, though it is not the organization's primary focus.

At the SASS stall, a posse of volunteers were dressed up in full cowboy attire. I chatted with a young-looking man with brown hair and spectacles to learn more about the sport of Cowboy action shooting. He introduced himself as Jim.[65] Telling him I was from Canada, he looked in their directory, informing me that there is indeed a club in my hometown of Ottawa.

"What kind of gear would I need to get involved in Cowboy Action? Is it expensive?" I asked Jim. He chuckled.

"Yeah, it can be a bit of a doozy starting up. The first thing you're going to need are your guns. You need two six shooters, most people use some version of the Colt Peacemaker."

"The gun that won the west?" I replied, echoing the famous Colt marketing slogan turned historical truism.

"Yessir. Then you're going to need a lever action rifle, and a shotgun. Most people use a double-barreled coach gun,[66] but you can also use a pump-action as long as it's a historical model, like the Winchester 1897."

"So, I need four guns just to start off?"

"Correct. Then you need your costume. No modern clothing allowed. You're going to need your leather as well. A good gun belt, holsters, something to carry around your ammunition. A lot of people buy wooden carts to carry around their guns from station to station during a competition."

Doing a quick mental tally, we concluded that the cost for the guns alone would be around $3,000–4,000 USD, if you purchased them new.

Participants in the sport also place a large emphasis on costuming and compete in full Western get-up. There are even prizes at SASS events associated with costuming. In her ethnography of Cowboy Action shooters, Kohn details the intense levels of passion, dedication, and financial investment that participants placed in their sport.[67]

Jim's red-haired boothmate, Beth, walked over and joined the conversation.

"Most people don't buy their gear before they attend their first event. You can just show up and ask to watch. People are pretty friendly, and most will lend out their equipment for new shooters to try. In fact, you should definitely attend a shoot first. I made the mistake of buying everything before I started and ended up regretting some of my choices. Try before you buy!"

Beth tried to sell me a SASS membership, but I said I would have to wait and try it first. Despite my rebuff, they were quite friendly, and Jim even exchanged his personal phone number with me in case I had any questions.

SASS was not the only historical association in attendance at the convention. Using the NRAAM phone app, I navigated my way to the section labelled "Collectors" on the map. This area of the convention center was made up of four rows of small booths occupied by different collector organizations. Some of these, like the Contemporary Longrifle Association, are devoted to certain time periods. Others are organized by geographic area, like the Virginia Gun Collectors Association. Others still are devoted to collecting specific makes and models, like Winchester Repeating Rifles. One booth was entirely dedicated to historical flare guns. As with the rest of the convention, these smaller booths made for better conversation. I chatted with the collectors quite a bit as they eagerly showed me their collections, many with quite valuable artifacts.

"This is a Kentucky Longrifle. It's a muzzle-loader, so you have to load it one shot at a time, from the front," said a hulking, bearded man dressed head-to-toe in buckskin, the spitting image of a rugged frontiersman. "These would have shot a .40 or .48 caliber lead ball. They were more accurate than muskets because they are rifled. The grooves in the barrel make the ball spin, sort of like a football, so it can travel further and straighter. These were used by frontiersmen, settlers, and American revolutionaries."

"Who makes these replicas?" I asked.

"Say that again." He was hard of hearing, a common ailment among older shooters, and the convention floor was quite loud. I repeated my question.

"I made this. I made it myself," he replied.

Many of the collectors were dressed in costumes: there were a few cowboys; my friend in buckskin, and others wearing the military uniforms of various historical armies. In general, the collectors were eager to share their passion for the past with anyone who stopped to talk.

Groups like the SASS and companies like Henry Repeating Arms form important pieces in the gun culture and the gun rights movement. When their sport, or their business, is threatened by regulation, they mobilize to resist that threat. While sporting groups like the SASS may seem apolitical, a key part of their mission statement is to protect their members' Second Amendment rights. Meanwhile, companies like Henry Repeating Arms provide material support to the gun rights movement, either through buying advertising space at the convention and in the NRA's publications, or through sponsoring fundraising events. One such event, the 1000 Man Shoot in 2016, was an attempt to break a world record by firing 1,000 guns at the same time. Henry Repeating Arms donated the 1,000 rifles that were used at the event, which raised money for the NRA.

Looking at groups like the SASS and companies like Henry Repeating Arms allows us to observe the power of selling the past, whether as a product or as an experience. They help us to better understand the complex answer to the question that Kohn poses at the beginning of her ethnography: "Why are so many Americans so attached to their guns?"[68] They also give us a window into the complex network that forms the gun-owning community and how these networks are mobilized by the NRA to pursue their goal of defending and expanding Second Amendment rights.

Entertainment and Education

There were deeper games at play at the NRAAM. Members of the media circulated, some quietly observing and taking pictures, others interviewing heavily made-up reps from the stalls under the gaze of large cameras and bright lights. As I admired a set of western revolvers, a waxed-mustached hipster in a brown waistcoat, whose Press Pass indicated that he was from a major left-leaning news publication, took my picture.

I silently wondered what my grandmother would think if she saw a picture like that of me in the newspaper.

Company representatives did not stay chained to their booths. They circulated around the showroom floor, greeting old friends from the gun show circuit and striking deals. While taking a break from the show at the nearby coffee shop, I witnessed a breakaway business meeting taking place. Later at the convention, I heard the representative from a firearms-related charity approach the booth of a major retailer, presumably to ask for a sponsorship. After years of gazing at the American gun culture from behind my screen, I was suddenly thrust onto the other side of the camera when I walked past a well-known firearms YouTuber, TFB TV, conducting interviews at a booth. I had seen a number of these interviews from other NRA conventions on YouTube and felt that feeling of surrealism that often accompanies gazing behind the media curtain.

Celebrities, both from the real world and the gun world, regularly made appearances at booths to sign autographs, greet fans, and promote brands. Chuck Norris, who had just been announced as a product ambassador for Glock, was signing autographs at their booth, wearing a black and white Glock baseball cap. The line to meet the famous actor and martial artist stretched all the way around the large Glock booth. Those unwilling or unable to brave the line satisfied themselves with crowding around, snapping photos with their smartphones. Given that Chuck Norris is now almost as famous among young people for the jokes that poke fun at his supposed invincibility, I heard several jokes being told as I strained to snap a picture of the red-bearded movie icon.

Colion Noir, then the NRA's most famous African American spokesperson and NRATV host, commanded what was probably the second longest line at the convention. I had hoped to be able to meet him, but those hopes were dashed when I saw the line to see him was at least 100 people long. I stood in line for ten minutes, but when it barely moved, I gave up my chance, knowing that he would be gone before I reached the front.

Those seeking a break from the exhibition hall did not want for entertainment. On the far side of the convention hall, there was small stage set up for NRA Country performers. Recognizing their need for allies in the cultural industries, the NRA profiles certain up-and-coming country music artists, giving them a platform to increase their support while also promoting the organization. The backdrop of the stage was set up to look like a Western-themed canteen. It had a bar, and a faux-red brick backdrop, covered with black and white photos of country stars, an American flag, a Gadson flag, and a large red show bill-style sign reading "Music City." The skirt of the stage was covered with the NRA Country logo, which features a guitar whose stem ends in shotgun barrels, with the words Music, Firearms, Freedom circling it. Emerging country star Payton Taylor, a former *American Idol* contestant, performed onstage to a small crowd. I listened for a few songs, one of which I had heard before though I had not recognized the performer's name beforehand.

Leisure and Community

The NRAAM is important because it provides spaces for interaction where members of the gun culture come together and deepen their involvement with the organization and its allies. For the NRA, this is an opportunity to harness the passion of the gun-owning community and encourage more engaged participation with the organization, either through donations, upgrading their membership, or getting involved with their various programs.

Looking at the NRAAM also helps us to clarify the relationship between the NRA and the rest of the gun culture and gun rights movement. Present at the convention were other sporting and advocacy organizations, like SASS; collectors' groups, like the Contemporary Longrifle Association; and companies, like Henry Repeating Arms. Cementing these alliances through the convention helps maintain the solidarity of the movement, deepen relationships between the industry and advocates, and create a sense of comradery amongst the membership.

By Sunday afternoon, with the convention about to close, my feet were aching from days of walking. The insole of my sneakers was almost completely worn away and it was readily apparent that my shoes would not survive my fieldwork. I limped to a nearby table to jot down some notes into my cellphone. Suddenly, I saw Jim and Beth, the couple working the SASS booth, walking towards me. They were out of costume and holding hands. They greeted me as though I were an old friend. Jim put his hand on my shoulder.

"I didn't even recognize you guys at first without your costumes," I said.

They laughed. Jim smiled.

"Yeah, that's a big problem at cowboy action events."

"Thanks again for your help before. It was great meeting you."

"Stay in touch, my friend."

We said goodbye, and I thought to myself how nice it felt to be greeted like an old friend by someone I barely knew.

Conventions serve a purpose for organizations. Like the agora of ancient Greece, they appear on the surface to be a marketplace. In reality they are much more. They allow like-minded people with a shared serious leisure pursuit to gather and to create a community – a powerful motivation priming attendees towards political action.

5   Storytelling and Lifeworlds

The right of law-abiding citizens to keep and bear arms is a freedom that is at the heart of the American story. Our founders won our independence with the power of their ideas and with the powder in their muskets.

– Vice President Mike Pence

Ethnographers look for patterns in a messy and complicated social world. Studying culture can at times seem like studying chaos, but to the careful observer, patterns emerge, leading to theoretical generalizations. One pattern I observed in my interviews with participants was the centrality of three core concepts to their view of gun ownership: liberty, American identity, and security. These concepts, or ideals, often repeat themselves in NRA communications material, and especially in the stories that they tell: stories about guns as essential to human freedom, about guns in American history and culture, and stories about good guys with guns.

In the last chapter, we explored how the NRA uses its annual meeting as an opportunity to shape the gun culture, and expand its potential audience. Another important aspect of the annual meeting is the political speeches. These speeches serve as a venue for the NRA to communicate with its core audience; not only those in attendance but those watching through the organization's website. As I will show, three key assumptions of the NPF, the "primacy of affect," "narrative transportation," and "the power of characters" can help us understand the impact of policy narratives on their audience.

The Speeches

The exhibition hall is the draw for members to attend the NRAAM and provides the funding for the event to take place, but the NRA-ILA

Leadership forum, the political speeches, is likely the most important point of contact that the NRA uses to communicate with its members at the convention.

The speeches took place across the street from the convention center in Lucas Oil Stadium, normally the home of the National Football League's Indianapolis Colts. The stadium was a monolith, its red brick facade blending neatly with its industrial surroundings. Crossing the street to the stadium, which was blocked off by police cars, I headed up to the queue where the security barriers had been erected, walking past a tent where members could check their prohibited items for a small charge.

"Next, please. Keep moving, folks."

A woman in a reflective vest scanned my ticket and directed me toward the security line, which was about five people long when I arrived. The security agents were a mix of Transportation Security Administration (TSA) and Secret Service. As the loudspeaker announcement repeated, the Secret Service had taken control of the stadium. The TSA agents announced to people to prepare to empty their pockets "just like at the airport." While the procedure was similar to airport security, the level of scrutiny was much higher. Rather than use an x-ray machine, agents inspected each person's metal items, looking through wallets, feeling cellphones and turning on the screens to make sure they worked. The man in front of me, a large fellow in his late 20s with black hair and thick glasses had a small multi tool attached to his key ring; so small it did not even have a knife attachment, but only a few screwdriver heads.

"You can either check it over there at the desk or we keep it," the agent informed the man briskly. He opted for the former.

Once we had passed through the metal detector, a secret service agent passed a wand over each of us. He was a young man with a clean-shaven head and a long blond beard. He wore a bulletproof vest and a black semi-automatic pistol at his side. Satisfied that I was unarmed, he curtly waved me forward.

Having cleared security, I headed inside. The cavernous NFL stadium was bisected for the event, with the stage and backstage section occupying half of the stadium and seating the rest. Seating was arranged into three sections. Seats on the pitch could be purchased for $50 or $30 depending on how close one wanted to be to the speakers. Seats in the bleachers would run you $10. I had opted for the middle way and reserved my seats ahead of time, so instead of the cold plastic stadium chairs, I sat 50 yards from the stage on a cushy blue fold-out chair. In front of me there was a couple in their 30s. The woman was tanned, with bright blue eyes and blond hair. Her partner had a shaved head underneath his baseball cap, and a long greying-blond goatee. Beside me, a middle-aged man in glasses was talking with his elderly father. I glanced around the stadium and saw that a greater number of attendees were wearing red MAGA hats than at the exhibition hall. The crowd was also older and whiter than inside the main convention center. I suspected many had come just to see the President speak.[1]

A jovial old veteran, both legs lost to war, sitting on a red-white and blue Rascal scooter with an American flag on the back chatted affably with the people next to him in a thick southern drawl. Though I was over an hour early for the event, the crowd was already starting to file in thanks to announcements inside the convention encouraging people to leave early and avoid long security lines.

The NRA had provided pre-entertainment for the show. The center stage was lit with red, white, and blue. The backdrop of the stage was decorated in the baby blue color scheme that the NRA had adopted for this year's meeting. Three jumbo screens played a rotation of ads, some of which were for the event's sponsors, like Henry Repeating Arms, while others were political NRA ads. An ad featuring then-NRA spokeswoman Dana Loesch, received a smattering of applause. This was followed by an ad which showed Trump's state of the Union Speech, in which he declared, "America will never be a socialist nation." This was greeted with even louder applause. The ads addressed a variety of subjects. Some featured individuals whose cause had been championed by the NRA, or people who had used their guns in self-defense. They addressed themes like heritage, showcased the diversity of the NRA, and played cuts of speeches by NRA executives, political allies like the President and spokespeople, including the late Charlton Heston.

The live speeches began at 11:15 a.m. and ran until late in the afternoon. The first speaker was Chris Cox, then the NRA-ILA Executive Director, though he would be removed a few months later following rumors of an attempted coup against Wayne Lapierre. A naturally charming and charismatic speaker, Cox was of average height with brown hair and blue eyes and was wearing a suit and purple tie. His speech largely took the form of political comedy, similar to the opening monologue used in shows by comedians like John Oliver or Bill Maher. Cox opened with a joke: "I actually have good news to report out of Chicago." He paused, and the crowd laughed nervously. Chicago is often used by the NRA as a symbol of urban gang violence and chaos that some of the nation's strictest gun control laws have proven unable to stem. Cox laughed at the crowd's response, pausing, and looking away to regain his composure. "For years we have talked about Chicago's absolute failure to prosecute its criminals. Well, they finally did it. They got one. The bad news is they let him go," Cox turned to the screen where a picture of Jussie Smollett was shown. Smollett is an African American actor and singer, most famous for his role in the show *Empire*. Days before the convention, he had been charged with hiring two men to stage a fake hate crime, and then filing a false police report, claiming that his attackers had used racist slurs and worn MAGA hats. The incident was big news, especially for those on the right who saw this as an example of a wider Hollywood conspiracy to label Trump supporters as racists.

Cox continued: "I don't know what's wrong with Jussie. Maybe he just needs a hug." He turned to the screen once again where a picture of an uncomfortable looking Smollett had been photoshopped to show the then Democratic presidential nominee candidate Joe Biden behind him, hands on his shoulder, sniffing his hair; a reference to allegations of inappropriate touching that haunted Biden's presidential candidacy. Cox moved on to admonish present day Hollywood, which: "Used to be filled with cool people who actually did cool things." As he said this, black and white photos of former Hollywood actors appeared on the screen. "I'm talking real icons, like Charlton Heston." A black and white photo appeared on the screen with Heston and several civil rights leaders in front of the Lincoln Memorial. "When he wasn't marching for civil rights, he was off doing what we do, enjoying our Second Amendment freedom. But most celebrities today ridicule us for that." Cox's demeanor changed, the humor draining from his voice, replaced with messianic fervor. "Instead they want to lecture us on how to live our lives. They hate us. They hate our trucks. They hate our plastic straws. And yes, they hate our guns. But what they fail to understand is we don't give a damn about what they think." His point was punctuated by a color photo of Heston wearing a cowboy hat with a break-action shotgun slung across his shoulder.

Cox's rhetorical style then moved back to humor, addressing the #MeToo scandals as further evidence of the moral failings of Hollywood celebrities, before pivoting to lambast anti-gun billionaires like Michael Bloomberg, and then again to address the alleged leftward movement of the democratic party: "The socialist wave we warned was coming is here. And it's not just the two coasts that are underwater. It's hitting the heartland of America." Cox warned that "socialists" like Nancy Pelosi and Alexandria Ocasio-Cortez are in for "a rude awakening in November, when the real America goes to the polls."

The most powerful part of his speech, however, was saved for the end.

> There's a single mother living with her kids in a trailer park somewhere near Indianapolis right now. Her husband beat her, so she took the kids and ran. She's out on her own. Trying to build a new life for her family. She works two jobs. The trailer parks not safe but it's all she can afford. No one in this room's ever met her, and the media will never talk about her. She'll never be famous. Maybe she's a Republican, maybe she's a Democrat. Truthfully, she's got more important things to worry about. But without the National Rifle Association of America, there's no one in the world waking up to make sure she has the same right to protect herself and her family as elitist billionaires like Michael Bloomberg. That's who we are. That's what we do. When you fight for freedom you fight on the most principled ground.

He concluded with a message of hope for his supporters, acknowledging that times were tough but that, "we don't exist for the good times."

Stories like that of the fictitious single mother recurred throughout the speeches and were highly effective. These are narratives that draw on deep cultural understandings. Policy narratives, have four central elements: a central character or characters, a setting, a plot, and a policy-relevant moral.[2] In this example, the setting is an impoverished trailer park, the principal character is the single mother, but other characters are brought in as well. The antagonist is Michael Bloomberg in name, though here he is used as a token to represent "anti-gun elites." The hero of the story is the NRA, who protects the mother's ability to protect herself with firearms. The moral of this story is that without the NRA, this innocent woman would be defenseless, unable to afford the same protection as the wealthy celebrities calling for the removal of her rights.

Three key theoretical assumptions within the NPF help to understand the impact of these narratives. The first is the concept of narrative transportation, the idea that narratives will be more impactful to their audience if "the reader/viewer/listener can imagine him-/herself surrounded by the scene and embroiled in the plot alongside the character."[3] The second assumption is called the "power of characters." The more an audience relates to, and likes, the hero of a policy narrative, the more likely they are to be amenable to the policy moral of that story. Narratives are effective because of their emotional impact, and their ability to connect the political message to wider cultural images and collective memories.[4] A third key theoretical assumption within the NPF that applies to this case study is called the "primacy of affect." This assumption holds that human beings are driven by emotion, and that narratives that strike an emotional chord with the listener have a greater impact than those that do not.[5]

Further, a key assertion of this book is that narratives are more powerful when they are connected by groups or political actors to larger cultural narratives. Though we have not heard this specific story of the woman in the trailer park, it is familiar to us as it draws on distinct cultural tropes. The listener may not know this single mother, but they might know a single mother in their own life, or a victim of intimate partner violence. Perhaps they have read about them in the paper or in fiction or seen depictions on a television drama. This character's status as a victim of violence gives her an inherent virtue. The audience wants to root for an underdog, and here is a clear underdog for them to empathize with.

Vice President Mike Pence, who followed Cox's speech, embodied another form of past presencing that the organization uses to present narratives about the past: discussing American history. While Pence's speech was likely not written by the NRA, it mirrored some of their rhetorical strategies in an attempt to pitch to their supporters. Pence's speech covered the gamut of conservative and NRA talking points, touching on religious faith, freedom, the threat to the rights of law-abiding citizens, and others. But he began his speech by grounding these talking points in a discussion of American history, referring to several of the key historical periods often drawn on by the NRA.

"The right of law-abiding citizens to keep and bear arms is a freedom that is at the heart of the American story. Our founders won our independence with the power of their ideas and with the powder in their muskets." Here, once again, firearms are connected to liberty, drawing historical gravitas from the image of the founders. This connects to another common NRA refrain that the Second Amendment protects the First Amendment. That is, that free speech cannot exist without an armed populace to keep the government in check. Pence continued: "Our pioneers won the West with their daring, their courage and their Springfields, Winchesters, and Colts." Here was a reference to pioneers and the Wild West, connected directly to the iconic firearms of that era. "Our forebearers fought our nation's wars, defended our way of life with the skills they learned on the rifle range, in the deer stand, at the knee of a father, a mother, a grandparent back home." The final historical reference here refers to the two World Wars, once again intimately connected to American liberty. These historical narratives were then connected by Pence to the present struggle: "And in our own day, there are no greater champions of America's tradition of responsible gun ownership then all of you and the 5 million proud men and women of the NRA. Thank you for your stand." Towards the end of his speech, Pence once again pivoted to the past. He acknowledged that stopping the threat posed by "anti-gun Democrats" would not be easy, "but it never has been":

> Thomas Payne explained during the American founding, that the battle for freedom is always arduous. As he said, quote, "the harder the conflict the more glorious the triumph." Then Thomas Payne added "what we obtain too cheap we esteem too lightly, and that heaven knows how to put a price upon its good. And it would be strange indeed if so celestial an article as freedom should not be highly rated." It's really about freedom that we gather here today. Preserving the freedom that is at the heart of America.

Connecting the struggle of the NRA to the struggle of America's founders gives their cause a sense of gravitas and historical continuity. Firearms, the tools that preserve freedom, are positioned once again as a key part of America's heritage, one in need of preservation.

As Pence exited the stage to music, waving goodbye, the anticipation in the crowd grew. People began to whisper to one another, sensing that the man that they had *really* come to see was about to speak. They were not disappointed. Chris Cox swiftly retook the stage to introduce the President of the United States. Cox used his introduction to compliment Trump, extolling his sacrifice of becoming president instead of retiring to enjoy a life of success.

The crowd, who had cheered wildly during Cox and Pence's speeches, reached a new climax of excitement as Trump entered to Lee Greenwood's "God Bless the U.S.A." The energy in the room was palpable as the president's supporters stood and clapped. There are few issue-based interest groups that both the President and Vice President would speak to directly. The presence of both of these politicians indicates the important role that the organization plays in mobilizing voters for the Republican Party. The Republicans recognize the role that NRA support can have in mobilizing voters and work hard to cater to the organization. In return, the Republican's advance the policy agenda of the NRA.[6]

Most of President Trump's speech was a rather characteristic mix of attacks on his rivals and lauding his administration's accomplishments. As someone who does not regularly watch Fox News, it felt to me like turning on a film halfway through. I was not familiar with many of the characters the president was attacking, or the incidents he was referencing. The most impactful portion of the speech was not given by the President. Rather, the President's speech itself featured three guest speakers, likely at the request of the NRA. Though these speakers came from different parts of the country and ticked different demographic boxes, they all shared a common characteristic: they were all "good guys with guns," the most famous of the NRA's three core narratives.

The first speaker, April Evans, was introduced by the President. "April Evans joins us from Virginia. One night, in 2015 she was home alone with her two-year old daughter when an intruder broke into her home violently. April took care of it." April walked across the stage looking nervous but determined. She was a heavy-set, middle-aged woman with long, wavy black hair. The audience stood up and cheered as she came on. Dwarfed by the President standing behind her, her head was barely visible above the special podium that POTUS had brought in for the event. She looked visibly nervous, and spoke with a wavering voice, but her story was no less powerful for it.

"My husband is a police officer, and he works night shift," her voice trembled audibly as she started her speech. "One night he was at work and my daughter and I were home alone. Someone started banging so hard on the door it broke in two places. He demanded that I let him in." The audience was presented with the personification of Cox's hypothetical mother, forced to defend her home against an intruder. "I called 911 and I went to my room to get the gun. I heard a loud crash and when I came out to the hallway to see, he was running towards me with a look in his eyes that I will never forget. I shot him twice, and I held him at gunpoint until the police arrived." This proclamation was greeted with loud cheers from the audience, many of whom stood up to give the speaker a standing ovation. April smiled nervously. "This event was something that changed my life. I've never been more afraid, but I've been standing strong and I've been telling my story again and again, because with each person I told they stood a little taller knowing that if I could protect myself and my family, that they could too." Transitioning to the moral of the story, April said, "Protecting my family would not be possible without the right to bear arms. It's an issue that is obviously close to my heart. If these rights had been taken from us, I may not be standing here today, and I may not have a healthy, now six-year old daughter." More applause. "I'd like to thank you Mr. President for your unapologetic stance on our right to bear arms. I truly believe those rights saved my life and the life of my daughter that night." Concluding her speech April gave the President a hug, then shook his hand. She walked off stage, giving a small, nervous wave to the cheering supporters who once again rose to their feet.

April's performance stole the show and not because her speech was particularly polished. Her prose were simple and to the point. Nor was it because of her rhetorical abilities, as she was visibly nervous to be reliving such an awful trauma in front of thousands of people. April's speech was impactful because of her relatability. Audience members could see themselves, or a loved one, in her story. It reinforced that the threat of criminal violence that they have spent so much of their lives thinking about is real, not imagined as their political opponents would have them think. It buttressed the importance of their political position, putting a human face on their cause. There were still two more examples to come.

Following April's exit, President Trump once again took the stage to introduce the next speaker. "Also with us is Mark Vaughn, who owns a meat processing plant in Oklahoma. When an employee began attacking coworkers with a knife viciously and violently, Mark drew his gun and ended the assault immediately, saving countless innocent lives."[7] Mark walked onto the stage, waving at the audience. It was instantly obvious that he was much more at ease in front of the crowd than April. Mark was a middle-aged man with short brown gelled hair wearing a grey suit and blue tie. A small American flag was pinned to his left side. His dress, posture, and composure created the sense of a polished businessman, someone used to talking in front of big crowds. He warmly shook President Trump's hands, smiling, and whispered "thank you." He removed his speaking notes from his jacket pocket and began:

"I got a call late one Thursday afternoon while sitting at my office. A frantic call from our customer service group, said an attacker with a knife was victimizing people in our office." The stage is set. Once again, the audience is presented with a relatable scenario, sitting in our office. That scenario is then transformed by the central action of the narrative. "I ran to my vehicle, ran the 100 yards to the other end of our complex, it was a very chaotic scene. Screaming, crying, blood everywhere. I immediately entered the building, ran down a hallway, and saw a man attacking a woman in the neck and head with a large knife. I yelled. He stopped, paused for a moment, and ran at full speed before me. At about 18 feet I fired three rounds from my AR-15 carbine …" Here he paused as cheers rose up from the audience. "Immediately incapacitating the subject. He was a determined attacker, unbeknownst to me, moments before he had decapitated a co-worker and had targeted several others in our operation to be attacked that day." Like April, Mark then pivoted to the moral of the story. "I was able to take that action because I had a gun, and I was prepared to use it. These are central missions of the NRA, and I thank you, the NRA for that, and everyone here." Like in April's story, the NRA is a silent protagonist here. The heroes of each story's central actions are premised on their ability to own and use firearms, which the NRA, we are told, safeguards. "We have but one true thing, one true mission before us today, and that's to come together like we never have before to preserve our foundational freedom to bear arms in the defense of ourselves, those we love, those we seek to protect, and, most importantly, our liberty." Mark appealed to the values of the audience. "Lastly, I'd like to express gratitude … No other President in our lifetime has stood with us so strongly in defense of our Second Amendment rights.[8] Thank you, Mr. President." He turned, shook the president's hand, and walked off stage.

While the first two speakers were relatively unknown outside, and even inside, of pro-gun circles, the organizers had held back the most famous testimonial for last. Shaking Trump's hand, Mark left the stage and POTUS introduced his final guest. "Finally, Stephen Willeford joins us from Sutherland Springs Texas. The great state of Texas. Where a mass shooter opened fire at the First Baptist Church, you all read about it, in November of 2017, taking many innocent lives. Wonderful, wonderful people. Stephen heroically risked his life to bring the horrible violence to an end. Stephen, please come up and say a few words."[9]

Stephen walked onto the stage to the loudest wave of applause yet. A barrel-chested and grey bearded man, he wore a black suit, tie, and white cowboy hat. His beard was neatly trimmed into a grey goatee and a pair of rectangular black glasses were perched on his nose. On his left side, he wore a pin with the crossed flags of the United States and Texas. He shook the President's hand, took the podium, and began, thanking the NRA and the President for the opportunity to speak. "On November 5th, 2017 I was home because I normally … I was going to start my on call at the hospital where I work as an emergency plumber and could be called a lot. So, I stayed home from church that day because I wanted to get rest. It wasn't to happen." Stephen's speaking style was an effective mix of the previous two speakers. While not quite as polished as Mark, Stephen was more down-to-earth and relatable. At the same time, he spoke with confidence.

"My daughter came into my bedroom and said 'dad, doesn't that sound like gunfire to you'." Once again, our protagonist begins in an everyday situation, in the home surrounded by family.

My daughter was an NRA distinguished expert when she was 8 years old … I was an NRA instructor. I ran to my safe and my daughter ran outside, ran out to her car, and ran reconnaissance for me. She ran up to the corner and came back while I was getting a gun out of my safe and loading it. She said: "dad there is a man in black tactical gear, shooting up the church." I said: "Did you call 9-1-1?" She said: "I did, they're aware of it." Right away that told me the police were coming, but I couldn't wait. I couldn't wait.

Stephen then pivoted into what has become a common note of caution. "Our Police Department in Wilson County has some of the best officers in this world, and they were racing as fast as they could, but my community couldn't wait for them." This is a common refrain in NRA material, captured by the saying, "When seconds count, the police are only minutes away." There is some evidence to support this talking point. The average police response time in certain communities, especially rural areas, can be quite long, with one study putting the median response time in rural areas at 14 minutes.[10]

Stephen continued: "I ran out the door and I told my daughter to load another magazine for me. I gave her busy work. I didn't want her to be there if I failed and I didn't want her to be there for a target for him. The Holy Spirit took over me at that moment, and as I ran across the street I yelled out." This was the first of the narratives to explicitly mention religion or contain overtly religious themes.

"The gunman heard me inside, so did some of the people from the church. So did my own daughter. He came running out of the church and started shooting at me. I put two shots center mass." This was a reference to aiming for the center of the assailant's chest. Despite how easy movies make it look, hitting a moving target in a high-stakes situation, when your heart is racing and your adrenaline rushing, is difficult. Law enforcement, the military, and concealed carriers are trained to shoot for the largest target on the human body and that which is most likely to stop the assailant quickly – the chest.

"He stopped shooting at me, ran to his vehicle. The two shots, center mass ... he had class-3 body armor on they made no difference. But when he ran and turned around his door to his vehicle, I put one in his side, and one in his legs." Stephen continued to describe his pursuit of the church shooter, who attempted to make an escape in his truck. "I met up with a man that was just parked and watched the whole thing, and everybody in this world would have driven on. But this is Texas, we aren't known for our sanity." The audience laughed, easing the tension somewhat. "I found out later his name is Johnny, and I got in the truck with Johnny, and we gave chase ... and at the end the gunman being the coward that he was, took his own life."

The action of the story complete, Stephen pivoted to the moral. "Inside the church were more heroes than we can even talk about in a limited amount of time. But I'm here today to talk about the fact that I used my own AR-15 to confront a shooter that had dropped 15 30-round magazines in my church. He murdered 26 people and injured 20 more. There were only seven people that walked out of that church without a gunshot wound. If it were not for our Second Amendment rights, and the right to carry an AR-15 – the same style gun that he had – then I would have been outgunned myself."

Once gain the NRA joins the narrative as a principal character, albeit off-screen. Further, the AR-15 that Stephen used to fight off the church attacker becomes a character in and of itself, allowing Stephen to accomplish his act of heroism. "I want to thank the NRA for being relentless in protecting our Second Amendment rights. And I would like to thank this president for defending the Second Amendment. And I would like to say today, he says Make America Great Again, and he's including you. You will make America great again with him." Here the speech took on an almost religious feeling. "But he needs you, he needs your vote, and if you do not get out there and vote for this man, then it's on you."

These three narratives contain several analogous elements. First, each takes place at two levels. The first level, the primary narrative, is the direct action of the story, while the second takes place in the shadows, behind the scenes. Each story has a setting that would be familiar to its intended audience: the narrator's homes, their office, their church. The stories all have villains. The villains that appear in the primary narrative are the violent assailants armed with their fists, knives, and guns. The listener is presented with little information on these villains, other than their malicious intent. We are not told their race, their gender, their motivations, or any of their back story. This is intentional. They are intended to represent evil. The unmentioned villains occupying the secondary narrative of these stories are, of course, those seeking to disarm the heroes. Though never mentioned directly, their actions are implied. As each speaker indicated, should these true villains prevail, the heroes would be unable to defend their lives.

The primary heroes of the story are, of course, the storytellers themselves. They represent not only themselves but take on the status of "good guy with a gun," a larger meta-narrative presented and cultivated by the NRA. This analysis is not meant to belittle these individuals. The three speakers that I saw truly are heroes: people who risked their lives to defend others, and accomplished things that many people would not have the courage or ability to do. But it is the narrative of the good guy with a gun that connects their stories together and gives them political meaning.

The heroes of these stories' secondary narratives are the NRA and the President. The common formula of each speech ended with the speaker thanking the organization and the President for their commitment to defending the Second Amendment. They are presented as the heroes that stand up for heroes. This leads to the moral of each story. First, that good guys with guns exist and save lives. Second, that for these heroes to be heroes, they need to be armed. Finally, that the NRA and the President are the key figures keeping these good guys armed.

But how does this connect to history, memory, and heritage? What does it have to do with the gun culture? In these stories we see yet again the Second Amendment being presented as heritage. As we explored in previous chapters, heritage establishes ownership over parts of the past,[11] and the tradition of gun ownership in America is often presented by the NRA as a form of heritage that needs to be protected. Heritage always needs to be owned, guarded, and preserved. The protectors of this heritage change depending on the message the organization is trying to send with a particular narrative. If the organization wishes to mobilize individuals to act, they will often present ordinary people as the defenders of this heritage. In the stories of April, Mark, and Stephen, however, the NRA, and their ally President Trump, are positioned as the key guardians of the historical tradition of the Second Amendment.

These stories also highlight the connection between individual memory, collective memory, and affect. It is difficult to convey the emotional impact of these stories in writing, especially to many readers who I assume find the idea of the "good guy with a gun" to be propaganda, or a right-wing talking point. Yet the emotion conveyed through these shared memories was a deeply impactful narrative strategy. As NPF scholars note, the "primacy of affect" is an important principle in understanding how narratives influence their audience. Narratives that employ emotion are generally more persuasive given the importance of affect in "focusing attention in human cognition."[12] In other words, emotions help people to decide what is important. It was evident from their reactions that these stories had a strong emotional resonance with the audience, myself included.

These speeches also give us an interesting opportunity to explore the interplay between meso and macro-level narratives. Macro-level narratives, as we have discussed, are sacred stories that exist at the broader societal and cultural level.[13] They shape how a given audience will understand the social world, and thus how they will interpret narratives. The policy narratives that the NRA is disseminating through these stories make sense in an American context given the macro-level narratives surrounding individuality and heroism in the wider American culture, which often draws on the image of the lone hero saving the day, sometimes with a firearm. It is through this macro-narrative that the NRA connects these stories to the figure of the good guy with a gun. In each, the hero acted alone, or mostly alone, given that help was far away. In Stephen's case, he rejected the help of his daughter to protect her from danger, though he establishes that she is also proficient with firearms. Most importantly, in each story the hero was armed.

Lifeworlds

The NRAAM provides the group with a chance to tell stories to its members. The stories they tell draw from America's past, as well as the collective memories of its members. They connect to key macro-level narratives about American history and culture, like the story of the nation's founding, or the image of the good guy with a gun. They help to solidify the relationship between the organization and its members, and rally members to support the cause. What often surprised me when conducting my interviews was how often the core ideas embedded within these narratives: liberty, American identity, and security, came up in my conversations with gun owners.

The NRA works very hard to connect the idea of liberty and American identity to firearms' ownership to great effect. Several authors note this connection in their own research on American gun owners.[14] Interestingly in Canada, a very similar country with a significant population of gun owners, these political meanings are largely absent from the public conversation.[15] The American gun owners that I spoke to often connected firearms to independence, freedom, and personal responsibility. For some, guns were positioned as a form of civic responsibility as carrying a gun means you are participating in the defense of the community. Owning or carrying a gun can also represent the exercising of a constitutional right, or a form of political communication or resistance to one's political opponents.

The NRA's three core meta-narratives, the good guy with a gun, guns as freedom, and guns as essentially American, have become incredibly persuasive through their constant repetition in NRA material. My research participants expressed similar views, each, for example, mentioning individual liberty or freedom in reference to firearms at least once, and this despite their socio-economic and demographic background, or their political beliefs.

I met Susan, a white woman, during my first NRA course. Susan is a triathlete who wore a humorous, triathlon themed t-shirt and drank from a mug with the logo of a local race on it. She was taking the NRA class to become more familiar with and proficient with her handguns, which she acquired for recreation and self-defense. I went to the range with Susan three times and met her for coffee to conduct an interview. During our chats, she did not strike me as politically conservative. While I avoiding asking her directly about her political views, those that she did express seemed moderate, and she spoke favorably of reproductive rights. Despite this, when I asked Susan: "What does firearms ownership mean to you?" she responded, quite simply, "Freedom."[16]

Bucky better fit the traditional image of an American gun owner. I met him during my concealed-carry class in late May. Bucky is a grey-haired, white man with a short-trimmed beard in his early 60s. He is also a veteran, but since leaving the military, he has had considerable success in the private sector and as a government consultant. He is the president and CEO of a consulting business and a manager for a large government agency. After getting to know Bucky during the firearm safety course, he agreed to sit down with me and chat over coffee. He framed his answer on the meaning of guns with a discussion of the American Revolution, concluded with "So I think to me owning a firearm, not just for me, but I think for people in general, that right is there in order to protect your individual liberty."[17]

Timothy and Sam were a father and son that I sat down with on separate occasions. Timothy was also taking the NRA course where I met Susan. He is an African American man in his late forties, seldom seen without his baseball cap, round glasses, and affable smile. Timothy was taking the basic class to qualify for the instructor level courses, so that he could teach his own firearm safety courses in his spare time. He is a veteran of the Air Force and now works as a pilot. He is heavily involved in the Boy Scout's movement and with his church. Given his employment, Timothy is often away from home, but we managed to get to the range twice together and sat down for an interview over coffee. Through Timothy, I was connected with his son, Sam.

While his father is large and muscular, Sam is slighter and his skin lighter, yet he inherited his father's infectious laugh and good humor. Like his father, Sam is heavily involved with the Boy Scouts and with his church. I met Sam when I was out shooting with Timothy. Sam joined us for the end of the range session and then stayed to try out his father's newly purchased AR-15. We later sat down to talk over ice cream. Sam is a university student studying in Alaska but was home for the summer.

I asked both father and son about the meaning of firearms to them. Sam noted that: "You can't own a firearm in a lot of other countries. For America it means a lot because it's another way for us to show that we have freedom. Really that's what it means."[18] Timothy drew on historical narratives to connect firearms to these ideals of freedom and liberty, seeing them as an antidote to despotism.

The reason why the Japanese did not want to do a land invasion of the United States was because they knew our citizens are armed. Other countries, you know Korea, the Samoas, the Mariana islands, that whole section of the south pacific, they didn't have firearms. So, all they had to do was overcome the military. Here, they try to overcome the military but after a little while they're going to be overcoming the whole fricken country. They knew they couldn't do that. That's why they didn't want to do a land invasion into the United States ... It was US firearms that stopped the despotic abuse of authority that we call World War I and World War II. It was the US firearms, or the fear of its use, that brought halt to countless conflicts around the world.[19]

Those who completed my online survey expressed similar ideas. When asked what firearms mean to them, respondents said things like, "Owning a firearm is a symbol of freedom. It means the government trusts you." Another participant said that firearms symbolize, "Independence, self-sufficiency, and a continual testament to the will of the individual being morally superior to the will of the collective." This same participant later wrote "honestly, as long as there are authoritarians who want to dictate how I live, why wouldn't I do everything to frustrate their efforts?"

Looked at from the perspective of those deeply involved in the gun culture, gun control is seen as a misguided, and often politically motivated, attack on this freedom; an attempt to restrain the behavior of the criminal elements of society by removing rights from the collective. They see firearms as neutral tools and argue vehemently that government should focus on controlling the behavior of criminals rather than attempt to regulate a tool which they use peacefully in their everyday lives. Sam expressed this view quite concisely:

> Yeah. A firearm is a tool. Just like a hammer, just like a nail gun ... just like skis. You can use it for something good, you can use it for something bad, it's up to the holder to decide what to use it for. Just like you research how you ski, just like you study what a car can do, the same thing comes too with a firearm. You have to study it. You have to know it. I think that's yeah. Final thought is that a firearm is a tool. It's not the gun that kills the person it's the person holding the darn thing.[20]

Similarly, gun control proposals are often seen through this lens. Several gun owners that I met noted how gun control propositions are meant to make firearms ownership either too expensive or too inconvenient for firearms owners, to concentrate firearms in the hands of the elite. There is something to the idea that many firearms regulations price people out of gun ownership. For example, when asked why he joined the NRA, Timothy responded:

> Well, I noticed a movement amongst financial elites, people that want to try to strip these rights from us, and I think that ... uh ... what do you call it ... an

interesting part is it's very disingenuous because they'll keep it for themselves, they'll have security guards and so and so ... They don't want us to have it. So you sit back and you go, I'm hoping that the small donations of a large group of people can outweigh the financial power of these few elite people.[21]

The narrative of the good guy, or gal, with a gun is also central to tying firearms to ideas of personal security, which, along with legislative changes, has led to an explosion of gun carry around the United States. The fastest growing segment of the gun-owning community are those that own firearms for self-defense. For some, this may involve simply leaving a firearm at home to deal with potential intruders. Others, however, carry firearms regularly. Currently, about 26 per cent of handgun owners carry "most of the time" and 31 per cent carry "some of the time."[22] As of November 2020, there were almost 20 million concealed carry permits issued in the United States.[23] This has been made possible by the expansion of "shall issue" and "permitless carry" laws.

Statistics on defensive gun use have produced widely varying estimates as to the amount of times firearms are used to defend life and limb. The Center for Disease Control (CDC) defines defensive gun use as "the use of a firearm to protect and defend oneself, family, others, and/or property against crime or victimization." Estimates on rates of defensive gun use vary from lower estimates of 60,000 times per year, up to the higher estimates of 2.5 million times per year. These numbers suffer from several methodological issues related to operationalization, false positives, underreporting, and survey design. Most defensive gun uses do not actually involve a gun being fired but simply brandished. As a result, they are often unreported to authorities. At the same time, violent encounters are not always as cut and dry as Hollywood would have us believe. One person's "self-defense" can be another's "act of aggression."[24]

Several of my participants were, or had been, regular concealed carriers, or owned guns for the purposes of self-defense. Though he was not carrying during our interview, Bucky discussed being a regular gun carrier for the past 25 years:

> BUCKY: ... of course it's not necessarily a nice world out there, and sometimes unfortunately you need to protect yourself from people who would do you harm. Sam Colt said ... you know ... Or as people would say ... How was that exactly said ... Like the Colt revolver made all men equal. Remember that quote? It was something ...
> NOAH: G-d[25] created man but Sam Colt made them equal, or something like that?
> BUCKY: Yeah something like that. So, you know that's certainly a part of it.[26]

Rick was the instructor for my NRA rifle course and that is how we met. He later sat down with me at a coffee shop above his local grocery store in suburban Virginia. A middle-aged white man and father of several children, Rick has brown hair, a stern jaw, and fierce, proud eyes. He is a veteran and his demeanor betrays his military experience. Rick has a thick southern accent and a direct way of speaking. Given there were only two other students in the class that he had taught me (one of whom was Rick's father), we got to know each other quite well throughout the day. While Rick does not carry now (he lives in what he describes as a safe gated community far away from the troubles faced by the nearby big cities of Washington and Baltimore), he did own a pistol for self-defense while living in the south. Though he was in the military at the time, he lived off-base in a rougher neighborhood.

> That was strictly ... when we were stationed there we weren't in a nice neigh-borhood, but it was close to base, so we wanted to be able to go walking. Also, there had been some incidences of some break-ins and things in the area. So I bought a Glock 23, .40 caliber, just for home and self-protection.[27]

Self-defense was very important to another of my participants, Steve. I met Steve while taking his NRA Shotgun Course in southern Maryland. He is a middle-aged white man with a short, grey goatee and a west coast accent. Steve is a veteran of the United States Navy. The course I took with him was another small group, with only two other students, and we had plenty of time to chat. Steve agreed to sit down and speak with me over video conference from his home in southern Maryland.

Steve spoke about how firearms empowered people to defend themselves: "As we have evolved as a people and as a human race we have always had this inalienable right to defend ourselves. And ... you know if you attacked me, I would have a right to defend myself because I didn't want to die that day." Steve is a firearms instructor and told me that a few weeks after the Virginia Beach Shooting, a friend of one of the victims joined his shooting class. When describing her friend: "She said that if ... she knew that if he were there, and if he had a gun, he would do anything to protect somebody or even himself. So, we talked about that for a little bit, because I said you know isn't that just the basic human instinct is to protect yourself." Discussing a lawsuit against the city government for making the office a gun-free zone, Steve said:

> I think hallelujah that somebody has had the brains to challenge that stu-pidity. Because criminals really don't give a rat's (*participant self-censors the word ass*) about gun free zones. That's why they're criminals. Why do we law-

abiding citizens have to die to prove that point constantly? I think it's irre-
sponsible and I think it's horrendously disgusting that good people have
to die at the hands of bad people who could care less about following the
law … I think that Second Amendment has got to be enforced so that we
have the right to protect … our right to defend ourselves from criminals
who don't care about our rights. We want to live, and if you look at the number of people who have their concealed carries that are getting arrested
every day because they're breaking the law, it's like point zero zero zero
zero zero zero four six per cent. So that tells me that concealed carry people
are, for the most part, law-abiding citizens that are doing the right things
and making the right decisions with their guns. So isn't that what we are
trying to promote, law & order? I think that that's … when you have guns
and people choose to keep them for their protection, in this country that's
a necessity. We should have the same right that the criminal does.[28]

Given the complex political geography of American firearms regulations, concealed carrying a firearm can create a variety of everyday
nuisances, especially for those who regularly cross state or county lines.
Given the location of my fieldwork in the DC, Maryland, Virginia (DMV)
area, this was especially problematic for my participants, many of whom
crossed state lines on a weekly if not daily basis. Bucky described the challenges of complying with the patchwork of firearms legislation as part of
his daily commute:

But yeah, so it's a problem, particularly for me because I work in DC, so
obviously I can't, you know, on my normal day I can't carry obviously. And
then on that off chance that you have to go into Maryland for some reason,
you know, then you have to be … if you have the firearm on you then you
know you have to … well what I do is I stop, take the gun apart, put the
ammunition in one place. Literally I will do a basic disassembly of the firearm, so there's not, you know for some reason a police officer, for whatever
reason, might want to … like there's something wrong with your license and
he's going through the car, he doesn't find a gun. He may find a barrel, he
may find the slide over there, but he's not going to find a gun. So, I do my
absolute best to be sure I don't violate any jurisdiction's firearm laws. You've
got to respect them, whether you agree with them or not, right you've got
to respect them.[29]

A person's ability to take advantage of liberalized concealed or open
carry can also be shaped by their positionality. While a white, middle-class
male may only be impacted by legal boundaries, racialized minorities
face deeper, systemic barriers to full participation in the gun culture.

This came out when I asked Sam, who is of legal age to purchase certain firearms, why he had not done so:

> But actually, for Virginia, as an individual such as myself it would be unwise to open carry. Just simply because it is Virginia and unfortunately, I am not white (*sarcasm*). So that poses a lot of questions. I'm a young ... young not white person. So, it's just unneeded attention. In my family, we are waiting until I turn 21, when I can conceal carry, so it's one, less noticeable and two, if I do get stopped I have the training, I have the papers, I have the card, so there's not much in the way of negotiating. Because unfortunately, even me having a pocketknife could be considered a concealed weapon. So, if someone is having a bad day and wants to make my day really bad ... I mean just having a pocketknife it could go south.[30]

Though their positionality and life experiences differed widely, all of my participants, regardless of race, gender, or political affiliation, saw firearms as an essential tool for security, much like a fire extinguisher. They agreed that firearms were a tool to manage one's personal safety in a dangerous world, where one could not necessarily count on the police or wider community for help.

The NRA uses narratives about America's and Americans' pasts to construct a political community of gun owners. As I have shown in this chapter, they draw on three central meta-narratives: the good guy with a gun, guns as essentially American, and guns as bulwark of liberty. These narratives have a profound impact in shaping the lifeworlds of those within the community of gun owners.

This grassroots support is translated by the NRA into political advocacy. The organization uses their communications materials and events to try to attract new members and new gun owners to join the cause, and to motivate existing members to deepen their involvement with the organization. These members then provide the organization with the financial and human resources needed to advance their policy agenda.

6 Home on the Range

You can't take someone to the anti-gun range.[1]

– Jon Hauptman

While it was still technically spring, you would not have known it standing under the scorching West Virginia sun. The rays seared my exposed skin, my sunscreen long since sweated away. I blinked the perspiration out of my stinging eyes and struggled to aim the borrowed Glock handgun at the center of the dark silhouette target in front of me. It was still morning, but the temperatures were in the high 80s. Regardless, our instructor put us through a series of rigorous shooting drills. "Draw. Hold. Fire." These drills are designed to inculcate the critical components of using a handgun to defend your life. We practiced shooting, of course, but also honed other key skills like reloading on the fly or drawing and re-holstering the firearm. At the beginning of the class, I was terrified that I was going to shoot my foot while drawing the gun from the holster. Once I had gone through the motions a hundred times with empty guns, I felt a lot more confident.

I walked up to within five feet of the target, as our next drill was close-range shooting. In Hollywood shootouts, opponents are separated by large distances, but most real-world defensive handgun encounters, we are told, happen within less than ten feet. I had never shot at such a close distance before. Wiping the fog off my glasses with the sleeve of my shirt, I prepared for the instructor's call. On his signal, I emptied five rounds into the center of the target. *Pop. Pop. Pop. Pop. Pop.*

The classroom, the gun range, and the gun show are some of the key sites where gun culture is practiced and constructed by those within the gun-owning community, and the NRA maintains a strong presence in all three. The NRA has several important points of contact with members and potential members, gun enthusiasts and the gun-curious, such as the organization's network of instructors, their communications materials, and major NRA events. The organization uses these points of contact to attract new members and new gun owners and motivate existing members to deepen their involvement in the cause. These points of contact provide a venue for the NRA to disseminate narratives and frame the gun debate. Gathering and galvanizing members is important for the organization, as the grassroots membership provides the financial and human resources capacity the NRA needs to advance their desired policy agenda.

The NRA understands that participation in the gun culture is a strong motivating force behind the gun rights movement, and that these everyday cultural practices play an important part in this. In the classroom, gun owners learn the skills, knowledge, and values involved with membership in the gun-owning community. On the range, they socialize, trade stories, and shoot guns. At gun shows, they talk with peers, making connections, and engage with material culture: gazing, buying, selling, and trading.

The gun rights movement is successful because of the passion that gun owners, who are standing up for something dear to them, bring to the fight. Gun rights advocates and the NRA understand that bringing people into this culture is an important way to grow the movement. This is because of the major differences between casual gun owners and those deeply involved in the gun culture. Using the number of guns owned as a proxy for attachment to the gun culture, Joslyn[2] notes that, in the 2016 election, the deeper an individual's involvement in the gun culture, the more likely they are to have voted Republican. For those who only owned one gun, the probability of them having voted for Donald Trump was 0.49. For those with four or more guns, this number increased to 0.64.[3] The NRA, and other pro-gun organizations, understand that the key to getting the gun vote is to deepen people's involvement in the gun culture, and thus, they hope, in the movement.

We have seen this reflected in the recent initiatives put forward by both larger and smaller gun organizations, the NRA included, encouraging gun owners to bring friends and family members out to the range. This includes things like the NSSF's "Take Your First Shot" program, or the NRA's various instructional videos that teach gun owners how to initiate new shooters.[4] Gun rights activists understand that getting people hooked on shooting will help to win hearts and minds and that this is an advantage that they hold over pro-control activists, who do not have a central activity, sport, or culture that their membership can rally around. As Second Amendment advocate Jon Hauptman says: "You can't bring someone to the anti-gun range."

This is also why NRA courses are an important tool for the organization to expand their membership. Given the scale and pedigree of the NRA's course offerings, it attracts people who want to learn to shoot, either for self-defense, competition, or as a hobby. These individuals are not necessarily NRA members. They may never have fired a gun before and are simply interested. NRA firearms safety courses are one of the first points of contact that people will have with the organization, beyond the digital world or news media. These courses seem to be quite popular, and the NRA notes that they teach over 1 million Americans every year. Firearms safety courses are not required to purchase a gun in most US states like they are in Canada, but they are required in some states if an individual is to apply for a concealed carry permit. Other people take these courses out of interest, out of a desire to become more comfortable with guns, or are brought along by a family member or friend.

Gun shows are also an important meeting place for the community of gun owners. They are a place to meet and trade stories as well as goods. For gun rights organizations like the NRA, gun shows provide an excellent point of contact with their current and potential membership. This chapter looks at three key sites where the gun culture is practiced, drawing from my participant observation in five NRA courses, going to the range with my participants and experiencing two gun shows, from both sides of the table. I show how the NRA leverages these points of contact with its active and potential members to grow the organization and harness the gun-owning community.

NRA Firearm Safety Classes

During the first half of my fieldwork, I rented a room in a small townhouse in suburban Fairfax, Virginia. The neighborhood was a crescent of several hundred duplexes, mostly filled with blue collar families, retirees, and new Americans. The street was often full of children riding bikes or playing tag. At a nearby park, groups of teenagers played basketball. The architectural style of the houses was eerily similar to that of the neighborhood I grew up in in suburban Ottawa, giving the whole place a strange sense of familiarity.

The evening before my first NRA course, I walked to the community mailbox to send some postcards I had bought while visiting DC. Ahead of me, a father in his late 30s bent down to check his mail. His loose-fitting t-shirt shifted forward as he bent over, revealing a concealed handgun. The moment broke the sense of familiarity, imbuing it with a new feeling of similar difference. A year before, I would have shied away, uncomfortable, but I was deep enough inside the gun culture by that time that my overriding emotion was curiosity. *Was that a Glock or a Smith*

& Wesson? I can't tell at this angle. Should I warn him that he is showing? I wonder if he would do an interview if I asked him? In the end, I just mailed my postcards and walked away, but the experience drove home to me a point that scholar David Yamane often makes in his work. In many places: "guns are normal, and normal people use guns."

With firearms ownership so commonplace, firearms safety education becomes an important service. The NRA's firearms education programs, a key part of the organization's original mandate from the 1870s, is one of the most overlooked elements of the organization's influence. The NRA has an extensive network of training programs offered in most US states and online, and trains over one million Americans every year.[5] Carlson, one of the few authors to examine this element of the NRA, argues that this represents a key part of the organization's success. She notes that: "the NRA continues to enjoy favor among many people because they view the organization as empowering Americans with a basic community service (firearms training)." Looking at this training is an important part of "a bottom-up" perspective on the organization.[6] NRA instructors are certified by the organization through a lengthy qualification process but most are not actually employed by the NRA. Most of the instructors I met had other jobs, or were retired, and didn't expect to make money as instructors. For them, it was a matter of sharing their serious leisure passion with others. Yet these instructors serve an important role within firearms regulations. In several states, Virginia included, taking a firearms course is a prerequisite to obtaining a concealed carry permit. Given that the NRA is often one of the few major outfits in many states to offer firearms training, these instructors often serve as the "gatekeepers of gun carry."[7] Carlson is careful to note that these classes not only teach students the mechanics of gun safety but are key points to teach students values and discursive practices, socializing them into the gun culture. NRA classes "Provide a critical space in which to shape gun culture from the ground up."[8] This was something that I observed during my participant observation in five NRA firearms safety classes.

While each class was a bit different, reflecting the personal style of the instructor, they all followed a similar, basic format, with half of the day devoted to theory and dry practice[9] and the other half spent shooting. On top of the course fee – usually around $200 USD – students had to bring their own food, ammunition, and equipment.

Framing the Gun Debate

My first course was the NRA Basics of Pistol class. It took place in an indoor gun range in Northern Virginia. I parked my car and walked into the main lobby, which looked like the front desk of an auto-body shop.

"Morning, I'm here for the NRA pistol class," I said. The range attendant, an East Asian man in his 30s with a mustache and long ponytail, checked me in, surrounded by gear for sale. Everything one might need for a day at the range was there, from ammunition to eye protection to targets, minus the guns, which can only be sold by federally licensed dealers. A clear glass window behind the desk gave me a peek at the actual range, though I could not hear what was going on inside thanks to a two-door airlock system that kept hearing levels inside the lobby at a safe level. "Just head down the hall," the attendant said, pointing me in the right direction.

I was one of the first students to arrive at the class. The room had exactly ten seats for the ten participants and was covered with NRA posters. Two hunting trophies stared down at us with unmoving eyes. At the front of the classroom was a projector showing a standardized NRA PowerPoint presentation. Though the instructors were self-employed, the curriculum of the courses was tightly controlled by the NRA. The instructors received PowerPoint decks, books, and exams from the organization.

Entering the room, I introduced myself to the instructor – I will call her Maggie – and briefly explained my project. There were three rows of tables and I took a seat at the back. While waiting for class to begin, I tried to strike up a conversation with some of the people around me. "Hi, I'm Noah," I said, turning to the woman beside me. Straight to the point. She turned towards me and I saw her travel mug, advertising a triathlon she participated in. She was in her 30s, thin with brown hair.

"Hi, I'm Susan."

"Is this your first class?" I asked.

"Yeah! I got a gun from my dad. Figured I should learn how to shoot it."

Most people in the class were shy in the beginning, and we soon lapsed into an awkward silence that any teacher or student will recognize as the pre-class stupor.

Maggie began the class by canvassing the students on our background and interest in firearms. "Why are you interested in owning a handgun?" she asked.

"To protect myself," a man two seats down from me answered curtly. He was older and held himself like an ex-military fellow. He had a short haircut and looked remarkably like a cross between Donald Trump and Martin Sheen. I did not see him smile the entire day.

Most of the other students cited recreation or self-defense as their reason for wanting to own a handgun. We were then asked about other firearm-related activities we participated in. No one mentioned hunting, which was not exactly surprising given that this was a handgun class being held in a suburban neighborhood. Yet this adds further credence to Yamane et al.'s[10] assertion regarding the shifting center of gravity in the American gun culture from hunting to self-defense.

As my classmates introduced themselves, I learned a bit more about the people surrounding me. The man next to me, Albert, was a middle-aged computer programmer with a grey beard and curly hair. Throughout the day, I got to know a few more people in the class, who I would later go shooting with and interview. Susan, who I had briefly spoken to, introduced herself to the class as an office worker and passionate triathlete.

In my years as a teaching assistant and instructor, I have come to notice certain archetypes in every class. Every year there are a few students that stand out because of their relentlessly positive attitude and work ethic. Timothy, who sat next to Susan, was one such student. A middle-aged, bespectacled, African American man who I seldom saw without his baseball cap, Timothy worked as a pilot and was often away from home. A proud veteran, Timothy is very involved in the Boy Scouts of America and was taking the class, amongst others, to try to qualify for the NRA instructor program so that he could teach with the Boy Scouts. Unlike Canadian scouts, some American Boy Scouts troops still offer firearms training.

John sat a few rows in front of me. He was probably only a few years older than me and worked as a bodyguard for some of Washington's higher-ups. He was also taking the course to try to qualify as an instructor. In the middle row was a husband and wife, who looked to be within a decade of retirement. The woman had long, greying brown hair and was all smiles. Her husband, an Indigenous man, was quiet and pensive behind his large glasses. As the class progressed, we learned that he was an avowed anti-consumer, preferring to make things himself, like his wallet which he showed us proudly. Finally, in the front row was a father and son. The father oozed military, with short-cropped grey hair, impeccable posture, and a stern demeanor. His son was in his early 20s, a college student, and wore a backward baseball cap. Had I seen him in the streets, I would have guessed that hacky-sack or skateboarding was his pastime of choice, rather than target shooting.

The course material itself was mostly focused on firearms safety. The first section was entirely devoted to memorizing the key safety rules. Topics included safely handling firearms, the different types of firearm malfunctions and how to fix them, and gun cleaning. The instructor used a combination of PowerPoint and multi-media to make her point.

"Never point your gun at anything you are not willing to destroy." Maggie repeated this often and was not shy about illustrating the point. At one point, she showed a YouTube video where a man came within inches of blowing his own head off because he looked down his shotgun barrel during a hangfire.[11] Luckily, he only ended up with a hole in his baseball cap.

Topics like safely storing one's firearms were also covered. An NRA image of three children who had blown up condoms like balloons were shown with a caption to the tune of: "If they can find it, they will play with it." The instructor drove this home further with her lecture.

"You are responsible for your guns 24 hours a day, seven days a week, no matter where you are. That's a big responsibility. Do not take it lightly."

Given the popular image of the NRA, I was initially surprised to see the focus on safe storage, considering that the organization is opposed to laws that require individuals to safely store their firearms. In reality, this is consistent with the organization's position that firearms responsibility should be managed by the individual, rather than mandated by the state. The NRA, and many gun rights supporters, see laws like safe-storage laws as incremental attacks on the right to bear arms. They would say that safe-storage laws do not prevent accidents but simply punish people after an accident has occurred.

The course was also used to promote further involvement with the NRA. This included a very brief history of the organization.

"Who knows how the NRA was founded?" Maggie asked.

I raised my hand and looked around. I was the only one.

Students were asked whether or not they were NRA members. A few were members, but most were not. Those who were not were encouraged to buy memberships by the instructor. It was emphasized that, on top of providing firearm safety training, the NRA was helping to defend their rights.

Words are the building blocks of stories. The NRA recognizes the power of words to shape the political debate. Further, given that gun owners enjoy an exclusive technical knowledge of firearms, a favorite game of gun owners is pointing out the mistakes in terminology that politicians and would-be regulators make. Maggie had an interesting method of socializing students into the linguistic practices of the gun culture. After registering for the course, we were instructed by e-mail to bring spare change with us to class. Maggie had a jar on the table, with a label that listed the three forbidden words in the classroom: "bullet," "clip," and "weapon." The first two are common gripes amongst gun owners. The term "bullet" is often misused by the public to refer to a cartridge. A cartridge is what the user loads into a firearm. A cartridge contains a casing, which is filled with powder and fitted with a primer that ignites the powder when struck by the firearm's hammer. It also contains the bullet, which is the projectile that leaves the gun once fired. Those less familiar with firearms often accidentally refer to cartridges as "bullets."

The second banned word, "clip," refers to a short strip of metal that latches on to the grooves at the back of a cartridge, allowing the operator to load multiple cartridges into a gun with a fixed magazine. It is an outdated loading device that is generally only used for older bolt-action rifles and the first generation of semi-automatic firearms. It was mostly used in guns from the First and Second World Wars, like the German Mauser rifles or the famous American M1 Garand that Marines carried in the Second World War. For some reason, the terminology stuck despite the fact that virtually all modern bolt-action and semi-automatic firearms are not loaded with clips. Gun owners often enjoy mocking the (mostly) Democratic politicians who use the term incorrectly. For example, Breitbart news poked fun at Joe Biden, who during the 2020 Democratic Primary race argued gun owners do not need a "magazine with 100 clips in it."[12]

Though these distinctions seem rather petty and technical, they represent a political tactic that the NRA uses to delegitimize their opponents. By attacking anti-gun politicians who misuse gun terminology, the organization casts aspersions on their ability to regulate objects that they seemingly know very little about. Someone who is pro-choice, for example, might empathize with this by thinking about how they feel about having their reproductive rights legislated away by someone who knows very little about gestation periods or reproductive anatomy.

The final banned word, "weapon," was offensive for more overtly political reasons. It was explained to us that the class we were taking was *not* a defensive shooting class, though passing the class does qualify you to apply for the Virginia Concealed Carry License. What we were learning was target shooting. We were thus not dealing with weapons but tools. This is an important distinction within the NRA's communications strategy. The argument goes that a firearm, like any other object, can be used for a multiplicity of purposes. Much like a baseball bat can be a piece of sporting equipment or a deadly bludgeon, the essential nature of the object is not inherent in its construction, but its use. The counterargument to this, of course, is that firearms were designed to be effective at killing, to which gun owners counter that, regardless of this, firearms are used most often by peaceful people for sporting purposes, hunting, and self-defense. Further, guns like those chambered in small cartridges like .22LR are not very effective at killing, but make excellent target guns. What is interesting is the extent to which the organization understands the power of language and knowledge in shaping the debate and uses their firearms safety courses as a medium to help make ordinary gun owners and NRA members into more effective advocates.

The NPF recognizes framing as an important narrative strategy that actors use to shape debates.[13] Frames serve to highlight sections of reality and bracket off others. Shaping the language that advocates use is an important way to frame the gun debate. It adds to some of the overarching narratives the organization disseminates through its other mediums. Thinking back to the NRAAM, and the secondary villains of the stories that Donald Trump's "good guy with a gun" guest speakers shared, we see how this works. The narratives that the good guys and gals with guns shared involved primary villains, the attackers, but also secondary villains, the politicians and activists operating in the background to try to disarm the heroes. Playing the language game is an important framing strategy that the organization can use to discredit these villains.

Following the classroom instruction, we were split into several small groups. While some of us trained on how to safely load and handle dummy firearms and ammunition, the rest wrote the multiple-choice qualifying test. When each group had passed the test and been introduced to the basics of safe firearms handling, it was time to head to the firing range. We were all sent back to the front desk to pay our range fees and buy any ammunition we needed. Those of us who were newer to handguns started with small bore, .22LR pistols, while those taking the course as part of their instructor training, who had more experience, had brought their guns from home, mostly 9mm polymer pistols like the Glock 19.

For the live fire portion of the course, we were once again split into groups, each led by a different instructor. Maggie led the first group, while two new instructors joined us to lead the other groups. One was a blond-haired, muscular young man and the other an older gentleman with a camo baseball cap and a long black beard. We were divided into three groups, with Timothy, Susan, John, and I grouped with Maggie. We waited in the lobby as the other two groups went in first. Eye and ear protection on, we continued to chit chat as we waited, struggling to hear one another with our ears plugged.

"So, what got you into guns?" I asked Timothy.

"What?" he said.

I repeated the question.

"I started shooting in the Air Force. We all had to be trained in basic firearm use. I realized I enjoyed target shooting and wanted to keep going after."

Later, over coffee, Timothy would expand on his journey into the world of guns. Since starting to target shoot recreationally, Timothy and his son Sam have fallen down the "rabbit hole," purchasing several handguns and now an AR-15 platform rifle. Sam, who got into shooting with his father, talks about how addictive this habit can be "you go down that rabbit hole and you really don't find a way back up ... You just go deeper and deeper."[14] Like many engaged in serious leisure pursuits, Timothy is aiming to turn his hobby into a side gig by becoming a firearms instructor. He does not wish to turn a profit from this, but merely use it to cover the cost of his involvement in the shooting sports.[15]

"We're up," Maggie interrupted our conversation.

She led us into the "sound lock." Indoor ranges always have two sets of doors. You walk through the first door, make sure that it is completely closed, and then enter the second door. This is to prevent the loud noise from entering the lobby where it could damage a patron's hearing.

Gun ranges tend to look quite similar. Most are concrete structures with thick walls. The range is divided into separate bays separated by steel dividers. These dividers are meant to deflect some of the sounds of your neighbor's shooting, and any empty cartridge casings that are ejected from the gun. This is much appreciated, as semi-automatic guns eject the bullet's casing after every shot, sending it flying out of the side of the gun. Getting hit with someone's "brass," while not painful, can be annoying. Further, if you fail to follow the direction of wearing a tight-fitting, collared shirt, and doing up your top button, hot, ejected brass can easily end up down your shirt, which I am told is a painful experience.

Each shooting bay in the range was outfitted with a table so that the shooter could set down their gun, ammunition, and any accessories they needed. The range featured the latest high-tech target system. This allowed the user to electronically adjust the distance that the target would be placed, and to call back the target holder to change paper targets. Paper targets can quickly fill up with holes, making it difficult to remember where your last shot was placed.

My group pulled up chairs behind the firing line, while Maggie took us up one by one to shoot. "For this round," Maggie shouted over the din of the shooting range, "just focus on putting your shots on paper." When it was clear that everyone was able to do this, we were given another practice round before shooting our qualifications. Maggie stood by each of us as we shot, correcting our stances and helping when we hit a snag. If she noticed a student mishandling a firearm or pointing it in 'a dangerous direction, she was ready to jump in, though she did not end up having to do so with our group.

The NRA has a system for measuring target shooting proficiency. Each level requires being able to shoot the target accurately and consistently from a further distance. Timothy and John were qualifying for their instructor level and had to take the shots from further away while Susan and I were simply going for our basic-level qualifications. Our shots were taken from ten feet away, at targets the size of a small tea saucer. You had to shoot each saucer five times consecutively. If you missed, you had to start again.

The experience of the firing range drove home to me the power of these courses as community-building tools. While some students had been chatting politely during the class, the experience of shooting brought our group together. When each of us would go up one by one to shoot, the rest of us would chat. When the person returned, we would cheer them on, high five and fist bump, especially when they were successful. We had gone from strangers to teammates in six hours.

When it was my turn, I walked up to the shooting bay. Maggie had placed the .22LR semi-automatic handgun on the table, the barrel pointing down-range. I had loaded my magazine while waiting and was ready to roll.

"Load the firearm," she said. I followed her orders and took up the shooting stance; hands extended in front of me, forming a triangle, knees relaxed but slightly bent, leaning forward to absorb any recoil from the gun.

"Go for it."

I took my shots slowly, one at a time. I remembered to fire at the bottom of my breath, so that the movement of chest expanding or contracting would not throw me off target. *Pop.* A small hole appeared in the black circle. I took another deep breath, waiting for the natural pause between exhaling and inhaling, steadying my hands. *Pop.* "Good!" Maggie said. Another breath. Another shot. Another breath. Another shot. This was it. One more to go. I relaxed my arms, keeping the gun pointing down-range. I shook out my shoulders to release some of the tension, then went back into my stance. I lined up my sights, concentrated on my breathing, and fired. *Pop.* Another hole in the black circle. I had qualified. I felt a rush of exhilaration and a sense of accomplishment and relief. In reality, the stakes could not have been lower for me. I did not need to qualify and when I returned home the certificate would be useless. Yet the experience of the classroom, the social dynamic and perhaps my innate competitive nature had made me deeply invested. Target shooting is a sport, and it is fun.

Once we had finished, we were free to leave. Leaving the range through a separate set of doors, we immediately went to the sink as instructed where we washed our hands and faces to remove any clinging lead particles. I exchanged information with Timothy, Susan, and John who had expressed interest in my project, and we discussed all going shooting together.

"You have to try this range near me," Timothy said. "It's state of the art!"

We agreed to meet later at Timothy's home range.

I left the class around four in the afternoon, exhausted but with a distinct sense of accomplishment. I had made contact. I had set up interviews. I was making progress. My next course would prove far more challenging.

Gun Culture: A Moving Target

As Yamane et al.[16] note, while the gun culture in the United States was originally centered around hunting and sports shooting. This began to shift towards self-defense, a shift which was accelerated rapidly in the 1980s due to legislative changes. The primary factor causing this rise was the concealed carry movement. But what was this movement, and how has it impacted the gun culture?

Before the 1980s, the majority of US states restricted gun carry. Many operated on a discretionary, or may-issue system for granting concealed carry permits. This means that those states had a large amount of discretion in deciding who was granted a permit and who was rejected.[17] Only ten states, clustered in the south and west of the country had *shall-issue* laws in place.[18] In a shall-issue system, the state must grant permits to anyone who can meet the basic requirements set out by the state, often related to training, residency, and the ability to pass a background check.[19]

Yet, the rising crime rates of the 1970s and 1980s, spurred on by the crack-cocaine epidemic, created a moral panic. This led to the creation of a movement to expand concealed carry. Washington was the first state to implement shall issue laws in 1961, though it remained an outlier until 1980 when Indiana joined the movement, followed a few years later by a growing number of states.[20] In 1987, Florida, which was experiencing higher crime rates than the rest of the country, shifted to shall-issue laws adding tremendous momentum to the movement.[21]

This movement paradoxically gained further momentum following the 1994 Federal assault-weapons ban, which left consumers seeking a new product and companies working hard to meet the demand. Seeking to make up lost ground, the NRA led the gun rights movement on an all-out charge to expand shall-issue laws at the state level. Between 1994 and 1995, 11 states brought in shall-issue laws.[22] At the time of writing, only nine states retain a may-issue system, and 21 states have gone so far as to bring in permitless carry laws, which do not require any type of license to carry a concealed handgun.[23]

Estimates suggest that, as of 2015, nine million Americans carry a handgun with them every month and three million do so daily.[24] This statistic becomes even more impressive when one reflects on the lifestyle changes that carrying a loaded handgun involves. To begin with, choosing to concealed carry generally involves drastic changes to an individual's wardrobe. On top of purchasing special holsters, concealed carriers need to avoid certain types of clothing. Tight-fitting clothing, for example, does not properly conceal a firearm and can cause a gun to snag when drawing it. As a concealed carrier, ordinary life events like going to the gym or the beach now involve complex logistics. For men, even using a urinal while concealed carrying becomes more complicated.

The patchwork geography of carry legislation is another major obstacle. On the micro-scale, there are many places where one cannot carry a firearm. From private businesses seeking to signal their opposition to guns by making their office a gun-free zone, to federal buildings and schools, these zones create complex landscapes for gun carriers to navigate. Encountering such a sign, a gun owner must choose between leaving their gun in their car, not entering the building, or flaunting the rules. Complex differences in state and county laws also pose a barrier. Most of my participants lived in the DMV: the DC-Maryland-Virginia area. This made crossing into states, or a federal district, with vastly different gun laws an everyday reality for them. Finally, gun carry opens up significant legal liability for gun owners, and has led to an entire industry of gun carry insurance that the NRA briefly engaged in.

Given all of this complexity, why do so many Americans choose to carry a gun? The common-sense answer to this question is fear of crime. This is seemingly supported by survey data, which shows that, when asked, the majority of respondents note "protection" as their main reason for carrying a gun.[25] Yet, the answer to this question is more complicated than survey data can capture, suffering as it does from a lack of depth and the problem of social desirability bias.

Authors writing from the field of sociology generally posit that masculinity is a large part of this equation. Though an increasing number of women are choosing to conceal carry, men still make up the lion's share of carry permit holders. Only 11 states have data available to the public on the gender of carry permit holders, making up a sample of about 5.4 million gun owners of which 26.5 per cent identified as women.[26] Melzer[27] sees the American tradition of "frontier masculinity" as being largely responsible for the existence of the gun culture. Carlson[28] explains this movement as part of a broader crisis of masculinity triggered by the erosion of the masculine bread-winner model. This crisis was brought about by neoliberal and post-industrial shifts in the US economy, which have unseated men from their traditional roles, which they then seek to recapture through the practice of firearms carry. I suspect that this is part of the equation, but I think these explanations miss out on other important elements: empowerment, enacting values, and pleasure.

The gun owners I spoke to generally positioned the outside world as dangerous and saw firearms, and the practice of gun carry, as empowering them to deal with the dangers that the world poses. Gun ownership and carry is often rhetorically positioned as another piece of safety equipment, like a fire extinguisher, which one keeps on hand to deal with a possibility, however remote, but hopes to never have to use. This came out in my interviews. Bucky noted that "of course it's not necessarily a nice world out there, and sometimes, unfortunately, you need to protect yourself from people who would do you harm."[29]

Just as carrying a firearm was a way to deal with an unfriendly world, it is also a way of enacting certain values. These values relate to the idea of gun ownership as a right. While most countries do not recognize gun ownership as a human right, gun rights advocates see this right as an extension of the human right to self-protection. The logic goes that virtually every society recognizes the right to self-defense. If criminals use firearms, then average people should have the right to defend themselves with equally powerful tools. Just as participants spoke of firearms ownership as the exercising of a right, they often framed gun carry, or the possession of loaded guns in the home for self-defense, as the exercising of that right. In an interview, my participant Susan summed this up neatly: "To me though it just means the right for me to be able to lawfully have a gun and to do what I wish with it as long as it's lawfully as well. Self-defense, to be able to have one in my house if I want to, loaded, which I don't keep mine loaded in the house but if I wanted that right to have it. If I wanted to, you know go running with my gun but I also just don't."[30] This quotation indicates that Susan's support for gun carry comes more from her core political values than her fear of crime. If Susan were fearful, she would keep a loaded gun in her household. However, she notes that she does not. What is important to her is the right to be able to do so should she choose.

Timothy also spoke of the importance of this right as it relates to self-defense: "We have the right to provide for ourselves while other nations' citizens must depend on the magnanimous nature of their government. We also have the right to defend ourselves. Again, a right not enjoyed by citizens in other countries. These other countries (governments) provide only an illusion to provide security for their citizens, but only really provide it for themselves."[31] The final reason for gun carry is joy or pleasure. This is probably the most difficult reason for non-gun owners to comprehend, but journalist and ethnographer Dan Baum captures the appeal of gun carry when he talks about the pleasure that gun enthusiasts get from handling firearms. He notes that gun owners derive a distinct pleasure from handling, thinking about, or seeing firearms, in the same way that a car enthusiast enjoys looking at pictures of cars online or in calendars, tinkering in their garage, or taking a car for a spin. "Most of us, though, seldom enjoy the pleasure of handling them – perhaps only when we take them from the safe for hunting season, plus a few sessions of target practice. The rest of the time, we read about them, think about them, and watch movies full of them. But we don't handle them. Imagine a musician who got to touch a guitar for one week a year."[32]

This sentiment was echoed by several of my participants. I suspect it is true that people who carry do fear crime. But I question the artificial distinction between leisure and preparedness. In many ways, being prepared, taking armed self-defense classes, or participating in other areas of gun culture related to self-defense are enjoyable to those who participate in them. As with other passions, from Yoga to music to skiing, these areas of our life resist being put away in boxes and seep through into our broader social relations. Anyone who has ever endured a conversation with a colleague or friend about the benefits of their latest exercise regime is familiar with this. Concealed carry allows gun owners to incorporate their serious leisure passion into other parts of their lives, and to embody or perform their political values. In the same way *Star Wars* fans plaster their cars with decals, carrying a firearm becomes another way of performing the social role of gun-owner and gun-enthusiast.

This sentiment came through clearly in my interviews. Though most of my participants spoke of having carry licenses, none were carrying when we met. When I asked Bucky if he was carrying, he said that though he has had his permit for 25 years, he often leaves his gun at home when running errands in his neighborhood, or when traveling into a different political jurisdiction, which he must do often for work.[33] Similarly, Timothy got into guns as a hobby, and then later ended up getting his concealed carry permit, suggesting that fear of crime was not his main motivation for gun ownership.[34] Susan, who often goes for early morning runs, discussed talking with her other running buddies about carrying while running. She described a conversation with a friend who lives in the same neighborhood who chastised Susan for not carrying when running. Susan responded:

> I mean I know you run early in the morning, but do you really think that like you're going to be like you need to carry your gun ... Not to say that something couldn't happen, but I have runner's mace that I carry with me when its warm, and or I'm alone or its night, I can just spray somebody in the face. I'd rather spray somebody in the face then shoot somebody ...

You have to worry more about people's dogs then people usually, based on where we live. It's not like were running in Southeast DC or in Baltimore.[35]

Rick admitted to carrying a gun for self-protection when he lived in a bad area. Now living in a gated community, far away from the troubles of nearby DC and Baltimore, he sees gun ownership as a recreational pursuit and so rarely carries:

> It's more of a hobby now at this point. It's not quite so much about self-protection because I'm in a fairly decent area. We live in … you know there's not a lot of crime in this area. I live in an upscale gated community house now, where I'm not having to live near a base or anything. So it's really more, after my retirement now, it's more about a hobby more than anything else. It's something else for me to tinker with. Whether I'm working on motorcycles or cars or doing stuff around the house. It's just one more thing for me to fill some time with. It's something I enjoy. There are some advantages to it. It's kind of calming. There's something about trying to put a little small, inch and a half long bullet into a target, you know, three-quarters of a mile to a mile away. That's pretty calming and relaxing and there's a lot of studying that goes to it. But it keeps me active.[36]

None of this is meant to suggest that fear of crime is not an important reason why many people, my participants included, own or carry firearms. Safety or security concerns were often mentioned by participants. Alvin, a participant who answered my online survey, responded to a question on the personal meaning of firearms by saying "Means Safety when carried." Barry noted, "it also means security in my hands." Carl listed "Self-Defense Preparedness" as a key reason for owning a gun.

But fear cannot tell the whole story. Looking at the full responses from the online survey, for example, Alvin followed up his comment on guns as safety with, "It also means fun when used in competition or shot at the range." Presented in full, Barry's answer reads: "It's mostly a sport/hobby, but it also means security in my hands." For Carl, "Self-Defense Preparedness" was listed six out of his seven motivations for owning a gun behind "Going to the range. Backyard plinking. Sports shooting … Hunting" and followed by "Firearms Collecting." Fear is not the whole picture.

Appadurai[37] is careful to note that while structuralist explanations are important for explaining the context of social action, it is important to be attuned to the agency of participants. Joy and pleasure are areas where we can directly observe the agency of participants at work.

Regardless of the motivations behind it, concealed carry is a significant and growing part of the gun culture.[38] Seeking to expand the gamut of training it offers millions of Americans in concealed carry, the NRA had recently revamped their basic concealed carry weapon (CCW)[39] course. As a result, I was amongst the first wave of students to get a chance to try the new curriculum.

To get to the class, I found myself driving along a backroad highway. Four lane expressways had long since given way to tree-lined backroads. I had left behind the mansions and suburban bungalows of Fairfax, finding instead farmhouses, trailers, and humble country homes. The speed limit was 50 mph, but the road twisted and turned so often I doubt that I ever got above forty. My GPS went haywire, alternating between welcoming me to Virginia and West Virginia as the road snaked along the state line. For me, it was an arbitrary boundary, but I could not help but reflect that, for many of my participants who choose to concealed carry firearms, it could be the difference between a Sunday drive and a hefty prison sentence, depending on the laws of the state they crossed into. This is the nature of the many-colored patchwork that is US Firearms Policy.

I walked into the class and introduced myself to the instructor, Bill. Bill was an older man, in his 60s, with short grey hair and a wide grin. He wore glasses, Gore-Tex hiking pants, and a black polo shirt with a shooting vest[40] over top. We had spoken several times over the phone when I explained my project to him and given that I was the only one in the class that he didn't know personally, he guessed who I was right away.

"You must be Noah," he said, smiling. "Now, you said you don't have your own gun, right?"

Since I was the only one without my own pistol, Bill was kind enough to lend me one from his collection, along with three spare magazines and a holster. After checking my passport to verify that I was indeed a US citizen, he handed me the unloaded firearm and holster and told me to wear it for the duration of the class. It was a Glock 19, the smaller, concealable version of the Glock 17 that I had tried in my previous class. Once again, no live ammunition was allowed in the classroom, but even having the unloaded gun on my belt I felt the weight of responsibility. It was unsettling at first. I kept reaching my hand down to make sure it had not moved. I grew accustomed to it as the day went on.

Bill introduced me to my three classmates. Given that this was a trial run of the new curriculum, the class size was kept small. All were ex-military or had worked in defense-related branches of the US government. All were interested in becoming instructors and approached the course from a pedagogical perspective, since they were familiar with most of the content already, had their CCW licenses, and carried regularly. I was clearly the outsider; a feeling that was only exacerbated after I introduced myself as a PhD student and dual citizen living in Canada.

Given that the day was quickly heating up, even at eight o'clock in the morning, Bill elected to switch the order for the class, conducting our practical training in the morning and leaving the book learning for the afternoon. After a short briefing, we went outside, fetched our eye and ear protection, and lined up along the shooting bench. The row of wooden benches, covered with an awning, was positioned 15 yards from several targets. These targets took the shape of a human silhouette rather than the circular targets that I had shot at the previous weekend during the pistol course. Bill explained that getting into the world of concealed carry was new for the NRA. Until recently, the "w word" (weapon) was completely forbidden. The NRA also refused to use silhouette targets for many years, given their humanoid appearance. As a large and old organization, the NRA is by its very nature conservative in both senses of the word. As such, they have been slower to adapt to the new realities of gun culture 2.0, which includes a shift in emphasis from recreation to self-defense. The new curriculum and course offerings were part of this shift.

The first 30 minutes outside were spent performing dry practice exercises. We practiced being able to draw the gun from the holster while keeping the muzzle pointed in a safe direction at all times. We had to practice moving aside an article of clothing to get at our concealed firearm, and Bill once again lent me a spare shooting vest to simulate having to clear away a shirt or jacket that I would be carrying the pistol under. Every single movement involved in drawing the gun was drilled into us. Bill walked behind us, checking to make sure our grip was correct, that we were doing the right movements and, most importantly, that our firearm was *always* pointed in a safe direction even when unloaded.

"Keep your pistol close to your chest when you draw, then extend out. Real self-defense shootings are not like Hollywood, they happen close, and they happen fast. You may not be able to get the gun all the way out if you must shoot, but that's okay. You can fire from closer in."

Respect for safety is drilled into gun owners during these courses. A large part of this is due to the nature of the activity. Accidents are rare in the shooting sports, yet when they occur the results can be life-changing, or life-ending. As a result, most gun owners that I know tend to be safety fanatics, and it is not uncommon to see someone being yelled at or kicked-off a gun range for a relatively minor safety infraction. While this respect for safety is likely genuine, some of it is also performative and political, as gun owners know that any mistake that they make is likely to be used as ammunition against their right to own and use firearms.

"Load five rounds into your magazine," Bill barked.

The dry fire was over. It was time to practice the real thing. I had brought with me several boxes of 9mm Luger ammunition, purchased at a nearby Walmart. Since I did not have a US driver's license, I had shown the cashier my passport, verifying that I was a US citizen and of age, and he had unlocked the case and handed me the ammunition. I carefully loaded five rounds into the Glock's detachable magazine, hand shaking slightly. Standing in front of the target, I slid the magazine into the gun and racked the slide to put a round into the chamber. There is no manual safety on a Glock, as it was originally designed with law enforcement officers in mind. Its manufacturers found that in self-defense scenarios, manual safeties often created problems for police officers, who would leave them on accidentally or worse, forget that they had not engaged them and act recklessly.[41] As soon as the round was chambered, the gun was ready to go. Arms extended in front of me, forming a triangle, I squeezed the trigger and dotted the silhouette target with five holes.

When we had run through all of the drills, and several hundred rounds of ammunition, it was time to take the test to qualify. "To get your certification," Bill explained, "80% of your shots must hit within the center zone of the target." This included the head and most of the torso. This was easy from three yards away. When the distance increased to seven, then 15 yards, however, it became more challenging. Though I am a relatively new pistol shooter, under Bill's tutelage I was able to pass the course, albeit with the lowest score of the group. At the end of the qualification test, however, one of the more experienced shooters approached me: "You did really well." He was impressed that this bespectacled and soft-spoken scholar could keep up with seasoned shooters. Though Bill constantly gave me pointers and corrections, he too admitted that I was shooting better than he had expected.

By the time we had finished the test I was sweating buckets and at the brink of heat exhaustion. We cleared[42] and holstered our guns, spent a good ten minutes picking up brass casings from the ground, and headed inside to the classroom. Post-shooting, the mood in the classroom had shifted perceptibly. Though not unfriendly, the other students in the class had largely ignored me in the morning. Now they were chatting more freely. "So, what exactly are you studying?" the man next to me asked. They were curious about gun laws in Canada, and we got into a long conversation about the wide variation of state-level gun laws in America, and what this meant for the Second Amendment. Shooting together, like other sports, creates a bond between people. The shared physical, emotional, and chemical experience of shooting creates a special sense of comradery, and community, amongst those that take part.

Overcoming suspicion would become a major hurdle in throughout my project, as gun owners tend to be suspicious of academics, journalists, or other members of the social elite that they see as a threat to the right to bear arms. Gun owners often share what I have labelled narratives of suppression. These narratives usually involve a powerful individual, group, or industry that has targeted the gun-owning community in some way. This came out in many of my interviews. Bucky, for example, casually alluded to the fact that the grocery store we were meeting in had stopped carrying firearm-related magazines: "But like a lot of places don't carry these magazines. I mean this place here stopped carrying, at least last time I checked, stopped carrying any gun related magazines." I asked him to expand on this and he said, "They used to. But the last time I looked – gone ... (pause) ... Not a good thing."[43] Bucky explained that he believed this was part of an increasing number of companies cutting ties with the firearms industry and gun-related groups.

Sam mentioned that, in Alaska where he studies, people are much more used to firearm ownership. I asked if he was able to talk guns with people his age in Virginia. He replied: "Oh, here in Virginia no I don't feel ... with people my age there is a lot of controversy." He lamented this fact, explaining that: "I wish it was more open, that people could talk about it, because I actually like hearing other people. Especially if their opinions aren't (like) mine, they are against my opinion. I like doing that. Because then we get to actually talk and have an educated conversation about why do I support mine, why do you support yours, and hopefully come out with a whole new perspective that's better."[44] Rick noted that this perceived suppression in the form of "credible threats" by the "previous presidential administration" motivated him to buy his first AR-15 and get involved with the NRA:

> When you have over restrictive stuff like that that makes zero sense, and these laws and regulations and things that they think are going to stop the violence, they're dead wrong. It hasn't worked in Chicago. It hasn't worked in New York. It just doesn't work. Because the only people you're going to restrict are the law-abiding people that are going to follow those restrictions. Uh ... Because of Barack Obama, and his administration, that's the only reason why I ever went out and bought an AR-15. When he threatened me with not being able to ever own one, I said well I better go get it now, just in case.[45]

An online participant expressed similar sentiments against wealthy businessmen who have lent support to gun control efforts. When asked why he joined a gun rights group, this individual answered: "The attempts in recent years by rich people (for example, Mike Bloomberg) to use their money and influence to deny poor people the comforts of security that the rich enjoy (in other words, a poor person cannot afford a body-guard, but they can afford a gun). This is just another way in which the rich are willing to victimize the poor for a vision of an (*sic*) utopia which will never be a reality." Serious leisure pursuits can become a major pil-lar of a participant's identity. This is even more true in the Great Gun Debate, where the language of life and death, and important political values like liberty and security, become attached to the debate. These narratives of suppression were an important way for gun owners to push back against the feeling of encroaching doom that is ever present in dis-cussions of gun politics. In a sense, they betray a feeling of powerlessness within the community, the sense that one is David staring down Goliath and unsure of the outcome of the fight.

The afternoon was spent on the theoretical portion of the course. This included things like choosing the right firearm and different ways of car-rying a concealed firearm. To the uninitiated, this probably seems rather pedantic but within the gun-owning community, it is the topic of endless vitriolic debate.

"Now, I hear a lot lately about appendix carry," Bill said.

Appendix carry is the newest gun carry fad, where the gun is placed in a holster between the bottom of one's belly button and one's pubis, facing downwards. Proponents argue that this is one of the most comfort-able and concealable carry methods, though I did not try it myself. This kicked off a heated debate in the class.

"I dunno," one of my classmates noted, interrupting Bill during a pause. "Whenever I think of appendix carrying, I always think of the first rule."

Everyone laughed. He was referring, of course, to the fact that when carrying appendix your holstered firearm is pointed directly at your geni-tals, running up against one of the central rules of firearms safety: "Never point your gun at anything you are not willing to destroy."

The discussion then shifted to defensive encounters. It covered proper situational awareness, which refers to changing how you navigate the world around you to be more mindful and aware of potential dangers, as well as how to avoid confrontation. The instructor ran us through some hypothetical situations to practice our situational awareness.

Hypothetical narratives present an interesting case study for scholars of storytelling. At the time of writing, I could find no NPF studies that look specifically at hypothetical narratives in public policy. While per-haps not as impactful as a true story, hypothetical narratives can still have an emotional draw on the listener and have the added benefit of allowing them to imagine themselves more literally in the scenario. These scenarios were often used in NRA courses, and occurred in online discussions about topics ranging from home or self-defense to preparing for apocalyptic scenarios.

During the class, we were presented with the hypothetical narrative of walking down a dark street toward a group of suspicious-looking men. The instructor took us through the escalation of force, emphasizing, like the textbook, that firearms are a tool of last resort, and that there are several steps to consider before using one's firearm. We were encouraged to cross the street when we saw the strangers approaching us. When the group crossed with us, we were told to try to hide inside a nearby business, in this case, a corner store. Eventually, when the ruffians cornered us, we had no choices left, it was do or die.

Hypothetical narratives and visualization strategies are tools used by professional athletes[46] and, in the 1990s, a special school was set up at West Point Academy to incorporate this training into the military.[47] These drills have since been incorporated into firearm's training to increase the mental readiness of carriers to deal with a real threat, and to help mitigate the inherent risks that come with carrying a firearm for self-defense.[48]

These hypothetical narratives are not only useful training tools but effective forms of political communication as well. As I discussed in the previous chapter, the hypothetical scenario of the single mother defending herself with a gun in the fictional trailer park outside of Indianapolis was an effective narrative strategy employed by Chris Cox during the NRAAM speeches. This strategy was effectively coupled with the three real-life testimonials of survivors of self-defense scenarios. This helps bridge the mental gap between the individual and these events.

The final portion of the CCW course covered what to do in the aftermath of a defensive encounter. This included both the legal and the emotional repercussions of a self-defense shooting. When we talked about the body's physiological responses to danger, other students shared stories of their experiences of adrenaline rushes and other physiological responses to fear. This included a discussion of Post-Traumatic Stress Disorder and the importance of seeking help afterward, whether through professional therapy or religious counselling.

As the day concluded, we handed in our completed exams and then graded them as a group. We finished up by discussing how to become more involved with the NRA. Bill went over some things that the NRA does for the firearms community and talked about ways that we could get more involved with the organization.

Cautionary Tales

Not all the courses that I took involved putting lead on target. They did not even all involve guns. The NRA's Refuse to Be a Victim Program is the organization's answer to the rising popularity of women's self-defense classes in the 1990s. Though the program is not explicitly aimed at women, it is clearly intended for a female audience. White, middle-class women make up the subject of nearly all of the pictures in the course textbook, for example. In the actual classroom, I was the only man.

The course was held at a private firearms school in the countryside. It took place in a portable classroom, evoking memories of my public elementary school education. I met the owner of the school when I arrived. She was a short, African American woman in her 50s, who was dressed like she was about to go play tennis, with the addition of a black, semi-auto handgun strapped to her waist. "Welcome," she smiled, and put her arm around me, as if greeting an old friend. "Just head outside across the parking lot. She's waiting for you there."

The instructor, Wanda, was an older African American woman in her early 60s. She was thin and walked slowly and cautiously due to a medical condition. She would have appeared almost frail were it not for the no-nonsense attitude that oozed from her persona. This attitude, however, masked a deep well of kindness. She had a piercing gaze and a facial expression that warned you that she was not someone to be trifled with. When her smile broke through the tough exterior, though, it was warm and gentle. This contradiction was embodied when she spoke about her grandchildren, which she did often. Her voice became soft in these moments then hardened again when she told us what she would do to keep them safe.

There was a wide age range of students in the class, and it was the most diverse NRA class that I took during my fieldwork. The first student to arrive was a middle-aged, African American woman with pink hair, a backward baseball cap, and prominent tattoos and piercings. She was a tow-truck driver and arrived with her truck fully loaded with a pickup truck on the back, much to the consternation of the school's owner. The next to arrive was a younger white woman, probably in her early 30s, with brown hair and an ostentatiously large wedding ring. She wore a red-orange Columbia hiking shirt, not uncommon shooting range attire. She introduced herself to the instructor as an instructor in training, who was supposed to shadow Wanda, whom she called "the best in the business."

Behind me sat a woman in her 50s who had brought along her mother, Betty, a spritely senior citizen whose spunky attitude reminded me of the characters that Betty White often plays on television. "I'm from New

York," she later told us. "People don't mess with me." She was also quite tough and talked about carrying a knife and pepper spray, and what she would do to criminals who tried to cross her. When we were introducing ourselves, Betty said that she had several guns already but wanted more training: "I'm armed to the teeth, but I don't know what to do with the darned things." When Wanda later talked about not carrying assisted opening knives, as they are illegal in Maryland, Betty joked: "I'm a little old lady, the cops aren't going to bother me," and winked.

The last row was occupied by a larger African American woman with short-cropped hair named Christina. She would later introduce herself as a parole officer. Finally, next to her and the last to arrive was a woman wearing a colorful floral hijab and black glasses, Salma. Salma had brought her young son who was no older than 10. This raised some eyebrows around the room.

The NRA Refuse to Be a Victim program highlights some of the contradictions in the organization, as it attempts to evolve with the times. On the one hand, the NRA has gone to great lengths to rebrand itself, hiring and prominently displaying diverse spokespeople like Dana Loesch and Colion Noir, and producing many publications and programs focused on getting women, people of color, and people with disabilities involved in the shooting sports. The organization recognizes that without expanding its appeal beyond its core demographic of older white men, it will not survive.[49] Yet, the Refuse to Be a Victim program seems to contravene this image. Firearms were barely mentioned during the course, as the curricular designers seemed to assume that women would be less comfortable with armed self-defense and chose to focus instead on prevention and less-than-lethal defense techniques.[50] Further, the pictures and examples in the textbook and course curriculum focus mostly on middle-class, white women. The instructor supplemented the curriculum, drawing on her own experiences living in low-income inner-city neighborhoods, but the main curriculum is missing out on a large segment of the market for the course.

Wanda began the course by explaining that the Refuse to Be a Victim seminar is about being prepared for any situation, using common sense solutions. "This is one of the NRA's only non-firearms courses," she said. "This is important because, in a self-defense situation, you usually only have three seconds to react, and sometimes this is not enough time to get to your gun."

Given the lack of gunplay in the course, narrative and mental training became even more important. Throughout the day, Wanda would often throw scenarios at us to ask how we would react. "You get back to your car in a parking lot to find that a white, unmarked van has parked next to you." She fixed her piercing glare at me. "What do you do?"

Taken aback, I panicked and said, "I would try to look into the front windows?"

"Wrong!" Wanda barked, in her matter-of-fact way.

She explained that in most snatch and grab situations, the criminal will hide in the back seat of the van and grab you from there. The correct answer, provided by Betty, was to ask a friend to escort you out. This was one of the many times throughout the day where I was forced to come to terms with the blind spots that my male privilege had left in my perception of the world. Blushing, I reflected on the fact that it would never occur to me to ask someone to walk me to my car. The risks we were discussing were much more real in the lives of these women than in my own.

Once again, these hypothetical narratives were extremely emotionally impactful. By placing the listener in the driver's seat of the narrative, the stories are imbued with a sense of realism and urgency.

On top of the hypothetical narratives, the workshop became a space for people to share their own personal stories of crime and victimization. Wanda would sometimes interject, correcting or commending the behavior that the people in the stories displayed. Quite unusually, I was the quietest student in the class. Occasionally, I was able to share some of my own stories, such as an incident that had happened earlier that week when a man tried to trick me into letting him into my car at a gas station. "Oh, that happened to a friend of mine!" someone interjected.

I am quite soft-spoken personally and did not have much of a problem blending in with the rest of the class. Wanda noted this later when talking about how the way that you carry yourself, and visual cues like eye contact, can communicate subconsciously to criminals that you are a soft target. When commenting on my unconscious communications, Wanda fumbled her words, clearly worried about offending my masculinity: "You … uh … you have a gentle and polite demeanor." I blushed, more worried that she would worry that I was offended than offended myself.

"What's your personal space?" Wanda later asked.

"About arm's length," one student said, most of us nodding in agreement.

"Wrong!" Wanda barked again. "Your personal space is as far as you can see. *You* are responsible for knowing what is in that space. The best strategy for personal safety is to avoid confrontation. When in doubt, get out."

Like in the Concealed Carry class, Wanda constantly stressed the importance of situational awareness. "Everybody is walking around outside, distracted all the time. Smartphones, iPods, video games …" She trailed off, shaking her head.

Surprisingly, quite a large portion of the course was taken up discussing non-physical threats, like scams and cyber-crime. Wanda also addressed the influence of technology on people's behavior. Few people in the class spoke positively about the digital revolution.

"If something happens, you can't count on people to step in and help you. These days, they're just gonna pull out their phones and videotape you."

There was, I must admit, quite a bit of truth to that.

The overall themes of the course were vigilance and responsibility. We put these into action later, when our guest speaker came in. Erik was an African American man in his late forties. He was tall and broad-chested, built like a linebacker, but with a long grey and black beard. He was wearing a dark red polo. He introduced himself as an ex-US marine who now trains law enforcement in self-defense techniques.

Erik once again emphasized visualization during our practice, talking us through the self-defense mindset. He said that most people do not want to think that bad things can happen to them.

"Just like people don't go to the doctor, because they don't wanna hear bad medical news."

He took us through a visualization exercise.

"Picture someone attacking you, how are you going to respond? Okay, now picture someone attacking someone you love?"

We all agreed that we were more aggressive in the later visualization.

"Why do you value your own lives so little?" he wondered.

Erik told us that, in many cases, people who resist violent attacks fare better than those who submit. He shared stories of break-ins and famous serial killers, and how people would submit to the criminals hoping to be spared.

"Why will we fight for others but not ourselves?" He then took us through body mechanics exercises and showed us a few self-defense strategies, before shifting into a conversation about how to pick the right pepper spray.

Toward the end of the class, we finally talked about guns. Wanda noted that the use of firearms as a means of self-protection depends on your living situation. Most of the women in the room seemed to already have firearms in their homes. Christina, who works as a parole officer with sex offenders in a rough city, mentioned she lived alone, and that her job puts her at significant risk. She described sleeping with a shotgun and having strategic caches of weapons staged[51] throughout the house.

This story drove home to me the complex ways that privilege can blind those on both sides of the Great Gun Debate. Though it is working to appeal to new groups, the NRA material is still very much shaped and motivated by the perspective of white men of privilege. This is not a particularly controversial or revolutionary statement to make and I do not expect that it will ruffle the feathers of many readers. What those of us who approach the debate from an academic perspective often fail to recognize, and especially those of us coming at this debate from outside of the United States, is how our own privilege can color the pro-control perspective. I have been guilty of this in the past, skeptical that anyone would need a firearm for self-protection. What my experiences within the gun culture have shown me is the extent to which this view reflects my having grown up in middle-class Canadian suburbs. Christina's positionality, and her employment, placed her at considerable risk. For her, firearms were a risk management tool in an uncertain world. Would she be safer if firearms were less widely available in the United States? If Americans invested in public institutions to improve policing, fight substance abuse, and support those in need? Perhaps. But these questions are academic.

Despite the somewhat macabre topics of conversation, the atmosphere of the class was quite convivial and warm. We became fast friends as people were eager to share their stories and experiences, to learn from one another and to tell jokes. The school, and the firearms range with which it was associated next store, was a family business, and several people, including Wanda's brother, popped in and out of the class at varying intervals to smile at Wanda and joke around with us. I once again felt the sense of community among a group of like-minded people. You could tell that people appreciated the space to discuss a topic that they might not share with others, and how the experience strengthened and reaffirmed their core political beliefs.

The NRA Basic Rifle Shooting Course and the NRA Basic Shotgun Shooting Course took on a similar rhythm to the other courses I had taken. The mornings were taken up with the theoretical portion, where we learned how to own and operate a firearm safely. I must somewhat reticently note that these classes put the Canadian Firearms Safety Course (CFSC),[52] which I had completed in preparation for my fieldwork, to shame. While much of CFSC is taken up with complex and counterproductive acronyms and dated material, the NRA courses cover a lot more ground and are updated regularly. For example, the Canadian course offered no instruction for students on how to clean their firearms, a major component of firearms safety. This was covered in depth in the NRA courses. Further, the Canadian course has no live-fire component. Students handle de-activated firearms in class but never go to the range under the supervision of an instructor. Students taking the NRA course cannot pass without demonstrating both theoretical knowledge of firearms safety, and the ability to safely handle firearms on the range.

The live-fire portion of the NRA Rifle Course took place at the NRA's dedicated range. The instructor, Rick, who I would later interview, took us through the qualification, which we completed using his rifles. Afterward, we were invited to stay late and try out a few of Rick's firearms, including his AR-15. Interestingly, Rick had mentioned that he had never been interested in owning an AR-15 until Barack Obama raised the idea of banning assault weapons. He saw the ownership of the much-maligned firearm as a form of protest. As a veteran, he was also familiar with the platform, as the controls of the AR-15 are similar to the M4 Carbine used by the US military, though the two guns are functionally different. I had never fired an AR-15 before, and I must admit its notoriety made the experience feel taboo in a way that shooting the bolt action .22 had not. At the same time, I could appreciate the qualities that make the rifle so popular. It was easy to handle, the recoil was manageable, and the rifle had been customized extensively.

For the practical component of the NRA shotgun course, the instructor Steve took us to his large property in rural Maryland. He had a Trap Thrower, a machine that launches clay-pigeons into the air, which allowed us to practice skeet and trap shooting. We had completed the theoretical portion of the course in a boardroom in suburban Baltimore which belonged to a small business owner who was a friend of Steve. After lunch, we formed a caravan and drove to his property. Parking our cars, Steve joined us with his fully loaded ATV. We threw our bags in the trailer and walked alongside it to the middle of the field. It was hot, and Steve had loaded the trailer with water bottles and sports drinks, which we chugged between shots.

Once again, Steve took us all through the qualifications to pass the course and then allowed us to keep shooting together. He gave us tips and pointers on our technique. Unlike the rifle and pistol shooting I had done so far, clay pigeon shooting involves firing at a moving target. This introduces some different techniques and mental calculations into your practice, making it both more challenging and more engaging.

In both the rifle and shotgun course, the practical portion of the course once again inspired a sense of comradery amongst participants. We had started the day as shy, silent strangers, and finished as fast friends. The cultural practices of the gun culture, target shooting, hunting, and self-defense preparedness are *social* practices. Incorporating people into these practices makes it more likely that they will contribute to the gun rights movement. The gun rights movement, and the NRA, understand that bringing people into the gun culture strengthens the movement by giving people a stake in the fight. They use venues like their firearms classes as community-building tools, employing modalities like narratives to build a political community of gun owners.

Range Days

The glossy handle of the small revolver made it difficult to grip with my naturally sweaty palms. After a few shots, I decided to put on my leather and nylon shooting gloves to give me more traction. The heavy trigger pull of the revolver rotated the cylinder, lining up a single round of .357 Magnum with the chamber of the gun. As the trigger clicked, the firing pin struck the primer and for a fraction of a section I held in my hands a miniaturized, controlled explosion. I directed that explosion at the paper target ten yards ahead of me, and then looked up to admire my handiwork. As my participant, Timothy would later describe it, at that moment "it's just you and the paper (target) trying to control the laws of physics."[53]

Going to the shooting range is a central cultural practice in the gun culture. During my research, I went to the range four times with my participants, not counting the visits to the range during the NRA courses. Engaging in this practice helped build a rapport with my participants, and a trip to the range was often followed by an interview.

I took my first trip to the range after my NRA Pistol Course. I had agreed to meet Timothy and Susan at a shooting range in northern Virginia. We went in the evening, just after dinnertime. Like many indoor ranges, it occupied a fairly non-descript building in a large industrial park. From the outside, the building looked like a FedEx Depot, except for the large sign with the name and logo of the business. I ran into Susan in the parking lot, and we walked in together. This was Timothy's favorite place to shoot, but neither Susan nor I had been there before.

Entering the lobby, we both looked around in bemusement. The facility was part of a growing trend of boutique shooting ranges – dubbed "guntry clubs." These ranges are generally quite upscale, featuring a large pro shop and state-of-the-art amenities like electronic target holders, advanced air filtration systems, and other add-ons.

As Susan and I approached the front desk, we were greeted by two young women wearing black polos with the range's logo on them. They checked us in, verified our IDs, and had us sign the range's long liability waiver. Before being able to shoot, we had to watch a safety briefing in a large conference room with a big-screen television. Timothy was already there when we arrived, and greeted us warmly, like an old friend. Timothy is one of those people who has a way of connecting with anyone he meets. His warm smile, genuinely sunny disposition, and positive attitude make him a very difficult person to dislike. We watched the safety briefing while he arranged our shooting lanes. The video was about ten minutes long and covered the basic dos and don'ts of shooting, as well as rules for the range, like which caliber, ammo type, and type of firearm were approved for use.

Once the video was done, we headed to the counter to pay our range fees. We then put on our eye and ear protection and passed through the two-door airlock and onto the range. This shooting range was much bigger than the one where we had taken our pistol course. The facility was divided into three separate ranges of varying distances, all indoors, divided into separate bays. Heading towards our pre-assigned section, we passed a group of two men and two women shooting together on a double-date. Timothy placed his gun cases on the table and started to unpack the firearms we would be using, careful to place the pistols with the barrel facing downrange. While he set up, I looked around. Next to us, a uniformed police officer practiced drawing from the holster and firing. To our right, at the end of the range, a young couple were taking turns firing a 12-gauge shotgun. The blast of the shotgun was rather unnerving in the indoor space, even with the double layer of ear protection I was wearing.[54]

"You can borrow my Glock," Timothy shouted over the din of the range. He gestured to his Glock 17 pistol lying on the shooting table, action open to show that it was unloaded. "Who wants to go first?"

Timothy seemed genuinely excited to have new range buddies, as he often goes shooting alone. He is also a natural born teacher, which is part of the reason he is trying to become a firearms instructor. With his children away at university, he was excited to have people to share his knowledge with, and I was very eager for his pointers. He had brought targets, which we clipped into the caddy. Typing seven yards into the computer screen, our target was whisked off downrange.

"Susan, you go first," I said.

She had brought her compact Smith & Wesson semi-automatic pistol, as well as her revolver, which had belonged to her late father. She stepped up to the table, loaded her handgun, and got to it. While she shot, Timothy handed me a Glock magazine to load with 9mm target rounds.

Once Susan was done, she made her gun safe and turned to Timothy, who gave her a high five.

"Great group!" he said, always encouraging and enthusiastic.

I stepped up to the booth, with Timothy standing next to me to offer advice. I did well. The Glock fit naturally in my hand and had a very positive grip. Having shot a few Glocks throughout my fieldwork, I can understand why the firearm is now ubiquitous in American gun culture. It is like the Mac computers of the gun world, sleek, simple, and easy to use right out of the box.

"Great job!" Timothy said. "Next time focus on your trigger pull. I could see you anticipating the recoil. Pull back slowly. Remember, you want the bang to surprise you a bit."

When shooting, trigger control is incredibly important. Jerking the trigger too hard causes the muzzle of the gun to move when you shoot and can affect where your shot lands by several inches.

We ended up staying until the range closed for the evening, firing at least a hundred rounds each. After washing up, we agreed to meet again to go shooting and would head to the range together a few times during my fieldwork. These visits to the gun range impressed upon me the role that these spaces play in the gun-owning community. They serve a major function as gathering spaces for gun owners, and the site of one of the most important cultural practices associated with the gun culture: shooting. These ranges also often work like community centers; they have cafes where members can socialize, and they organize events, socials, and classes. While the indoor ranges we shot in were run by private companies, others are run by non-profit associations or conservation groups and operated by volunteers. The NRA itself runs several ranges, including one in its headquarters in Fairfax.

The NRA recognizes that gun ranges are spaces where they can gain access to their potential members and advertise their organization and programs. Some ranges and gun shops, for example, give out NRA pamphlets advertising the organization. Other ranges partner with them, offering discounted range fees or memberships for NRA members. You would be hard-pressed to walk into a gun range and not see an NRA logo somewhere in the background.

Gun Shows

The gun show is yet another institution and cultural practice of the gun-owning community. Since the 1930s, gun shows have been "local gatherings for the display, sale, and exchange of firearms."[55] They are held anywhere from convention centers to malls, churches to community centers. Though they have a long history, early gun shows were much smaller affairs. In 1986, however, the Firearms Owner's Protection Act was passed by Ronald Reagan, easing the regulations around where gun businesses could sell to customers. This led to a boom in gun shows.[56] The Bureau of Alcohol, Tobacco, Firearms, and Explosives (ATF) estimates that there are now more than 5,000 gun shows every year in the United States.[57]

Gun shows are also popular in Canada, especially in rural and western communities, though I could find no official statistics on how many are held annually.

Gun shows have been at the center of the gun debate in recently years, due to what is colloquially called the "gun show loophole." This refers to the fact that some states do not require a background check to be conducted for the *private* sale of a firearm. While businesses that possess a Federal Firearms License must put all customers through a background check, individuals conducting private gun sales are not required to do so. Pro-control advocates argue that closing this loophole is common sense and would help keep guns out of the hands of mass shooters and criminals.

On the other side, pro-gun advocates note the logistical difficulties that attempting to regulate private firearms transfers could raise. First, they argue that these regulations would only impact people who already want to follow the law, and the ban would be unenforceable. Further, they note that being able to transfer firearms between family members is a part of American heritage and tradition, as many young men receive their first gun from their parents or a family member. Finally, loaning guns to a friend during a time of personal crisis is used as a way to reduce the risk of gun-related suicide in many rural communities.[58]

While gun shows are at the center of the gun debate, it is unclear how much they contribute to the circulation of illicit firearms. A 1999 report conducted by the ATF warns that "gun shows provide a forum for illegal firearms sales and trafficking." They note that their investigations "reveal a diversity of Federal firearms violations associated with gun shows."[59] Survey data gathered amongst convicted criminals paints a different picture. Criminals, it seems, prefer to source guns through family members, friends, or illicit networks. A survey of prison inmates conducted by the US Department of Justice, for example, found that only 0.7 per cent of criminals sourced their guns from gun shows, while 39.6 per cent acquired them from family or friends.[60]

Throughout my fieldwork, I had the opportunity to conduct participant observation at two gun shows and on both sides of the table. As those who have done fieldwork can attest, often the biggest breakthroughs are not a part of your original research design. While talking to a colleague at George Mason University, where I was a visiting scholar, he mentioned radio ads that he had heard for a gun show near Dulles airport. I decided that it would be worth my while to check it out.

The gun show took place over three days at an airport convention center located in a suburban mall. I arrived on Saturday morning, a few hours after the show opened. The parking lot was already full, and I had to park in the reserved parking which was slightly further away. The lot was mostly filled with large SUVs and a sea of pickup trucks. A significant percentage of the cars were adorned with gun-related bumper stickers, featuring parts of the Second Amendment, the logos of gun brands, or political witticisms.

Though this gun show was organized by a private company, the NRA was very much present. Two NRA booths were set up, one at each main entrance to the convention center. Volunteers at the booths were promoting the NRA and its various programs and encouraging convention-goers to sign up to become members.

I walked inside and purchased my ticket to the show for $16 from a blonde, middle-aged woman in a straw hat covered in flowers. She had the demeanor of a bubbly kindergarten teacher, and greeted me warmly: "Good morning, hun. Just one ticket then?" I showed the security guard my stamped hand and walked past the gun inspection booth, a safety precaution at most gun shows. Given the number of guns being handled at the show, allowing unboxed, live ammunition, or loaded guns, is a recipe for an accident.

The gun show occupied most of the convention center. It was made up of a large central room, and a smaller side room, though even the smaller room was about the size of two high school gymnasiums. The show claimed to contain over 1,300 booths, most of which were filled by smaller businesses and mom and pop shops. Many of the people operating the booths had brought their children with them or even put them to work.

My time at the NRAAM had given me the chance to develop an order of operations, or methodology, for conducting participant observation at the gun show. My first step is always to take a quick initial lap around the convention center and collect my first impressions. During this lap I focused on the large crowd surrounding me. The booths had been arranged in a tight formation, which made wading through the large crowd difficult. It did, however, give me lots of time to observe. Though predominantly white and male, the crowd was still quite diverse. There were a large number of African American men and families, as well as many Asian Americans. The older generation in attendance seemed to be mostly white, however, the younger crowd was a lot more diverse in terms of race and gender. Many women in attendance seemed to be with their partners, though I saw a few women flying solo or visiting with their girlfriends.

Walking around, I spotted a man in a cowboy hat and camo cargo pants, with a long brown beard and shoulder-length hair examining a pistol. Across from him, a small group of 20-something Southeast Asian

American men with bulging muscles and tattoos were ogling Sig Sauer's latest take on the AR-15 platform. Their years of experience with firearms showed in the way they handled the rifle on the showroom floor, inspecting the chamber before picking it up, and always controlling the direction of the muzzle. At a nearby booth, an African American woman with long dreadlocks unsheathed a Samurai sword, examining the blade. Like Dulles airport itself, the gun show stood at a crossroads between urbanized DC and the suburbs and countryside of Northern Virginia. But it also reflected the crossroads in the gun culture, between old and young, Gun Culture 1.0 and Gun Culture 2.0.[61]

While reflecting on this, one booth in particular caught my eye. It was run by a small non-profit organization devoted to women's self-defense. The bright pink design of the stall was quite eye-catching, as well as the colored hair and bright eye-makeup of the young African American woman minding the booth. I introduced myself and she confessed: "We don't get a lot of men stopping by this stall."

"I'm a researcher," I said, "I sometimes look at the intersections between gender and gun culture."[62]

This made her smile.

"Well, you've come to the right booth. We are a small organization. We focus on empowering women to take responsibility for self-defense. We have pamphlets and books for kids, all kind of great stuff!"

She gave me a quick tour of the booth then turned to another patron while I continued to look around. The booth sold accessories like self-defense key chains, personal alarms, pepper spray, and tasers, all available in black or pink.

This booth was yet another example of the emerging nexus between women's self-defense and the world of guns, a connection that the NRA is working hard to forge through their communications material[63] and their courses. As I later discovered, booths at gun shows can be rented by virtually anyone, subject to the approval of the organization or company running the show. It was clear that this women's self-defense group saw the show as a way to reach its core demographic, women who might be concerned about self-protection.

The gun show was a hive of activity. Like at the NRAAM, there were a multitude of products for sale. Beyond the obvious firearms of every type and caliber, there were other products as well. Certain booths specialized in antique and used firearms, some selling for vast sums. The most expensive item I saw was an antique revolver from the old west that was priced at $18,000. Other booths specialized in selling knives for hunting or everyday carry as well as less-than-lethal self-defense tools for the less gun-friendly jurisdictions in the vicinity of Dulles. Every once in a while, the general din of the showroom was pierced by the crackling of a taser demonstration.[64] The first time I heard the loud *zap* I almost jumped out of my skin, but I soon became accustomed to it.

This was not the only initially shocking practice I would become used to as the show progressed. Given that a large part of attending the gun show is buying, swapping, and selling used guns, it is common to see people walking around with shouldered rifles and holstered pistols. This was quite surprising at first. Given the size of the NRA show, and the level of professionalization, guns were not permitted to be taken from the booths. At these smaller shows, however, a sizeable minority of attendees were walking around packing unloaded guns. I found this particularly striking where children were involved. At one point a younger boy, probably twelve, walked past me with a shouldered pump-action, .22 rifle. While stunned, I was impressed by how well he carried himself and how attentive he was with it. This drove home Yamane's important observation about guns in America,[65] and I would argue much of rural Canada as well: for large parts of the continent, firearms are a normal piece of their everyday life. The whole thing, so foreign and exciting to me, was a normal part of these peoples' lifeworld.

At the center of the showroom, one of the largest booths was taken up by the NRA, which distributed literature and small trinkets to recruit members. They were not the only gun rights organization in attendance. At the show, I had my first encounter with the Virginia Citizens Defense League (VCDL). The legislative battles in the great gun debate are fought at multiple levels of government: the municipal level, the county level, the state level, and the federal level. As a result, a slew of state-level gun rights organizations have emerged to lobby at these lower levels. After a quick internet search, I found that at least 42 states have at least one state-level gun rights organizations, with most having more than one (see Table 6.1).

The VCDL is a small gun rights organization that advocates for the Second Amendment in the Commonwealth of Virginia. The attendant at the booth looked like the archetype of a suburban dad with greying hair, a short beard, and khaki cargo shorts.

"We are like the NRA but at the state level," he noted. "We're a grass-roots organization, run by volunteers, and we send out newsletters to try to get citizens together to protest unjust laws."

The logo of the VCDL is a colonial-era militiaman holding a musket. The logo's color scheme is red, white, and blue. The minuteman is depicted gazing off in the distance, eyes focusing on an unseen threat, as he pours gunpowder from his powder horn into the priming pan of his musket. This would not be the last I heard of the VCDL during and after my fieldwork.

Table 6.1. State-level pro-gun organizations

State	Groups	State	Groups
Alabama	1	Missouri	2
Alaska	0	Montana	1
Arizona	2	Nebraska	1
Arkansas	0	Nevada	0
California	5	New Hampshire	2
Colorado	2	New Jersey	1
Connecticut	1	New Mexico	1
Delaware	1	New York	3
Florida	2	North Carolina	2
Georgia	2	North Dakota	0
Hawaii	1	Ohio	2
Idaho	1	Oklahoma	0
Illinois	3	Oregon	3
Indiana	1	Pennsylvania	3
Iowa	2	Rhode Island	0
Kansas	1	South Carolina	2
Kentucky	1	South Dakota	1
Louisiana	1	Tennessee	1
Maine	1	Texas	2
Maryland	2	Utah	2
Massachusetts	1	Vermont	1
Michigan	4	Virginia	2
Minnesota	1	Washington	1
Mississippi	0	West Virginia	1
Missouri	2	Wisconsin	2
Montana	1	Wyoming	1

The gun show at Dulles gave me an idea. If businesses and gun rights organizations can use the venue of the gun show to promote their products and advocacy, why not use it to promote my research? I went onto the website of the show's organizer to see which upcoming shows were nearby. The closest show to me that would take place during my fieldwork was in Lynchburg, VA. I put in an application and was soon put into contact with an employee of the company. My request for a booth was unusual, to say the least, but after explaining my research project over the phone, the organizers agreed to let me rent a booth. With only a few weeks before the show, I rushed to amend my ethics protocol, book a hotel, and prepare an online survey that I could promote at the show.

Lynchburg is about three hours south of my main field site in Fairfax. Rather than take the interstate, the GPS directed me to take a smaller state highway. While Fairfax felt very familiar, things changed quickly after heading south. The homes became less affluent and more modest. Accents changed, picking up a slight twang. The fast-food businesses changed, and I started to notice more southern fare on the menu. I stopped at a fast-food joint outside of Charlottesville and ordered the biscuits and gravy to fill my belly for the rest of the drive. As I ate, I reflected on the fact that only a few years before a white supremacist rally had shocked the world and resulted in the death of a counter protestor and two state troopers. This event seemed emblematic of the growing political divide confronting America; a divide that I was poised to dive deeper into in the coming days.

Lynchburg itself is a town with a close connection to the American right. Home to Liberty University, founded by Evangelical preacher and right-wing activist Jerry Falwell, the area is much more conservative than Fairfax, which tends to be one of the liberal enclaves in Virginian politics. The city itself is home to just over 80,000 people and is known colloquially as the "City of the Seven Hills" given its topography.

I pulled into the parking lot of my hotel in the late afternoon. The hotel was perched on top of a small hill, and even from my ground floor room, I had a good view of the city's outskirts, and Liberty University. The university had shaved its initials, LU, into the top of a nearby hill, which dominated the skyline. I had selected the hotel because it was located directly across the parking lot from the mall where the gun show would take place. I stayed in that evening, tired from the road and nervous for the next morning's work. Coming back from the hotel gym, I glanced at the tourist brochures in the lobby. A brochure for the Liberty University Creation Hall caught my eye, the school's creation science museum.

I woke up early on Saturday morning to set up my booth at the show. A travel cup of free hotel coffee in hand, I shuffled across the parking lot with my poster, sign-up list, business cards, and a bag of candy to give out to my booth visitors. The show was being hosted in an abandoned department store on the far end of the shopping mall. I showed my confirmation sheet to the attendant at the door, and they directed me to the sign-up table, where I could pay my fee and get my booth number. The sign-up desk was being run by a seemingly overwhelmed older woman in her late

60s or 70s. She seemed swamped by the sheer volume of booth members queuing up to register.

"I'm so sorry," she said, "This is the first time we've run a show here in twenty years. We're all a bit frazzled."

After a few minutes of confusion, she was able to sign me in and direct me to my table. Given the historical focus of my project, I had been placed in the section of the show devoted to historical firearms and militaria sellers.[66]

The booths at the show were arranged in rows, with three aisles, and tables backing onto one another. My booth was in the center aisle, and I busied myself setting it up as I waited for the doors to open to the public. The booth to my right was being operated by an older woman and her husband, whose business was devoted almost entirely to selling antique German Luger pistols from the Second World War. Given the popularity of these pistols in Hollywood movies and video games, they command a high price.

To the right of my booth, Liam, a middle-aged man from Ohio sold Second World War memorabilia. He was quite knowledgeable about different artifacts and made a business of buying old heirlooms at estate sales, garage sales, or through word of mouth and then reselling them to collectors.

"I do a few of these shows a year," he explained. "Some of 'em are gun shows, and others are just for the militaria folks."

Despite the age gap, Liam and I became fast friends throughout the day, chatting during lulls in the crowd and watching one another's tables when going for lunch or bathroom breaks. When Liam complained the lines were too long for him to grab lunch, I shared some of my snacks, pretzels with Nutella dip, with him and he was very grateful. These things seem trifling, but when you are alone amongst strangers at a show like this, far from home, these small gestures and shows of friendship are quite meaningful.

The other tables in my row were mostly selling militaria or some older firearms. An older man behind me spent the whole day in his chair, having loud and opinionated conversations with his neighbors. Across from me, a tall and muscular African American man walked between his two booths at opposite ends of the room, while his wife staffed their soap and shampoo booth nearby. His table near me was entirely devoted to selling Trump paraphernalia, like Make America Great Again hats and flags.

The show was jam-packed. I later learned that thousands of people walked through during the two days of the show. Given that I was alone at my booth, I did not have a lot of time to explore, but anytime I left for a restroom break, the already thin laneways were clogged with people milling about and looking at the different items on display. The clientele in the morning was decidedly older and whiter than the show near Dulles. As the day progressed, however, the crowd grew larger and more diverse. While most people were white and over forty, the younger members of crowd were more diverse in terms of gender and race. There were some lone guys, but most were accompanied by friends, wives, girlfriends, and families. Like at the Dulles show, many visitors carried recently purchased guns, or firearms that they were trying to sell or exchange. Some would put sticks down the barrel, taping a piece of paper to the protruding end which listed the model and price of the gun. Some had lists taped to their backpacks. Later in the day, I even saw a man enter with two rifles over his shoulder and with his wife balancing two more on the stroller that held one of the two children they had with them.

Like at Dulles, all guns were safety checked at the door to make sure they were unloaded, and plastic zip ties were secured around the action of the firearm to render it temporarily inoperable, and to show that it had been safety checked. In the corner, an employee from the state of Virginia sat at a desk with a set of rugged, military-style laptops connected to the national background check system. Booth attendants could request that customers pass a background check before purchasing a firearm. The state employee was periodically relieved by two Virginia state troopers who patrolled the event. The troopers were in full uniform, their wide-brimmed hats held at an angle with leather straps. Both troopers were hulking men with shaved heads, and they were not the only law enforcement on the scene. Other police officers, some off-duty and some on, milled about occasionally, as well as the gun show's armed security team.

My table at the show consisted of my foam board posters, two ledger-sized laminated sheets explaining my study in ethics review board approved-language, and a bag of candy I bought at the grocery store to entice attention. I talked to over a hundred people throughout the day, handing out business cards with links to my survey and my email. As much as possible, I tried to encourage potential participants to sign up for a survey mailing list so I could send them a link directly. Most people were pleasant and curious about my research. Younger people tended to be more interested than older people, and several particularly curious visitors were former or current students at Liberty University. Many people just seemed genuinely happy to be able to have their voices heard and get a fair shake in academia, a venue which they perceive, rightly or wrongly, to be unfriendly to their lifestyle. Others were quite suspicious until they heard the details of my research. Very few people were rude. If they were not interested, they would usually just say no thanks and walk away.

Sunday was much slower than Saturday. Liam, a veteran of these shows, had correctly prophesized the rhythm of the day to me while we were setting up.

"It's Sunday morning, everyone's at church. You will see, people are gonna get out of church. They will go to lunch, meet up with friends, and things will pick up around 1 p.m."

He was spot on.

Taking advantage of the morning lull, I did a quick lap of the gun show to scope out what was there. The show was smaller than the one I had attended in Dulles, but still had a bewildering variety of items for sale. There were fewer medium-sized businesses at this show, and a lot more mom and pop outfits and individual collectors. There were also food vendors selling everything from pickles to dog treats. One stall only sold parts for AR-15s, including painted barrels and receivers. Others sold knives and self-defense equipment. One sold Velcro patches decorated with flags or pro-Second Amendment slogans. Another sold tactical-style vests for dogs.

The Virginia Citizens Defense League, who I had first encountered in Dulles, was out in force, offering free admission for those who signed up to be members. The NRA was not there, but an affiliated organization, the Virginia Friends of the NRA, were, as were the Virginians for Trump, who rolled up in an RV adorned with TRUMP in big white letters, and massive pictures of the then-President. These organizations clearly saw the show as a useful point of contact with their active and potential memberships.

Returning to the three central sites I argue are integral to the gun culture and, specifically, the NRA's efforts to expand the community of gun owners, the NRA firearms safety classes I attended teach students not just technical knowledge and firearm safety, but the values and discursive practices of the gun culture. In these classes, students are taught that guns are tools, not weapons, and engage in exercises involving hypothetical narratives that place themselves at the center of the action. Gun ranges are spaces where the community can interact and socialize, and they provide opportunities for gun rights organizations like the NRA to attract new members. Similarly, the organization uses venues like gun shows to reach its target community.

The NRA uses points of contact within the gun-owning community to disseminate narratives and frame the gun debate in particular ways. These points of contact include the NRA Firearm Safety Courses, gun shows, and gun ranges. These points of contact provide the organization with a venue to attract new members and motivate existing members to become more involved. The relationship between the NRA and the gun culture itself is a nexus at which much of the force behind the gun rights movement resides.

Participant observation is a useful technique for observing this phenomenon at work. It is one thing to read about NRA courses in a book, and quite another to experience them. For those outside of the gun culture, guns are objects of fear. They make people think of criminals, mass shooters, and danger. Through participating in the cultural practices of the gun culture, I have a better understanding of what guns mean to the ordinary people who own and use them. I understand that, to those within the community of gun owners, target shooting, self-defense preparedness, and even concealed carry are expressions of pleasure and empowerment as much as they are fear. I can better understand how this passion for their serious leisure pursuit could motivate someone to fight so hard to keep their firearms when they perceive them to be threatened by government intervention. More importantly, I witnessed firsthand the NRA turning this passion into advocacy.

In my short time at the gun show in Lynchburg, I spoke to many people. Most were wary at first but warmed up as we continued to talk. One man openly admitted that he and his friends were skeptical of me, but after talking with me had determined I was "okay." As I sat there, listening to story after story, meeting person after person, shaking hand after hand, I saw in their face a hesitance and mistrust that, as the conversation continued, melted away, replaced by a willingness, an eagerness even, to share. They told stories of afternoons at the range, self-defense situations, of perceived political marginalization, and gun shows of yesteryear. They talked about their hobbies, their re-enactments, and their collections. It soon became apparent to me that people do not just come to gun shows to shop but to socialize with likeminded people.

At that moment, I felt the full weight of the responsibility that had been creeping up on me since the beginning of my fieldwork. I saw with perfect clarity the immensity of the task before me. Here were a group of people, much maligned, declared deplorable, stereotyped, and hated; yet, they were eager to have their stories told and their perspectives shared, just as they were wary of being misrepresented. I realized how easy it would be for me, as many before me, either through bias, ignorance, or ill intention, to portray these people in the way they are used to being represented. To make them out as ignorant, stupid, or poorly educated. To fail to look beyond my own urban and class biases to understand who they truly are, and to try to show their humanity and their value. Therein lies the value of ethnography, and the task of the ethnographer.

As the show ended, I packed up my things and bid farewell to Liam and the various friends I had made over the weekend. It was after four o'clock and I wanted to make it back to my dorm room in Fairfax quickly to write up my notes. I had a long road ahead of me.

7   The NRA Firearms History Museum

Noah: What role do you think firearms have played in US history?
Sam: (*instantly*) They gave us our freedom.

The NRA National Firearms Museum is located inside of the organization's headquarters in Fairfax, a pair of non-descript office buildings. These two blue-green glass towers are flanked by a parking lot, with a larger covered parking garage in the rear. If you drove by it and did not see the stone and metal sign bearing the NRA's crest, you could be forgiven for assuming that it belonged to a tech company or accounting firm, like many of its neighbors. While much of the headquarters is taken up with office space and thus restricted to the public, a few sections are open for visitors. Members of the public can eat at the NRA Cafeteria, take in the National Firearms Museum, shop at the NRA gift shop, and take advantage of the NRA shooting range, where firearms safety classes and shooting competitions are held.

Pulling into the parking lot, a sign pointed me towards the dedicated museum parking. I shut the door to my car, locked it, and made my way towards the closest tower. I followed the instructions and clicked on the buzzer button, where I was greeted by the security guard. "I'm here for the museum," I said, nervously into the speaker. The guard buzzed me in and greeted me warmly.

"Welcome," he said. "You start off over there, just past Mr. Selleck."

He gestured to the large cardboard cut-out of actor Tom Selleck in full cowboy regalia, which held the museum's pamphlets. "The tour is at one-thirty, if you want to stick around."

I thanked the guard and walked around the corner into the museum, tipping my baseball cap to Selleck as I passed him by and whispered:

"Howdy partner."

The NRA National Firearms Museum is 15,000 square feet, containing 3,200 firearms, which I was told is a fraction of the museum's overall
collection, much of which is stored in large underground vaults or at
the NRA's other museums. The National Firearms Museum is one of
three NRA museums scattered across the United States. Collectively,
these museums attract 350,000 visitors every year.[1] The National Firearms
Museum has only five permanent employees and relies on help from
volunteers to run it and preserve the collection. Each of the collection's
thousands of firearms are cleaned and oiled regularly. Anyone who has
ever cleaned a gun, let alone an antique firearm, can appreciate what
a massive undertaking this represents. Gun owners I spoke to who had
been to the museum described being overwhelmed by the scale of the
collection. Though not as physically large as the great state-run museums
of the Smithsonian Institute, it is nevertheless packed with artifacts and
takes at least a full afternoon to take in, if not several days. My research,
for example, took place over four visits to the museum from May to June
of 2019, as well as an interview with the Director of the Museum, and the
NRA's Head of Research.

Why does the NRA have a museum and what is the role of the museum
in the organization's broader political communications strategy? A key
assertion of this book is that the NRA plays a leading role in the social
construction of gun culture in the United States and that a large amount
of its political power stems from its ability to build and mobilize the gun-
owning community. The organization targets three core groups; those
already involved with the NRA, gun owners who are not politically active,
and the gun curious. For a community to exist, it must have an identity.
As this chapter demonstrates, the institution of the museum has served as
a powerful tool for national communities, and increasingly local minority communities, to assert their identity. This is a key role for the National
Firearms Museum.

In this chapter, I argue that the NRA operates the National Firearms
Museum for the same reason that nation states, corporations, and minority communities operate museums. First, museums are powerful status
symbols for the organization, and the donors who contribute to it. They
serve as a public relations tool for the gun culture, establishing the
right of the gun-owning community to exist. Second, the NRA museum
serves internal purposes within the organization similar to a corporate
museum. These include preserving corporate memory, the organization's identity, and acting as a storehouse of knowledge for employees
to use in legal trials or articles. Third, and most important, the museum
helps to connect the gun-owning community and the meaning of firearms to the three central macro-level narratives emphasizing the role

that firearms have played in the country's sacred stories and thus reaffirming their importance.

I begin with a brief outline of the literature on museology, and the history of the museum, to illustrate the connection between museums, status, identity, and power. From there, I highlight the primary tools at work in the museum: narrative and artifact, and examine how the National Firearms Museum is used to legitimize the NRA's place in the gun-owning community. It does this, I argue, through a combination of narrative and artifact.

Museums as Political Spaces

For most ordinary people, the museum does not seem like a political space; rather they are thought of as places of education, entertainment, or even escape. You might remember having visited a museum as a child, or as a teenager taking a trip to a new city. Perhaps you remember gazing at the paintings in an art gallery or staring at a stuffed woolly mammoth at a nature museum.

Behind their apolitical artifice, however, museums are deeply political institutions; born of, shaped by, and implicated in the hot button issues of their time. The past is brought into the present for a variety of reasons: to help us to make sense of the world, to validate practices or beliefs, to create and affirm identity, to guide our lives and to enrich the present.[2] Museums are physical manifestations of the past. They impart new ways of seeing the world. They can be used to validate and reaffirm our practices and beliefs. Most importantly, they are powerful tools for the creation and affirmation of both our individual and group identities. Understanding this requires tracing the origin of the museum from a tool of nascent western nation-states during the Enlightenment to a globalized medium, employed by corporations and community groups alike.

Museums as Political Spaces

The museum can be traced back to the ancient world,[3] but it was not until the Enlightenment that the museum as we know it began to take shape. Before this time, collecting was the purview of the social elite, like Renaissance Princes or wealthy aristocrats. But the public philosophy of the Enlightenment, and its obsession with classification and ordering, led to an expansion of the practice of collecting, and later to the creation of the public museum to cater to the growing middle class.[4] The purpose of these new national collections was to take the collections of individuals and incorporate them into the nation state. These collections gave nations the ability to "amass and present evidence of their own pasts, so turning their histories into 'objective' fact and legitimizing their right to exist."[5] Put simply, museums were created to justify the existence of a national community.

The largest period of growth for museums occurred in the years following the Second World War, and especially in the decades since the 1970s. Approximately 95 per cent of modern museums were founded during this period.[6] As the world continued to change rapidly, people sought to cling to the past.[7]

During the 1970s and 1980s, a growing number of scholars began to interrogate the relationship between knowledge production and power in society. The expansion of the museum as an institution, as well as a slew of high-profile museum scandals, forced museums into the middle of the identity politics debate, turning museums into battlegrounds for the key public debates of the time.[8]

This movement resulted in the creation of a literature dubbed the New Museology, launched by Peter Vergo's with the publication of an edited volume in 1989. This intellectual movement sought to move the study of museums away from "museum methods" and towards a consideration of the foundational assumptions that underpinned the museum, and the power structures that these museums upheld.[9]

In the introduction to his volume, Vergo notes that: "The very act of collection has a political or ideological or aesthetic dimension which cannot be overlooked." This is because collections inevitably lead to questions regarding what is worthy of preservation, how we judge beauty or historical significance, and how we treat material from other cultures. The arrangement of the museum is based on the values of those who created the museum and the society from which they emerge.[10]

Since 1989, the literature has proliferated widely. Macdonald identifies three main themes in the literature of the new museology. The first is the desire of scholars to "understand the meanings of museum objects as situated and contextual rather than inherent." The second focuses on the increased role of "commercialism and entertainment" in the museum industry, and the ways in which the museum is connected to the market. Finally, this literature seeks to shed light on how visitors interact with and understand the museums that they visit.[11]

The state is not the only actor that recognizes the power that comes with operating a museum. The end of the twentieth century saw the emergence of the small, or local museum. These museums were collection-based, and generally run privately or by local government branches, or community groups.[12] Like states, these groups saw museums as tools to assert their identities and display them to fellow group members and to the world.[13] Museums have thus become "sites of persuasion" for communities and cultures.[14] They are prime battlegrounds in cultural and political conflicts and debates because museums are a way for groups to present themselves to the world. Further, museums institutionalize ideas, giving them "tangibility and weight."[15] Given that museums are "powerful identity-defining machines," having control of a museum meant having control of the self-identification of your community or movement.[16]

The medium of the firearms history museum emerged along a similar timeline as the museum itself. While the first deliberate firearms history display was the Grand Storehouse in London, which was opened in 1688, a wider explosion of museums featuring firearms occurred in the nineteenth century.[17] In the United States, the first firearm museum display was opened in 1840 at the National Institute for the Promotion of Science, which would later become the Smithsonian Institution.[18] Some of these early displays were commercial, like Samuel Colt's display at the Crystal Palace Exhibition in 1851 in London, England.[19] There are currently about 30 firearm museums in the United States, operated by federal, state, and private actors.[20]

Despite the history and popularity of firearms museums, the field of museology and public history have only recently begun to engage with these museums as distinct entities.[21] Two camps have emerged in the small literature on the museology of guns. The schism is representative of a wider divide in museum studies between those focused on studying museums from a technical perspective, and those focused on the critical theory side. The first camp, which I label the technicalists, is composed mainly of pieces written by curators and professionals. Given that these individuals are engaged actively in the museum enterprise, they grapple mainly with the logistical challenges of storing, curating, and presenting guns as "loaded" cultural objects. For example, authors in this camp note the problems of presenting firearms in a way that engages with their broader history of use, or appealing to audiences to whom firearms may have very different meanings.[22] They acknowledge the difficulties that emerge from displaying firearms designed for military use or self-defense alongside firearms intended to be works of art for display or sporting tools. Further, they grapple with the fact that firearms are contentious objects in the public discourse.[23]

The second camp within the literature is made up of critical artists and academics. This camp generally comes from the anti-gun culture, and seeks explicit pro-control policy change on the issue of guns, which it often euphemizes as "opening a conversation."[24] Curators and scholars engaging with gun museums from this perspective are highly critical of the technicalists, arguing that their neutrality is merely an attempt to avoid dealing with the political nature of their work.[25] Authors within this camp are critical of exhibitions that treat firearms as objects of art or historical artifacts, but instead frames them through the lens of "gun violence," which is signaled out as a particularly morally repugnant form of violence given its prevalence in American society. For example, Dell'Aria[26] is highly critical of the way that museums turn guns into objects of art, isolating them from the acts of violence that they were used to commit, asking "what would it mean to include a firearm in a museological display that dealt explicitly with its relationship to gun violence, suffering, and death?"[27] He goes so far as to argue that the presence of guns in society stifles conversation, and that artwork that speaks back to this can help to, "produce (rather than evade) conversations around complex issues, allowing us to move past the stalemate and comprehend how the material proliferation of guns intersects with broader social justice concerns."[28]

I use a third approach in this chapter. Rather than spend time critiquing the claims made by the National Firearms Museum, I instead attempt to uncover and analyze the instrumentality of the museum and how it fits within the organization's broader communications program.

Thus far we have seen that, since the Enlightenment, museums have served as powerful tools to assert the identity of communities, both national communities as well as smaller sub-national groups. Museums have two principal tools at their disposal to do this: the artifact and narrative.

The primary tool of the museum is the artifact. Artifacts are objects that are selected by museum curators as important and placed into the context of a museum. The primary function of the museum for most of its history has been to take artifacts from the social world in which they existed and recontextualize them within the context of the museum.[29] Within this perspective, museums then become spaces where objects can be ascribed value.[30] Artifacts serve similar functions to the relics or objects of meaning that I have discussed throughout this book. They serve as physical evidence of the past, lending it gravitas. These artifacts are given value and meaning by virtue of being placed in the museum. This value is often explained to the viewer using a label, which helps to guide the visitor in interpreting the significance of the artifact. The "space between object and label" is extremely important in the production of meanings. These labels do not describe objects neutrally. Rather, they communicate the meaning that the exhibitor wants the viewer to take from the object.[31]

Artifacts in a museum are rarely displayed on their own. Usually, they are part of a collection, which opens them up to further understandings.

Collecting in the context of museology is defined as "a self-aware process of creating a set of objects conceived to be meaningful as a group." The key idea is that the creation of the collection is self-conscious and intentional. This involves recontextualizing objects as parts of a collection rather than how the objects were originally intended to be used or thought of.[32]

Narrative is also a powerful tool for the museum, as museums are not just about displaying objects but about tying objects to a narrative. The narrative thus helps to convey the message or lessons that the museum is trying to impart, while the objects solidify that message, providing material evidence to support the message.[33] Like a lawyer presenting physical evidence to support their witness's testimony, this one-two punch of narrative and object impacts the viewer more strongly than simply reading about something in a book.[34]

This use of narrative makes museums important tools for the creation of community. In the nineteenth and twentieth centuries, museums told the stories of the nation, working make concrete the "shared history represented in the grand narrative of the nation."[35] In the era of globalization and the retreat of the state, other actors are beginning to use this identity-making tool for their own purposes.

Throughout their history, museums have been powerful tools for legitimizing or demonstrating authority, prestige, and status, creating communal identities, and spreading a message. Museums do this through the assemblage of artifacts into a collection and through the use of narrative.

Status, Community, Resonance and Wonder

It should be clear at this point that museums have been tied to conceptions of status and identity throughout their history. In Europe, the practice of museum creation was largely confined to nation states since the eighteenth century. Museums were a way for these new and emerging nations to show their status, their commitment to certain values and to showcase their identity. In America, where the state was less involved in this process, private associations of wealthy benefactors used museums for similar purposes.

The NRA National Firearms Museum serves as a symbol of status for the organization. Having a museum helps to project an image of the NRA's sophistication, commitment to education, and to showcase its power. This is demonstrated through the grandness of the museum. Though the individual sections of the museum have different themes, the overall decorative theme is that of a patrician hunting lodge. This is conveyed through the use of old-fashioned decorative wallpaper, low lighting, and wood paneling, as well as through the paintings, ivory décor, and mounted animals displayed throughout.

The Peterson Gallery, the newest section of the museum, and the first that the visitor sees when entering the museum, is a prime example of this. As I passed through the large glass doors of the museum into the exhibition proper, I was greeted by this gallery. My eyes, slowly adjusting to the dim light, were drawn to the large, diamond shaped case filled with some of the most expensive and rare artifacts in the museum. These elegantly engraved firearms were made for hunting, many of them for taking dangerous game in Africa. Behind the case and to the right was a hearth, surrounded by dark, wood paneled walls. Each of these walls contained either a painting of a hunting or nature scene, or a framed display of rare firearms. The hearth at the center of the display was flanked on both sides by elephant tusks, embellished with intricate carvings. To its right, there was an American flag and to the left the flag of the Commonwealth of Virginia.

The wood paneling and hunting lodge motif is a consistent theme throughout the museum. There are also pieces of art showcasing hunting and nature scenes, as well as various hunting trophies, including large stuffed bears, lions' heads, mountain goats, and deer. These displays help to not only link the organization to a tradition of American hunting that dates back beyond the nation's founding, but also assert the status and identity of the organization through portraying their patrician roots.

The décor of the museum also allows the organization to help assert the identity of the gun-owning community, and the place of the NRA as the head of that community, by showcasing its values and cultural practices. It is a way for the organization to say: "this is who we are, and this is what we stand for."

The connection between the gun culture and the family is a recurrent theme throughout the museum as it is in the organization more broadly, one that is likely highly effective given the centrality of the family unit to processes of remembering and identity construction.[36] This helps to not only emphasize that firearms ownership is a heritage deeply linked to the family unit, but also assert the fact that the gun-owning community is centered around the family.

One of the ways that this is done is through the use of symbolism. For example, the hearth is a common theme that popped up in the décor of the museum. There are no fewer than four hearths in the museum spread out throughout the various exhibitions. Both of the Peterson and Thurston galleries contain a hearth, as well as the exhibit on the American revolution and in the Civil War section. The hearth is a key symbol of family and home. Expressions like "gathering around the hearth," or "hearth and home" show the long history of the hearth as a family gathering place in western culture. Even though the hearth has been obsolete as a heating method since the mid-nineteenth century, it has retained its symbolic function, and remains a common feature of most homes, serving as a symbol of "domestic harmony, nostalgia and comfort."[37] A key example of this being mobilized in politics is Franklin D. Roosevelt's fireside chats. Roosevelt faced a unique challenge in adapting an American political system that had largely relied on personal connections to the new reality of an emerging mass public. He used the medium of the radio to address the public directly, drawing on the tropes of family to connect with his audience.[38] The fireplace was a key element of this symbolism.

The section of the museum devoted to the American childhood, which will be discussed in greater detail later, further ties the organization and the wider gun-owning community to the American family. For example, this part of the exhibition features a painting of a father and son on a hunting trip. Both are wearing blaze orange hunting uniforms, and the father is clearly instructing the son on what to do. A wall of air rifles and BB guns in this section is centered around an image of a 1950s father wearing a suit and fedora and kneeling beside his son, who is aiming a BB gun. The father's hand rests lovingly upon his son's shoulder.

Finally, this focus is also made quite clear in the twin family galleries, the Thurston Gallery and the Petersen Gallery. Both galleries were donated to the museum by prominent American families. A large painting at the entrance to the Thurston Gallery, for example, features the elder Thurston kneeling, rifle in hand, beside a downed Cape Buffalo on a hunting trip in Africa. His son is crouched down behind him. The painting captures an important family memory, a moment of bonding between father and son. The Petersen gallery also features numerous family photos mixed in amongst the ostentatiously decorated engraved firearms and on the mantle of the fireplace.

This focus on the family connection throughout the museum is clearly meant to evoke the personal memories of the firearms enthusiasts who visit the museum, emphasizing the connection between family, childhood, and firearms. It helps to establish firearms as a key part of American heritage, one that must be preserved so as to pass it on to the next generation. It also asserts the key role of the family as the center of gravity for the gun culture.

The NRA National Firearms Museums serves as a space for the NRA to present the gun culture to the world, showcasing its values and cultural practices. But the museum is also a space for members of the community to interact with the organization. Like the NRAAM, the NRA National Firearms Museum provides yet another point of contact between the organization and its current, latent, and potential members. The museum is promoted heavily through the NRA's website and its NRATV programs. Further, in each of the firearms safety courses I took, the instructors mentioned the museum and encouraged us to visit. During interviews, when I would ask my research participants if they had been to the museum, those who replied no always offered excuses and promises to go later, in the same way that someone might justify having missed church or visiting an elderly relative. The museum is further promoted through public road signs. The freeway exit closest to the museum has a sign that says: "National Firearms Museum this exit." Further, as one approaches the museum on Waples Mill Road, there is a worn green public road sign advertising the museum.

Upon entering the museum, there is a computer set up to help members renew their memberships, or sign up, showcasing the way that these points of contact help the NRA recruit and retain members. Visitors can also join the NRA at the museum's gift shop. During my last visit to the museum I saw a group of young men who were so motivated and excited by their visit, they all signed up to become members. The shop also allows supporters to display their affinity for the organization by purchasing NRA paraphernalia. The gift shop sells everything from firearm history books to NRA memorabilia like t-shirts, ball caps and mugs, as well as tactical gear like backpacks, and even souvenirs for children, like toy guns.

In my visits to the museum, I witnessed a surprising variety of visitors. The building was never packed, but there were always at least five to ten other visitors there with me. This may have been because I only visited the museum on weekdays when it is less busy, according to Google Maps analytics. The visitors to the museum were surprisingly diverse. Though there were usually several older white couples, as well as single white men, the museum is popular amongst families visiting the area, many speaking Mandarin, Hindi, and Spanish to one another.

The tour, conducted by one of the museum's curators every weekday at 1:00 pm, provides another opportunity for the organization to speak directly to its potential constituents. I took the tour on a particularly quiet day. For the most part I had the guide to myself, though various people joined in and branched off during the hour-long guided walk through the museum. The guide was a kindly, older gentlemen, wearing a yellow polo and beige cargo pants. He wore thick glasses, over which he peered at me as he took me through the gallery.

The tour provided the back story for many of the artifacts in the exhibition, as well as the stories behind the displays. The guide was exceptionally knowledgeable, obviously a long-time employee of the museum. He was close friends with many of the donors and often lapsed into tales about the history of the museum. For example, he told the story of the museum's move from the increasingly anti-gun District of Columbia to Fairfax in the winter of 1993, where a fleet of semi-trucks transported the entire collection through a blizzard.

He also gave the context for many of the objects which did not have panels devoted to explaining their origin. These stories were generally focused on the value of the artifact, or how it was used by the owner. The guide took particular joy in pointing out the many quirky guns along the way, like a double-barreled, bolt-action hunting rifle designed for dangerous game in Africa. It is very rare for a bolt-action rifle to appear in this configuration. Apparently, the firearm was commissioned after a close call with three charging elephants was narrowly averted using a regular double-barreled elephant gun. The owner wanted more fire-power in case the situation repeated itself.

The messages conveyed by artifacts in a museum collection are not always literal or textual. Often, they are emotional. Museums can employ affect in several ways. Most relevant to the NRA museum are the concepts of resonance and wonder. Wonder can be defined as "the power of the displayed object to stop the viewer in his or her tracks, to convey an arresting sense of uniqueness, to evoke an exalted attention."[39] Wonder, in objects, is characterized by the experience of "intense, indeed enchanted looking." This occurs when "the act of attention draws a circle around itself from which everything but the object is excluded, when intensity of regard blocks out all circumambient images, stills all murmuring voices."[40] This sense of wonder can be a result of the individual's personality or interests, but can also be cultivated by the museum itself. Often, museums use lighting to create this sense of wonder, a practice borrowed from retail shops.[41]

Resonance, on the other hand, refers to "the power of the displayed object to reach out beyond its formal boundaries to a larger world, to evoke in the viewer the complex, dynamic cultural forces from which it has emerged and for which it may be taken by a viewer to stand."[42] Resonance is not necessarily tied to the object itself, but the cultural meanings and stories surrounding the artifact, which change as the object moves through time. Thus, resonance can be created by the object itself, or by the narratives that the museum weaves around them.

A key component of the charm of the NRA museum for firearms enthusiasts is the sense of resonance and wonder that it inspires. This "cool factor" is a large part of what drives visitors to the museum and is usually the most powerful takeaway. Participants who spoke about the museum often used terms such as "awed" and "amazed" at how large the collection is, as well as the items within. What resonated with these visitors was the experience, however brief, of being surrounded by so many firearms and their history.

When I sat down with one of my participants, Timothy, I asked him about his experience of the museum. He described being awed by the sheer scale of it. "I was only there for about an hour ... that didn't give justice to the ... it's a huge collection. So ... uh ... My son and I we just laughed because we didn't have that much time, we were like there's no way we can enjoy this (properly)."[43] His son, Sam, echoed the sentiment: "We didn't have a lot of time to look around. It was more we just stopped and walked through it quickly. Uh ... There was still like ... We only walked like one-fourth of it. The museum is pretty big."[44]

Of course, the portions of the museum that will resonate or evoke feelings of wonder are deeply subjective and based on the personality of the visitor. For example, the prospect of seeing General Patton's revolver evokes curiosity, but not excitement for me. However, for a middle-aged white gentleman who interrupted our tour several times to ask about it, seeing this item was a singular obsession; the man even walked out of the museum after discovering the revolver was not there. Sam, one of my participants, was particularly drawn to the M1 Garand, the service rifle carried by American soldiers in the Second World War. When asked to elaborate, he talked about his interest in studying the war:

> My interest in firearms history is actually all over the place, but one of the conflicts I like to research and study the most is WWII, because I like the politics that were being played, how that tied into who got what firearms, to the supply routes. How different countries built up their armies. How there were still, during WWII, you had some countries still using cavalry while others were using tanks. So ... that time period is very interesting ... How the technology kind of took a jump and countries are trying to catch up but at the same time they are trying to fight a war. So, it just all got mixed up. There's a lot to study.[45]

Firearms owners often feel deep emotional ties to certain firearms, connections that can motivate them to read books about them, memorize their history, and spend money collecting, shooting, and maintaining them.

The parts of the museum that resonated with me the most, and provoked feelings of awe and wonder, were those that connected to key parts of history and popular culture. I was immediately drawn to the Winchester 1873 Repeating Rifle in the Wild West Section. This is because I find the history of the American west fascinating, probably because of my exposure to this period in popular culture growing up through movies and video games. The memories that this period of history evokes in my mind are childhood images of playing with a Cowboy Lego set, or teenage memories of watching the most recent remake of *3:10 to Yuma* with my best friend Nathan. The various Winchester Repeating Rifles, like the Colt Peacemaker, have a particular aura about them for me as a result, and I enjoy watching documentaries or reading books that tell the history of the production and use of these firearms.

Despite the fact that resonance and wonder are subjective, it is still possible to observe certain portions of the museum that are particularly designed to evoke these emotions in the viewer. A large portion of the museum is devoted to firearms curiosities and popular culture. The former category refers to strange or experimental firearms which never saw commercial success but were unique and curious. The latter refers to firearms popular in movies, television shows, and other media.

The most obvious manifestation of this in the museum was the section devoted to firearms used in Hollywood. This gallery is located in a separate room, directly following the section on the American childhood. One enters the gallery through a set of wooden double doors that are propped open. A life-sized cardboard cut-out of John Wayne dressed as a cowboy flanks the entrance. When one enters the gallery there is a full wall of glass cases facing the viewer. The back wall of the room is plastered with Hollywood movie posters for films featuring John Wayne, Ronald Reagan, and Clint Eastwood.

The glass cases are filled with movie memorabilia and firearms. Seeing the firearms used by famous action heroes transposed the aura of the Silver Screen to this museum display. The glass cases displayed firearms from historical films, such as muskets used in both the original and the remake of *The Alamo*. It held handguns from popular modern TV shows like *Criminal Minds* and older shows like *Magnum P.I.* A large portion was devoted to Western films, with various props from John Wayne movies, like the famous eyepatch he wore when portraying Rooster Cogburn in *True Grit*. There were even fantasy guns from sci-fi blockbusters, including a stormtrooper blaster from the *Star Wars* franchise. These movie artifacts bore labels, explaining which movie they were from and which actors used them. They were usually placed next to a small poster of the movie, or a picture of the actor wielding them.

Many of the unique pieces throughout the museum were similarly used to evoke resonance and wonder in the visitor. One of the most famous pieces in the museum, often used in its promotional material, is the Vampire Hunter's Revolver. When looking at this item in its case, Greenblatt's observation of an invisible circle of interest being drawn around the object can be felt; the artifact commands attention. The revolver, a short-barreled Colt Detective Special, is engraved with gothic motifs, including a cross and a bat hanging with its wings folded. The firearm came as part of a set, which was sold in a coffin-shaped gun box. The set included a small mirror (to confirm that your target is actually a vampire), a miniature wooden stake that attaches to the gun, a small container of holy water, and six silver bullets with vampire heads carved into them. The craftsmanship and attention to detail of this item are captivating in and of themselves. Yet the way that the revolver ties itself into Bram Stoker's Vampire lore, bringing the fantasy realm to life in an object as serious and solid as a firearm, blends whimsy and reality in the mind of the viewer, creating a powerful emotional pull.

While many individual objects in the museum evoke this sense of wonder, the museum resonates with firearms owners because of its uniqueness. There is a siege mentality in the gun-owning community. As more and more brands and celebrities come out as anti-gun, and the weight of America's massive cultural industry is being put behind gun control reform, there is a sense of impending peril within the community. The museum thus provides a space for gun owners to explore their interest, an unspoiled oasis free from the anti-gun forces that seem ever assembled and ready to attack.

The Corporate Museum

One way of looking at the NRA museum is through the concept of the corporate museum. The comparison will not be perfect, given that the NRA is not a for-profit corporation, but a collective actor. That being said, looking at the museum as a corporate museum can shed light on the strategic internal purposes that the National Firearms Museum serves.

Corporate museums are exhibits that are owned by companies, and generally form a part of their public relations strategy.[46] These museums are usually located in or near the headquarters or production facilities of the organization and are managed by the organization or by an affiliated non-profit group.[47] Corporate museums consist of several moving parts, like the artifacts on display, the written labels, the narrative of the tour guide, as well as the meanings created by the museum visitors. These museums began to appear in the English-speaking world at the beginning of the twentieth century, with companies like the Union Pacific Railroad opening their own museums. Like the wider post-war museum boom, however, the largest growth of corporate museums happened after the Second World War.[48]

Corporate museums serve several unique purposes. First, they tell the story of the company. They usually begin with the story of the organization's foundation and explain the way that the company grew, thus attempting to define the identity of the company. After all, who are we if not for our past? How do we move forward without knowing where we have been? To preserve the company's history, these museums collect and present notable artifacts in the company's production history, commemorate key moments and, overall, make the organization's history more "tangible."[49]

Second, corporate museums create a sense of identity and pride amongst the employees. They are not only used to project the company's image externally but internally as well, creating a sense of identity. Some companies, like the Coca Cola Museum, even use these museums as a tool to train new employees.[50]

Third, corporate museums serve as a form of advertisement for those visiting, and to build a sense of connection with the company's brand. They are tools for public relations and as such are political in that they choose which elements of the company's past they wish to highlight and those they choose to forget.[51]

Another important function of the corporate museum, which is especially relevant for the NRA, is the way they can serve as a "goods lounge," a place to store the impressive relics the company has collected during its history. This can help project the company's image during its interactions with business partners.[52]

Viewed through this lens, certain elements of the NRA museum begin to make more sense. First, while the story of the NRA is certainly downplayed in the museum, it is far from absent. The museum takes several opportunities to mention its advocacy efforts, weaving its own story into the displays. For example, the section of the museum devoted to telling the history of sports shooting in America highlights the role that the NRA has played in organizing shooting sports events in the United States.

Further, the museum takes several opportunities to commemorate key actors within the organization like actor, civil rights activist, and NRA spokesman Charlton Heston, who is commemorated in the form of a large bronze statue. There is also a bronze bust of Harlon B. Carter, a former NRA president and the first Executive Director of the ILA. Beside the bust of Carter, an information panel tells the story of his life and contributions to the NRA. It features an assemblage of pictures of Carter shooting or posing with family members, and contains his service revolver and badge from when he served in the US Border Patrol. Displays like this tell the story of the organization and its key members, serving as a repository of memory to be accessed by visitors and employees alike.

During my first visit to the museum, the function of the museum as a "goods lounge" also became apparent. On this visit, I ended up running into Chris Cox, then the Executive Director of the ILA, who I had seen speak at the NRAAM. Cox was visiting with several of his family members, who were receiving a private tour of the museum. It is not a far stretch to imagine the museum being used in a similar way for official visitors.

During my interviews with NRA officials, the function of the museum as an archive became apparent. When I sat down with Joshua Savani, the Director of Researcher for the ILA, the organization's advocacy wing, he noted that the information in the museum and archives are often useful for legal cases. "There have been times when I've actually literally gone down to the museum for a particular piece of legislation to show that a particular gun worked a particular way, which is really handy to have on site."[53] Jim Supica, the museum's curator, noted that the National Firearms Museum's archives and library provide information for employees that is simply not available at other libraries. Further, the museum staff's collective knowledge of firearms history is often valuable for employees as well. For example, Mr. Supica noted that NRA staff have served as expert witnesses on the history of firearms technology.[54]

Internally, the museum is seen by employees as an important part of fulfilling the organization's mandate of protecting the Second Amendment. That is because firearm's history is seen by the group as a form of American heritage, one that less and less people are interested in protecting. Conceptualized as a heritage that must be protected, preserving the history of firearms becomes an important part of defending this heritage.

> Maintaining the history of firearms is part of the mandate of defending the right, and maintaining information and an understanding about the firearms that existed ... a lot of American history is tied to arms bearing. Like the history of the world is. Most wars are pretty important events for the history of the world, so ... you know ... they're fought with weapons.
>
> Again, I think part of the mandate of the NRA is preserving firearms history. We feel like we have a pretty broad mandate as far as, you know, who else is going to do it? We have, between the museum that is here at headquarters and we have one other relatively large museum, and between those two museums we have one of the largest historical firearms collections in the world. It's kind of part of what we see as our job.[55]

Mr. Supica noted a similar theme in our discussion, when he discussed what he sees as the disarmament of museums. Given anti-gun trends in academia and the museum industry, he noted that less and less museums are including firearms in their exhibits or telling the story and history of firearms. The National Firearms Museum is thus seen by the organization as one of the lone actors protecting this heritage.[56]

America's Story and Soul

Perhaps the most important function of the NRA National Firearms Museum is as a communications tool for the organization. The museum helps the group to disseminate key narratives that work to tie firearms to American history and identity, emphasizing the role that guns have played in the country's sacred stories and thus demonstrating their importance. It serves as a communications tool not just to those who visit the organization, but also to those who watch NRATV or read the American Rifleman Magazine, where the museum is often featured.

As discussed in previous chapters, the NPF focuses on the way that political actors use storytelling to shape policy. To do this systematically, the NPF separates narratives into three levels: micro, meso, and macro. Those who have studied micro level narratives look at how these narratives impact individuals, while studies of meso-level narratives look at how political actors mobilize narratives within the policy subsystem.[57] In this chapter, I focus on the macro-level narrative, grand narratives or sacred stories that are shared by larger communities, like cultures, religions, or nations. These background ideas[58] are large truths that are rarely, if ever questioned by those within the political community.

The National Firearms Museum provides the NRA an opportunity to emphasize the role that firearms have played in pivotal or foundational moments in US history. In fact, this is a central element of the museum's mission statement: "to educate the public about firearms history, technology, and artistry in an accurate, accessible, responsible, and entertaining manner, with special focus on the role of firearms in American history and culture."[59] Connecting firearms to America's sacred stories helps to demonstrate their importance to American culture.

America's Story

The goal of the NRA National Firearms Museum is to tell the story of "Firearms, Freedom, and the American Experience." While the two private galleries of the museum described earlier tend to focus more on the objects themselves, the main body of the museum focuses on describing the role that firearms have played in America's story. Once again, the purpose of this analysis is not to question the veracity of these narratives, but to demonstrate that telling the story represents an effective political tactic for rallying supporters and upholding certain truths. Infrastructure of commemoration prevent political actors from rewriting the past, but they can always tell their side of the story.

As I continued to move through the museum, I left behind the newer Peterson Gallery and entered the largest section of the museum on the history of firearms. The barrier between the two is marked by a change in the carpeting on the floor. The first section of this gallery begins not in America but in Medieval China and Europe, telling the story of the history of the development of gunpowder and early firearms, and the role they played in helping to end Feudalism.

Following the trail laid out by the museum curators, I continued deeper into the section on historical firearms, which looks at the firearms used in the 13 colonies, emphasizing their utility for protection, trade, and survival. I passed through a doorway and entered what looked like the living room of a colonial home. The walls of this recreated colonial foyer have glass cases built into them like windows, which tell the story of the French & Indian War through the American Revolution. They tell the story of America's tumultuous entrance into nationhood, but place emphasis on the different firearms used by British and colonial forces. The display stresses the role that firearms played in the revolution, noting that a key inciting incident that ignited the revolution was the British attempt to seize gunpowder from the colonists. This is something that the NRA feels gets overlooked in the wider public discussion:

> I have a presentation that I give to university students about the purpose of the Second Amendment, and I always start with how most American history books talk about the Tea Party and the stamp acts and things. They don't often get as much into the fact that it was right at the time that arms seizures, so the powder seizures were literally the event ... the powder seizers in Virginia and Massachusetts ... were kind of the sparks that led to the beginning of the revolutionary war in the United States because when the English troops started to march to seize arms and powder the militia mustered and tried to stop them. So that's how the war started.[60]

The NRA sees itself as responsible for reminding people that the colonists, "understood that one of the things that was essential to their future liberty was the ability to defend themselves from the crown."[61] This is a key pillar of the organization's argument that the possession of arms by individuals serves as a check and balance, designed by the nation's framers, against tyrannical government. Here we can clearly see the interaction of background ideas, macro-level narratives, and foreground ideas (see Figure 7.1). If you understand the use of arms by ordinary citizens during the American Revolution as a key source of the revolution's success, it opens the door to seeing firearms as a check

Figure 7.1. Macro- and meso-level narratives

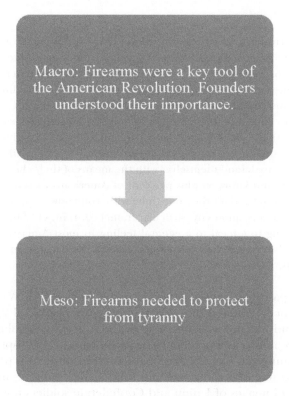

Macro: Firearms were a key tool of the American Revolution. Founders understood their importance.

Meso: Firearms needed to protect from tyranny

on excessive state power in the present day. It also helps to explain why citizens of other developed countries tend to find this argument unintelligible. Without this collective memory this argument makes no sense. Clearly this historical interpretation of the revolution cannot speak for itself and has been the topic of lively debate.[62] It is a macro-narrative that must be retold in order to survive, and the NRA sees itself as a key actor in its retelling.

The section on the American Revolution was particularly important, given that the nation's founding is a key and recurrent theme in NRA material. This is because the foundational story of a nation is often a pillar of that nation's identity and presents a powerful affective draw. Emphasizing the role that firearms played at this pivotal juncture in the nation's history helps to underscore their importance and connect them to ideas of freedom and liberty. By connecting the story of firearms rights to the story of the nation's founding, the NRA can thus not only mobilize its supporters but also appeal to a larger swath of Americans:

> Most Americans feel a strong connection to the founding of the United States and its especially people that value individualism, as kind of a general concept … you know a lot of the writings that are contemporaneous with the founding are focused on concepts of individual liberty and freedom and so … we're talking about defending a civil right and so we often try to appeal to that authority as much as possible. It's something that most Americans will agree with. The gun debate is a highly divisive debate in the United States, but if you talk broad policy, like people have a right to defend themselves with the means of their choosing, you start to get, you know, 80 plus per cent of Americans to agree on that, 75, 80 per cent. And it's the same thing with, you know, appealing to the constitution or to quotes by particular framers or things like that. Again, we are trying to appeal to a general feeling in most Americans about liberty and freedom that, you know we think the Second Amendment represents.[63]

Walking past the weapons of the Mexican War and the War of Texas Independence, I entered the section on the American Civil War, where the clear and unambiguous message of the American Revolution gives way to more murky and potentially divisive ground. This display is especially relevant given that the National Firearms Museum is perched on the dividing line between north and south. The conflict is introduced with a wall of images of Union and Confederate soldiers holding their weapons. This focus on everyday soldiers seems to be a key theme in Civil War commemoration; a way to depoliticize the conflict by focusing on common experiences of war rather than the reasons for which it was fought.

Just past the photos, I walked between two displays. On the right, I gazed through what appeared to be a small factory in an industrialized northern city in the mid-nineteenth century. It had red brick walls and green windowpanes. Reading the label, I learned that the shop had been made to look like the gun foundry at Harpers Ferry, which was famously seized by pre-civil war abolitionist John Brown. Brown sought to arm the slaves for an uprising. This incident added urgency to the national debate on slavery and led directly to the American Civil War. John Brown is an important historical figure in the region. The preserved old town of Harpers Ferry, a 30-minute drive from the museum, is now managed by the National Parks Service, and much of the historical information presented in the town focuses on Brown's attempted slave uprising, trial and eventual hanging, and the roll that this played as a catalyst to the American Civil War.

Gazing through the window of the recreated foundry, I examined the display of Union firearms from the war. The display emphasizes the industrial power and modernity of the Union, discussing the production process and standardization of their firearms. Most of the firearms on the display were muzzle loading,[64] percussion cap rifles like the 1861 Springfield Rifle Musket.

Directly across from the display of Union weaponry is the showcase of Confederate weaponry, which is housed in the recreated foyer of an antebellum southern mansion. The visitor peers through three sets of double patio doors, separated by white Greek columns. The firearms inside are laid out on the sumptuous wooden coffee table, perched on plush red chairs, or hung above the fireplace. My eye was immediately caught by a Confederate Lemat revolver sitting on top of a wooden box on a table in front of the hearth. Famously wielded by the Man in Black in HBO's *Westworld*, this cap and ball revolver[65] not only fired nine .42 caliber balls, but had a 20-gauge shotgun barrel underneath.

This display is quite captivating. On the one hand, it tells the viewer a lot about the two sides in the war, contrasting the industrial power of the north with the old-world agriculturalism of the south. Further, by paying homage to John Brown's attempted slave uprising, the museum once again subtly connects firearms to themes of freedom, liberty, and emancipation in American history. The message that the museum wants you to take from the display is that Brown understood that seizing firepower, something that slaves had been systematically denied, would be critical to winning their freedom from slaveholders.

Leaving behind the Civil War, a large bronze statue of Charlton Heston dressed as a cowboy ushered me into the history of the Wild West. The statue held a lasso in one hand and a Winchester rifle in the other and gazed sternly off to the side. The exhibition on this period of American history was centered around a large rectangular glass case filled with the iconic guns of the period, arranged in rows that mirrored the evolution of lever action rifle and single action revolver. At the end of the display is a plaque talking about Oliver Winchester and Sam Colt, which I will expand on later.

Another glass case lined the wall to the right of this display. It held a life-sized mannequin of an African American Buffalo Soldier standing behind a Gatling Gun in front of a large, mounted buffalo head. The panels on the display noted important events in the history of the wild American West. They discussed famous events Little Bighorn and the Battle of Wounded Knee, emphasizing the role that firearms played on both sides of the conflict. The displays are careful to mention that, because of US army bureaucracy, American troops were outgunned by the allied Indigenous tribes at Little Bighorn, many of whom owned Winchester Repeating Rifles which gave them an advantage of firepower. The display featured black and white photos of famous Indigenous leaders in the American Indian Wars like the famous Apache chief Geronimo, and examples of firearms, some decorated with feathers and animal skins, that these Indigenous warriors would have used.

This display represents yet another example of the NRA's efforts to universalize the gun culture. Corporations, like Nike, are increasingly realizing that adopting elements of progressive culture can be a powerful branding tool for reaching key demographics.[66] Advocacy organizations are not far behind, and are working hard to attract women and visible minorities.[67] The NRA clearly understand the need to speak to a wider public and diversify its support base in a changing America. Though it is often unsuccessful at this, and has garnered much criticism on this front, the museum's staff clearly realize the need to bring the museum in line with the times, and the rhetorical power that comes from connecting a political narrative to the struggles of a marginalized group. What these displays tell the viewer is that firearms have served as the tools of freedom for diverse people, not just white settlers.

The exhibit also focuses on the more glamorous aspects of the Wild West. A glass case to the left of the room is dedicated to the history of outlaws and lawmen, like the famous Wyatt Erp of OK Corral fame, while another emphasizes the exploits of Annie Oakley, Buffalo Bill Cody, and other gunslingers and showmen. A large panel is devoted to the exploits of Nat "Deadwood Dick" Love, a slave freed following the Civil War who would become a cowboy and famous marksman.

Firearms in the hands of individuals are central to the legend of the Wild West. Despite the fact that this period of history was less bloody and violent than popular culture would have us imagine,[68] the popular memory of the period, stoked by iconic western films has made the guns of the old west almost as famous, if not more famous, than the people who wielded them. Evoking this frame in the museum helps to strengthen the narrative of the Good Guy/Gal with a Gun, that the NRA evokes in its messaging. The displays on the Wild West set the image of a good guy with a gun against a familiar cultural backdrop, in which firearms in the hands of righteous and moral individuals helped to bring law and order to the American frontier. The modern concealed carrier can then imagine themselves continuing this American tradition.

America's Soul

Nations are imagined communities,[69] and these communities are built on stories. The macro-level narratives that form a part of national identities are powerful forces to which political actors can connect their cause. The National Firearms Museum is quite effective at emphasizing the role of firearms in broader American political culture and symbolism. This is done not only by evoking the narratives of American history we explored in the previous section, but through connecting firearms to the collective memories of visitors. Not only are firearms presented as a key element of America's past, but of her soul as well.

What better place to begin this narrative than with childhood? A section of the museum is devoted to the quintessential American childhood. This section is composed of four displays. When I entered this room, my eyes were first drawn to the large shooting gallery to my right. This is a recreation of an old carnival shooting gallery, where visitors would have paid to fire pellet guns at metal targets that move mechanically. The display now uses motion sensors, and as I approached it, it roared to life, filling the silent room with raucous carnival music as the targets danced in front of me. Compared to the relatively static displays in the rest of the museum, this one seizes your attention as if by force of arms.

Flanking this display are two walls. One is filled with children's BB guns, which are presented as a rite of passage for young American children. On the other side is a display of .22 caliber rifles, the next step in a young person's journey into the world of firearms. To the left is perhaps the most powerful display of memory in the museum: a recreation of a child's bedroom. Though the display uses the term child, the display will likely be read by the viewer as a young boy's bedroom. It is designed to evoke the essential American childhood and looks like the bedroom of a young, middle-class boy growing up in the 1950s or 1960s.

The room was plastered with blue wallpaper with cartoon images of saddles, cowboy hats, and horseshoes. The window of the room was flanked with beige curtains covered with images of horses. To the right of the room there was a bed, with a western themed bedspread, littered with old cowboy comics, several cap guns and BB guns, and a small triangular boy scouts' flag. A boy scouts' uniform hung on the top of the bed frame. There were several western paintings on the wall, depicting horses and cowboys set against the colorful landscape of the American west. Beside the bed sat a record player and bookshelf topped with an old wood-paneled radio, a gas lamp, and a globe. These objects worked to give the viewer a sense of the period the display was meant to evoke.

Tying firearms to visitors' collective memories of childhood has a powerful emotional impact. The display is obviously an embellishment, as there is no typical American childhood, rather childhood is "a name we give to a vastly complex and variable set of experiences."[70] Yet, representing childhood, or attempting to construct an image of a "universal childhood" is a vector used to communicate certain meanings and connect the visitor's personal memories to a larger collective conceptualization of childhood. Though few viewers would have grown up in a bedroom exactly like this, they can see pieces of themselves in it. For example, though I did not grow up in the time that the bedroom was representing, the cowboy imagery struck a chord with me, evoking images of playing with my Lego cowboy set as a child.

Further, this display ties into collective memories of childhood conveyed through popular culture. It evokes such sets as Andy's bedroom from the iconic *Toy Story* series, or Ralphie's room from the American classic *A Christmas Story* (1983). There is even a Red Ryder BB gun on display in this part of the museum. This connection to American popular culture and film is further reinforced in the Hollywood gallery, which was discussed earlier, though it bears repeating. The meaning that the visitor is meant to take from this exhibit is as clear as day: firearms are an essential part of a normal American childhood.

Narratives of progress and innovation are central to American culture, as are the stories of the enterprising individuals responsible for these inventions. Inventors, successful businesspeople, entrepreneurs, and innovators often attain a hero status in America. In contemporary society, people like Elon Musk, Jeff Bezos, Bill Gates, and Mark Zuckerberg are household names. In American history, people like Henry Ford, Thomas Edison, and John D. Rockefeller are legends. This image is also present in American popular culture, where heroes like Iron Man and Batman save the day not with the help of superpowers, but with wealth, scientific prowess, and their ability to wield industrial power.

These individuals become living symbols of the American faith in progress and scientific advancement. The faith that tomorrow will be better than today. The central promise of the American dream: the pursuit of happiness. The National Firearms Museum weaves the story of firearms, and the individuals who invented them, into the narratives of technological progress and the great innovators that represent such a large part of the "American experience." A key theme of the museum is technical innovation and the inventors who brought it about. This is done primarily in three displays. The labels of these displays evoke the language of a Science and Technology museum, highlighting the impact of great inventors on scientific progress in the field of arms development.

The first display, located in between the galleries on the American Revolution and the Civil War, focuses on one of the most pivotal periods in the history of the modern firearm. As a result of industrialization, firearms technology evolved by leaps and bounds in the nineteenth century. As the century opened, battles were fought, and game taken with single shot, breach-loading muskets and rifles that could fire at most a few shots every minute. By the end of the century, Gatling guns, repeating rifles, and semi-automatic pistols could hurl multiple shots downrange with significantly reduced reloading time. This period of technological progress made names like Colt, Winchester, Smith & Wesson, Remington, and Browning famous. This display highlighted the key innovations of this period, like the percussion cap,[71] which allowed for the development of repeating firearms. It highlights the accomplishments of the great inventors by telling their stories and tying them into the broader history of the United States. For example, one panel discusses the relationship between Samuel Colt and Texas Ranger Sam Walker. Walker, who understood the value of Colt's revolvers for cavalrymen due to his campaigns against the Comanche people in Southern Texas, worked with Colt to develop a revolver for the military.

While the guns of the west are largely uncontroversial in the American gun debate, the section entitled "America's Rifle" delves into a more controversial topic. The display shows the development of semi-automatic firearms, culminating in the AR-15. A series of firearms are placed in a timeline, though no dates are given this time. An information panel discusses the achievements of Eugene Stoner, founder of Armalite who was the inventor of the original AR-15.[72] Pictures next to the firearms show soldiers firing the M16, the military counterpart to the AR-15, as well as civilians using the AR-15 for target practice. Other famous modern firearms, like the AK-47 and FN-FAL are displayed bellow the AR-15. Given the controversial position that the AR-15 holds in the Great Gun Debate, the museum seeks to remove it from its political context and emphasize the technological aspects of its development, weaving it into the narrative of technological development and scientific progress. Further, by dubbing it "America's Rifle", the museum works to tie the controversial firearm to American identity.

The final key element of American culture and identity that the museum weaves together with the history of firearms is the mythos surrounding the American Presidency. This reverence for the figure of the President as a symbol of national identity is widespread in popular culture. It has even spawned a particular genre of action movies, which involve a threat to the President's life being thwarted by the actions of a heroic individual, whether it be Harrison Ford in *Air Force One* (1997),

Channing Tatum in *White House Down* (2013), or Gerard Butler in the saga that includes *Olympus Has Fallen* (2013), *London Has Fallen* (2016), and *Angel Has Fallen* (2019). The aura surrounding the Presidency is also put on display in shows like the *West Wing* (1999–2006).

There are several firearms in the museum that belonged to former US presidents, many of whom were members of, or involved with, the NRA. This includes a single-action .45 Colt revolver that belonged to President John F. Kennedy and Ronald Reagan's Kentucky Rifle. The largest display of Presidential firepower is devoted to America's outdoorsman president, Theodore Roosevelt. In a glass case devoted to the ascendency of America to global power, Roosevelt features prominently. Set against a blown up black and white photograph of Roosevelt posing with his Roughriders, a Winchester Model 1895 features prominently, as it is positioned just below the viewer's eye level. A small information panel explains that the rifle belonged to Roosevelt and was used during his service in Cuba. Below the rifle is a Colt single-action revolver, which lies next to a box of machine gun shells attached to a Colt 1895 belt-fed Machine gun. It is explained that both of these firearms were used by the Roughriders. Curiously out of place in the display is a small Teddy Bear, the popular children's toy named after Roosevelt, who famously refused to shoot a tied up black bear on a hunting trip to Mississippi.[73]

These objects serve to connect firearms to the aura surrounding the American Presidency, naturalizing firearms as quintessentially American. This narrative is almost an appeal to the authority of the institution of the Presidency, proving that firearms are a key part of American identity by showing them being owned, used, and gifted to the men elected by the people to symbolize the nation. My participant Sam noted that this part of the museum surprised him, as one does not often associate firearms with the presidency:

> Something that stuck out was that the presidents actually owned firearms. Yeah, they don't really talk about it, because politics, but the different presidents owned different firearms. Obviously, Teddy Roosevelt having a large collection, because of his hobbies. But I don't think the media or anybody really talks about it that much. Because you know the leader of our country owning their own firearms ... They could ... I don't know ... It's just politics in the end.[74]

This points to another narrative of suppression that was often raised by my participants. The idea that the mainstream of society, usually personified by the media, anti-gun billionaires, or large corporations, seeking to suppress the gun culture, consciously hides or skims over information that might normalize firearms ownership or the gun culture, such as the idea that presidents might own firearms.

Factories of Meaning

Firearms are objects of meaning. These meanings can be personal, such as the significance of a particular firearm to an individual or can be shared by broader communities. But these meanings must be produced. They do not spring from nothing. The NRA museum produces meaning, tying firearms to key narratives surrounding America's past and identity. These macro-level narratives then serve as the ideological backdrop against which the organization's political program can be set.

Much like museums have served the needs of nation-states, corporations, and community groups for hundreds of years, the NRA museum serves several functions for the organization. First, the museum is meant to assert the NRA's status, prestige, and identity. It does this through subtle elements like the patrician décor or the focus on the family. The museum serves as a repository of corporate memory, telling the NRA's story and serving as a treasure trove of evidence to be brought forward for trials and promotional material.

But the museum is also a powerful communication device for the organization. The tools that the museum uses to do this are artifacts and narratives, which, when paired together, are powerful instruments for storytelling and identity-building. The true power of the museum lies in its ability to resonate with, and inspire wonder in its visitors. This is the aspect of the museum that is most difficult to capture, even with thick description. The NRA National Firearms Museum represents a truly unique and captivating space for those within the community of gun owners. Museums allow communities to come together and represent themselves. Seeing one's serious leisure pursuit reflected in the glass case of a museum display is affirming, especially for a community that sees itself as at war with the powerful American cultural industry.

8 Ideas, Policy, and the Great Gun Debate

We may not live in the past, but the past lives in us.

– Samuel Pisar

This book has traced the ideational roots of the National Rifle Association's influence on the Great Gun Debate in America, and thus their ability to influence firearms policy in the United States. I began with the assertion that explanations of the NRA's influence that focus solely on lobbying or campaign donations miss out on the source of the NRA's power, which is its ability to mobilize its membership to provide human and financial resources for the organization. I then sought to explain how the NRA uses key points of contact with its membership, like its magazines, videos, classrooms, and events, to communicate important stories to its active and potential members. These narratives often take the form of macro-level policy narratives, which attempt to influence how Americans understand their past to justify a specific set of policies, and work towards the growth of the gun culture from which the NRA and their political allies draw political support.

Throughout this book, we have seen how the NRA works to influence the perceptions of the American public towards both their present and their past. Macro-level policy narratives surrounding the American Revolution, the Second World War, or Good Guys with Guns are intended to reinforce the idea that firearms have played an essential role in American history. This role includes not only the personal protection of Americans, but also a political safeguard against government overreach and tyrannical government. These narratives reinforce the idea that firearms are a key part of America's story and soul. They tie guns to key elements of America's identity, from what it means to have an American childhood to the defining characteristics of the American people – self-reliance, freedom, innovation, and a disdain for authority.

Given its long history and its size, the NRA has many tools at its disposal to disseminate these narratives. Particularly important are its written and audio-visual material, the *American Rifleman Magazine* and the former NRATV. There are key physical points of contact as well, explored in earlier chapters: the NRAAM, NRA Firearm Safety Classes, gun shows, and the National Firearms Museum. As we have seen, these narratives have three intended audiences. The first audience is the NRA's existing membership, which must be mobilized to ensure their continued participation in the NRA's advocacy efforts, be it financial contributions to the organizations, keeping one's membership current, getting out to vote, or engaging in advocacy work like letter writing. The second audience are gun owners who are not currently deeply engaged in gun culture. These owners likely own a single gun for the purpose of self-defense. They are not involved in the gun culture, and do not engage in practices like reading about guns, listening to or watching programs about guns, going to the range regularly, hunting, or participating in the shooting sports.

Deeper involvement in the gun culture is a predictor of political behavior,[1] and the NRA has a strong incentive to capture members of this group, who are primed to be sympathetic to its messaging. Finally, NRA programming targets the gun-curious, people who may be open to the idea of gun ownership but have simply never been drawn to guns or are unsure of how to proceed. This includes new groups of gun owners that the NRA now recognizes are essential for maintaining the Second Amendment: women and racialized minorities. Recruiting these people is a major focus for the wider gun rights movement, and the NRA is no exception.

This book has made three broad contributions to the literature. The first is to the literature on the policy process, specifically to the theoretical development of the NPF. Using the NPF as a scholarly lens allows us to empirically trace the influence of narratives in the Great Gun Debate. While the approach was initially intended to bridge empirical work and theory, scholars have tended to focus on empirical projects at the expense of theory development. As a result, the macro-level of the NPF remains underdeveloped. This project has worked towards righting this imbalance, drawing on insights from the field of history and memory studies to account theoretically for the influence of macro-level narratives.

Macro-level narratives about a nation's past and a nation's identity serve two purposes. The first is a repertoire of stories that allow ordinary people to make sense of the world around them, including the political world. These broad narratives serve as a heuristic that helps us navigate the complex barrage of political information that ordinary people are bombarded with on an everyday basis. Political actors can influence the meanings that people take from these narratives by engaging in past presencing, highlighting certain elements, and downplaying others. Though the past is not infinitely mutable, powerful actors with access to a well-funded and professional communications program can certainly influence the way that we see our past. As we have seen, the NRA works hard to control the way that Americans see key macro-level narratives about American history and identity, to make them amenable to the organization's policy preferences. For example, by utilizing the narrative of the Good Guy with a Gun in their magazines, online television programming, convention, museums, and courses, the organization creates the necessary ideological backdrop to make policies like concealed carry laws intelligible and desirable to a broader public.

The second function that macro-level narratives play is community building. The NRA both socially constructs and draws on macro-level policy narratives through what memory scholars call past presencing; drawing on history, public and personal memory, and heritage to build a political community of gun owners. The organization works to build the gun-owning community because they understand that participation in the gun culture is a powerful predictor of political behavior. Communities are built on shared stories, and those with the power to tell these stories to a wide audience gain the power to shape the meaning that people take from them. To those within the gun-owning community, gun ownership is about more than just self-protection. It is a serious leisure pursuit and a way of finding community and purpose in an increasingly fractured world. It is also a political act, an assertion of agency in an era where ordinary people are increasingly discmpowered by the forces of globalization; global capitalism, centralization, and bureaucratization.

The second contribution my project makes is to the literature surrounding the NRA and gun culture in the United States. This diverse literature spans several fields across the social sciences and humanities: history, political science, sociology, and anthropology. My book contributes to this literature through the addition of a holistic, bottom-up approach to understanding the influence of the NRA. It expands on the work of Melzer,[2] Carlson,[3] Lacombe,[4] and Spitzer[5] who have attempted to trace the cultural and grassroots influence of the NRA. It does this by exploring the role of narrative and memory in the organization's toolkit. Further, it expands on the work of scholars like Tonso,[6] Wright,[7] Kohn,[8] and more recently Yamane[9] by engaging with the gun culture on its own terms, and seeking to understand how the diverse meanings and understandings attached to firearms within the gun-owning community motivate political action in a way that other serious leisure pursuits do not.

Finally, this book contributes to the field of memory studies, museology, and the emerging literature on firearms' museums. Though the field no longer sees the state as the sole producer of historical material, the majority of the scholarship in this field has been state-centric in focus. This is understandable given that nation-states are often the largest producers or funders of historical material in a given country. The past is important for states, as it represents a major component of the nation-building project.[10] Comparatively little research has examined how advocacy groups mobilize memory to promote their cause. The NRA has several tools at its disposal to engage in past presencing and the practices of memorialization. It regularly presents historical content and personal memories in its magazines, through its museums, and during its conventions. NRA instructors further mobilize individual and hypothetical memory to promote the practice of self-defense preparedness.

Implications for the Great Gun Debate

Those expecting to find the usual scathing critique of the gun culture, gun-owning community, or NRA within this work have likely been disappointed. I do not see the value in attempting to judge and measure the NRA by the normative standards of academic critical perspectives. The NRA is a conservative political organization and will obviously fail to live up to those standards. This approach has been adopted by many other authors who I have cited in the preceding pages. I do not try to hide behind the artifice of neutrality, but the normative goal of my project has always been promoting rapprochement and understanding. Setting aside a discussion of various gun control policies and their consequences for a later time has been a necessary precondition to achieving this goal. Instead, I have attempted to address a gap in the academic understanding of the gun culture, a gap with consequences for our empirical understanding of the success of gun groups like the NRA.

The reality is that the overwhelming majority of academics approach this issue from the perspective of what Tonso[11] first labelled the "adversary culture" to which gun ownership is, at best, a strange curiosity, or, at worst, an unconscionable vice. I do not write this to pander to the fantasies of conspiracy theorists who see academics as ideological culture warriors doing the bidding of George Soros, but to acknowledge the empirically verifiable fact that most academics in the social sciences and humanities approach the world through a more "left leaning," "progressive," or "liberal"[12] worldview, especially on social issues like firearms policy.[13]

Further, while a small academic literature exists that approaches the issue from the perspective of the gun culture, this is generally relegated to the fields of econometrics or obscure legal journals. This literature speaks past the mainstream, and the two paths rarely cross. Adding a third voice to the conversation, one that is able to bring two vastly different world views into conversation, is normatively and analytically valuable. I hope that by now you will be convinced that we cannot fully understand the Great Gun Debate without knowing what guns represent, what they mean, to the people who own and use them. Approaching firearms through the lens of deviance and crime simply does not allow us to do that.

When it comes to the American gun debate, I do not see an end in sight. Regardless of the future of the NRA, which at the time I am writing this book faces significant legal trouble in the state of New York, the community of gun owners from which it drew its strength is not going anywhere. This community is highly motivated towards advocacy, and increasingly connected using social media and the internet. The pro-gun advocacy network grows seemingly by the day, with more and more pro-gun groups representing a more diverse segment of American society.

On the other side, the pro-control movement, criticized for years by opponents and academics as lackluster, is gaining strength, and benefits from key allies in the cultural industries, as well as virtually universal positive media coverage. The Parkland students, who have turned horrific personal tragedy into a social movement for gun reform, have brought a fresh face, and a new generation, into the fight. The odds of significant changes to American gun laws seem higher than they have been in a long time, though the short attention spans of media outlets and their readers could derail this momentum.

Ideas in Public Policy

This book adds further weight to the assertion that ideas and identities matter in public policy. The ability of key policy actors, whether advocacy groups like the NRA or political leaders like Barack Obama or Donald

Trump, to translate their interests into political action depends on their ability to persuade. Actors have many tools of persuasion that they can use in the modern media environment, but few are as persuasive as storytelling. Narratives are fundamental to what it means to be human. The stories that we hear and tell live inside of us, influencing our thoughts and behaviors in ways we are not always directly conscious of. As scholars of policy, understanding the power of storytelling is of the utmost importance, as is reaching beyond the artificial confines of our discipline for theorizing its influence.

Moving Forward

This book has raised several important questions for further research. The study of macro-level policy narratives is still in its infancy. More work is needed to determine how actors both draw on and shape key macro-level narratives to gather support for their cause. A possible case study might be the other side of the gun debate. How do pro-control activists draw on the past to support their program? What parts of the past do they focus on? How do pro-control groups draw on the public memory of tragic mass shootings as part of their advocacy mission? When it comes to the use of narrative, pro-control activists have some advantages. The stories of mass shootings, and the tales told by their survivors, can have a powerful impact on public attitudes. What role have these narratives played in the recent successes of the formerly "missing movement"[14] for gun control in the United States? How have movements like the March for Our Lives used storytelling to rally a new generation of young people to their cause?

Further, the shift from gun culture 1.0 to gun culture 2.0 has diversified the gun culture in the United States.[15] For example, looking at concealed handgun permit data from 2019 demonstrates that women now represent 26 per cent of permit holders in states that track the gender of applicants, compared to 16 per cent 20 years ago.[16] For further comparison, only 12 per cent of gun license holders in Canada, where a shift in gun culture has *not* occurred, are women.[17]

The gun buying spree of 2020 has served as a catalyst for this. The outbreak of the COVID-19 pandemic in 2020 created an enormous amount of global uncertainty. In the United States, it sparked a sharp uptick in sales for the small arms and ammunition industry. The year witnessed record gun sales and a massive influx of new gun owners. 21 million background checks were conducted for gun sales in 2020, compared to 13.2 million the year before, a significant jump.[18] At least five million

Americans purchased a gun for the first time in 2020,[19] including many groups that have traditionally been more averse to gun ownership like women and people of color. In one study of firearms purchases made during the pandemic, 64.8 per cent of first-time firearms owners were women.[20]

There has been intense debate about how this will impact gun politics in the United States. Research has demonstrated that gun ownership is a significant predictor of voting behavior. This would lead us to believe that an influx of new gun owners would mean more support for gun rights. That being said, this effect is not equal across all types of gun owners and is much less noticeable in "casual" gun owners. For example, research has demonstrated that the more guns a person owns, the more likely they were to have voted for Trump in the 2016 election. Those who owned three or four guns were much more likely to have voted for Trump than those who only owned a single gun. This suggests that the relationship between gun ownership and political behavior is cultural, rather than tied solely to ownership.[21] Gun culture is what accounts for the political effects of gun ownership, yet not all gun owners, and certainly not all Americans, are involved in this culture.

In addition to the increasing gender diversity in the gun culture, we also see increasing racial diversity, as groups with traditionally lower levels of gun ownership begin to exercise their Second Amendment rights. While only four states collect data on race, we see that African American and Asian American permit holders are the fastest growing groups.[22] We can see this reflected in the world of gun advocacy, where a new and diverse generation of advocates are taking advantage of social media to spread their message. This includes African American advocates like Colion Noir, Ursula Williams, and Maj Toure; Jewish American advocates like Ava Flanell, and Yehuda Remer, who goes by the moniker the Pew Pew Jew; white women like Eva Shockey and Dana Loesch; and Asian American activist Chris Cheng, who rose to prominence as an advocate after winning $100,000 on the shooting sports reality show *Top Shot*. We can see it in the growth of minority gun rights organizations, like the National African American Gun Association (NAAGA), which grew by 25 per cent in 2020 alone.[23]

The social and political turmoil of 2020, which led to one of the largest surges in gun sales in American history, served as a catalyst to this diversification. Initial studies have shown that women and visible minorities are making up larger percentages of new gun owners during the pandemic. For example, in one study of 1,000 participants, 64.8 per cent of people who had bought a gun for the first time during the pandemic were women.[24]

These events raise interesting questions for scholars moving forward. Considering much of American gun history involves the concentration of firearms in the hands of white, Protestant men, do these new groups draw on the past in their advocacy? If so, how? One interesting place to look is at the Black Tradition of Arms. While conducting this project, I came to discover two historians exploring this vein, Nicholas Johnson[25] and Kellie Carter Jackson.[26] While guns are generally framed as a threat to minorities, and gun control as a solution to inner-city violence which disproportionately impacts racialized minorities, these authors have written histories of African American armed protest and resistance, from slavery to the civil rights movement to the present. These texts seem to have had an impact on the discourse employed by African American gun advocates, with advocates like Maj Toure of the Black Guns Matter movement, and Philip Smith of NAAGA drawing on them in the public discussion of guns.

Further, do liberal gun owners fit within the gun culture? Liberal gun owners tend to exist on the periphery of scholarly analysis, yet as Yamane et al.[27] note, 20 per cent of gun owners identify as liberals and 37 per cent as political moderates. More work needs to be done to understand this silent majority of gun owners, and the role that they play, or do not play, in firearm advocacy.

Looking beyond America, we can see that the gun debate is global. This work raises questions of comparative analysis between the American gun rights movement and others. In Canada, the gun rights movement has been increasingly active since the election of Justin Trudeau in 2015. In response to the Trudeau government's ban on "assault-style weapons," the movement has spearheaded a large legal challenge and multi-million-dollar public relations campaign. How does the Canadian gun rights movement operate in an institutional environment much less friendly to its goals? Do Canadian gun rights groups tell stories about the nation's past? How does their rhetoric compare to that of the NRA?

My journey into the gun culture has now spanned half a decade. I have explored the gun culture through several mediums, from the pages of magazines to the gun ranges of Virginia. I have sat with thousands of cheering Trump supporters, walked the aisles of gun shows and fired the most mediatized objects in the Great Gun Debate: the Glock handgun and the AR-15. I have spoken to NRA supporters, ordinary gun owners, and employees of the organization. In the end, one lesson sticks in my mind: human beings are social creatures. We seek company and community. Communities form around shared activities, interests, and stories. If we are to understand the community of gun owners, we must look at it through this lens. Only then can we truly understand gun culture, and the advocacy that it inspires.

Appendices

Appendix A – NRA Tax Return Summary

Year	ILA – Lobbying	Communications	Programs/Services
2013 Spent	27,618,525[1]	41,409,374	34,063,015
2014 Spent	47,081,434	39,467,120	54,497,007
2015 Spent	24,851,934	35,465,774	45,404,733
2016 Spent	76,579,388	37,776,105	48,204,544
2017 Spent	27,086,771	145,759,099	

Appendix B – Methods: Ethnography

Ethnography is a relatively new tool in the toolkit of political scientists. As such, I thought it would be useful to include a short discussion of the craft of ethnography. It is my hope that this will be useful to future scholars, particularly graduate students, seeking to apply this method to prepare themselves for both the professional and personal challenges of performing such involved research.

Narrative analysis is a useful methodological tool to understand the political world, though there are some distinct challenges. Narratives are forms of communications that are deeply based in culture. Those reading narratives from outside of the culture face the risk of misunderstanding elements of the narrative. Ethnography is a useful tool to overcome this cultural barrier. If we want to glean meaning from stories, and the transformative political power they contain, we must endeavor to understand the people who tell them and the people who listen. As a bespectacled, city-dwelling, Jewish academic, descending from a proud lineage of lefties, neither hunting nor sports shooting had been a part of my upbringing. If I was to understand the group of people that I wanted to study, I needed to walk a mile in their shoes, or risk reproducing the tired cliché regularly trotted out on the evening news of a well-dressed, wealthy reporter going "undercover" to show the alleged depravity of American gun owners. Ethnographic research seemed the most appropriate venue through which to do this. It allowed me not only to understand the people who shared these stories, as well as the world they came from, but to also experience them firsthand.

Though originally the purview of anthropologists, an increasing number of political scientists are choosing to use ethnography to shed light on political problems. Having accepted that "ideas matter" in political science[2] it is only natural to want to study how these ideas impact the political thoughts and behavior of individuals. After all: "central to the anthropological perspective is the attempt to understand assumptions made by people when they organize their worlds in the ways that they do."[3] Understanding the way that people make sense of the world helps us to understand how that worldview influences their decision-making.

Political scientists have noted several advantages that ethnographic methods can offer the field of political science. First and foremost, because ethnography involves getting close to research subjects and attempting to gain an insider's view into their lives, known as the emic perspective, it allows scholars to gain a richer and more detailed understanding of the lifeworlds of their subjects.[4] This can help political scientists to ground theoretical assumptions, explain anomalies, and gain insight into a group's self-understanding. It is particularly useful for studying group politics, given the role that personal meanings play in motivating advocacy.[5] While statistics and surveys can offer us powerful snapshots into the gun debate, they have trouble capturing the complex thoughts, feelings and meanings that drive political behavior and thus can be well complemented with ethnographic research. For example, statistical accounts that focus on gun ownership amongst white, rural, middle-class men paint over the large minority of liberal or centrist gun owners.[6]

Further, ethnography is a useful tool to understand phenomena that would not have been considered by traditional political science.[7] This includes the politics of the everyday. Ethnography can help shed light on the fact that for gun owners, the simple choice to go to the gun range, buy a certain type of firearm, watch a pro-gun YouTube video or purchase coffee from a self-proclaimed Second Amendment friendly coffee company can be a political choice.

Ethnography differs slightly from auto-ethnography. Though the line between the two concepts is quite blurry, the generally accepted distinction is that autoethnography involves a researcher writing about a group to which they belong, rather than a group to which they are an outsider.[8]

Using ethnographic methods is not without its challenges and drawbacks. Given that ethnography is a detail-oriented research method, it is difficult to generalize from ethnographic research alone. Ethnography thus works best when connected to a solid theoretical framework, that allows the scholar to reach beyond the particularities of their case study. There is a social world that we can access, as intersubjective meanings that are socially constructed are by nature accessible to numerous people. Thus: "An ethnographic interpretation might underscore the tensions and contradictions of everyday life, but its burden is to maintain theoretical sovereignty over those complications."[9]

In sum, I chose ethnography as an appropriate methodology for my study of the NRA, as it is the most comprehensive method for getting an insider's perspective so as to properly understand not only how the NRA communicates narratives about America's past to its audience, but also how those messages are received and incorporated into the lifeworld of that audience.

Having explained why ethnographic research is useful, it is also appropriate to consider how to conduct it – or at least how I went about it. When we think about ethnography, our minds immediately jump to participant observation. While it is true that participant observation is the most important tool in the ethnographer's toolbelt, it is rarely used alone. Ethnographic research involves drawing on a range of research methods. For example, my research involved combining insights from content analysis, museum analysis, interviews, and participant observation. Some of these could be employed from the comfort of my own office, others in the field.

Before departing for your fieldwork, it is important to become as accustomed as possible to the social group you intend to study. My interest in studying the gun culture began in the winter of 2016, and since then I have spent much of my spare time absorbed in the world of firearms. My prep work began in cyber-space, where I listened to countless hours of firearms related podcasts, like *Gun Guy Radio*, the *Wasted Ammo Podcast*, *Gun Funny*, and others. I have also watched innumerable hours of YouTube videos from popular firearms channels, to immerse myself in the online culture, learn the jargon, and familiarize myself with firearms.

But my preparations were not only digital. To become more familiar with the workings of actual firearms I took the Canadian Firearms Safety Course (CFSC), the Canadian Restricted Firearms Safety Course (CRFSC), and acquired my Canadian Non-Restricted and Restricted Possession and Acquisition License (RPAL/PAL). This was important not just from a safety perspective, but also to help me to gain familiarity handling firearms and participating in the shooting sports, like skeet and trap shooting closer to home before heading to my field site.

After a thorough review of the literature, I thought the best place to begin my empirical analysis would be by using written and audio-visual material. I analyzed 100 *American Rifleman* articles, and 35 episodes of NRATV. This was useful for gaining an understanding of NRA messaging strategies, and of gun culture itself.

In the field, I conducted participant observation at the NRAAM over the course of three days in April of 2019. The process of writing field notes brings the tension of your position as a researcher to the forefront. As a result, there are several different approaches on how to go about recording them. Many ethnographers will record jottings throughout the day and turn these into longer fieldnotes during downtime or after leaving the field.[10] This is the method that I elected to use at the convention. This was different from the notetaking technique used by Melzer[11] for example, who was fearful of being observed, and chose to record his jottings in the bathroom of the convention. The proliferation of smart phones since he completed his ethnography gave me an easier solution. I took small jottings on my cellphone's notepad application. Given the amount of time most people spend glued to their phones, this method of notetaking was unobtrusive and went completely unnoticed by my participants. At the end of the day, I would use these jottings to jog my memory as I composed my fieldnotes. Sitting at my laptop in my hotel rooms, quick notes like "North – national anthem – Broadway" would become long passages: "I heard a speaker introduce Oliver North (of Iran-Contra fame), the current President of the NRA. I headed over to the doors to the convention center to see what was going on. North was giving a speech, though there was such a crowd around him I could hardly see him. I only caught the end of the speech, but afterward the mc introduced a young blond girl to sing the national anthem. The MC said she dreamed of one day singing on Broadway. Everyone removed their hats and sang the national anthem." Between May and July 2019, I participated in five NRA Firearm Safety Courses. These courses lasted between seven and nine hours. During the NRA courses, where the demands of the class forced me to become more participant than observer, I had to adapt. I usually did not take notes during the classes, except to jot down the most pressing of thoughts, which I recorded in shorthand. I am lucky in that my handwriting is almost illegible, thanks to my learning disability, so I was not worried about classmates deciphering my notes.

In these classes I had a very short time to build trust with potential participants, who were naturally skeptical of a researcher coming from anti-gun academia, especially one from Canada. The question of my citizenship came up several times. I am dual American-Canadian citizen. This provided me with a tremendous advantage, as I was told by my instructor that only American citizens are permitted to take NRA courses, or have access to shooting ranges in the US thanks to policy changes made after 9/11.[12] However, explaining my citizenship, even after proving it with my passport, was always a point of contention. I was usually able to gain participant trust, however, when they realized that my project was agnostic on questions of firearms policy evaluation and was not one of the numerous media hit pieces to which gun owners have become accustomed.

Thus, my fieldnotes for the NRA courses were taken after the fact. After driving home and taking a shower to wash off any lead or gun powder residue, I would sit down and write for a few hours. I would leave the notes to percolate for a few days, and then return to them, expanding on things that I had remembered once my brain had had time to process the information.

To expand the scope of my participant observation, I visited two gun shows. One was in the wider DC Area, which I visited for a full afternoon, and the other in Lynchburg, VA. This second gun show involved participant observation over a full weekend. I set up a booth at the show to talk to participants, and recruit for my online qualitative survey. The survey resulted in a small pool of responses (n=12) to compliment my interview data. Respondents generally wrote long paragraphs in answer to the question, which I treated as cultural texts, similar to the data gathered from my in-person interviews, and incorporated into my data.

I conducted interviews with two NRA executives; the NRA's head of research and the Director of the NRA National Firearms Museum. Elite interviews usually lasted under one hour. They took place at the NRA Headquarters. My interview with the museum director also included a tour of the museum's collection that is not on display.

I also conducted interviews with my six principal participants, who I recruited during the firearm safety classes. Interviews were semi-structured, and while I had a list of "prompts" for my participants (see Appendix C), I tried to let them lead the conversation as much as possible. Interviews lasted between 30 minutes and one hour. All but one participant consented to be tape recorded. I also took notes during the interview but kept the notetaking to a minimum to be as engaged as possible with participants. These interviews were often preceded by trips to the gun range with participants. Interviews were conducted over coffee, or in one case ice cream, and I always treated my participants to a coffee or tea to thank them for their time.

These interviews were useful for understanding how ordinary gun owners interact with and selectively incorporate or reject the NRA's narratives into their worldview. During interviews I was often taken aback by how closely the rhetoric of my participants mirrored that of the NRA. This is partially a reflection of the success that the NRA has had in shaping the discourse on gun policy. But it is also a reflection of the experience of speaking to a researcher. Some participants seemed to be uneasy about sharing their views with an academic. One even came with a pre-written prepared statement to ensure that they got their message across clearly. I believe that they saw themselves as ambassadors for their community. They saw me as a researcher as a vessel to have their voices and opinions passed onto a wider audience, though they were nervous about having these views misrepresented. Falling back on certain talking points was a way of protecting the integrity of their message. As interviews wore on, however, participants usually became more comfortable, and began to share more personal stories, opinions, and experiences that moved beyond these talking points.

My analysis of the NRA Museum was performed over four visits between May and June of 2019. These visits usually lasted between two and four hours. I conducted my initial visit to get used to the space. I took only brief notes, focusing on capturing my initial impressions of the museum. On the second visit I took a tour of the museum and conducted a more thorough visit. In addition to taking short form notes on my cellphone, I also took pictures of displays and information panels that I could come back to later when writing more detailed notes at my computer. These pictures proved useful for remembering key details of the different exhibits. For example, when remembering the display of Gatling guns in the museum, my mind had been so focused on the firearms that I had completely blocked out the wall of ammunition displays in the back, that were themselves interesting pieces of history.

Looking at the museum involved taking into consideration several perspectives. My academic hat was the easiest to don, as it is the one that I wear the most. For each exhibit I tried to puzzle the why and how of it all. Why was this included? Why was it presented like this? How does it fit into the broader narratives of the organization? The other hats were more difficult to adopt. Analyzing the museum also involved trying to imagine how a non-expert would interpret the displays and narratives. I simply did not have time or the institutional access to perform exit interviews of the museum, robbing me of an important perspective.

In addition to methodological challenges, it is important for researchers planning on conducting ethnographic field work to think about the personal, ethical, and emotional difficulties that this research entails. Ethnographic research can be lonely, stressful, and presents the researcher with moral and ethical quandaries that few other scholars need seriously engage with. Descending the so-called "ivory tower" and being close to your research, or your research subjects, very clearly problematizes the artificial boundary between researcher and subject. It is for this reason, however, that ethnographic research is so rewarding and so honest. Entering the world of your participants helps to break down some of the barriers, and power dynamics, between researcher and subject. It makes you feel vulnerable and forces you to try to understand your participants on their terms.[13] It is easy to disparage someone, or their belief system, in the comfort of your office, writing at your computer. But when you look someone in the eyes, and talk to them openly and honestly, you are forced to meet them halfway, and gain a more grounded view of the truth.

Researching a topic that you are passionate about poses its own challenges to your mental health. First, the boundary between work and life becomes extremely difficult to maintain. Every news story, conversation with friends and relatives, or snippy line in a once favorite television series brings you back into work mode. This phenomenon is compounded when you are in the field. Being somewhere for a short time to do research places one under a tremendous amount of strain and pressure. You are isolated from your normal social circle, and the challenges of adjusting to a new place are compounded by the pressures of research. I failed to appreciate, until I was in the field, how isolating it would feel to go days without a face-to-face conversation with another human being that did not involve the exchange of goods or services.[14]

Further, being in the field erases the delicate boundaries that academics fight to maintain between their personal lives and work. There are no family members, romantic partners, or old friends to take your mind off your work, no excuse for you to stop. In the field, your project is your first priority. As I would learn, carving out days to try to not think about my project would become exceptionally important to my well-being, and thus my ability to keep my mind sharp and do the best job that I could

Progress in the field came stochastically. Brief flurries of activity were followed with days of down time. I spent this time doing research, taking advantage of the George Mason Library, and trying to set up meetings to speak with other scholars. Yet despite this it was hard to shake the nagging feeling of failure, the pressure to justify my time spent away, the financial burden, and my loneliness.

The silence of the lulls was filled with self-doubt. What was I doing here? Was I wasting time and money? What was the point of all of this? During the flurries of action however, I was elated. Anyone who has done research knows the sense of exhilaration that a new discovery or lead can create within you. The closest experience I can compare it to, though one that people may find strange, is the experience of dating. You feel a simultaneous sense of excitement and nervousness at meeting someone new, yet this joy feels fragile. What if my interviewee cancels? What if they revoke my access? What if I lose participant trust? What if something happens to me and I do not get to finish my work? Thoughts like this flew through my head during these breakthroughs, making me oddly nostalgic for the melancholy and comforting gloom of the lulls.

The stress of ethical dilemmas was another factor that I had understood academically, if not emotionally, when planning my trip. It is one thing to consider ethics when planning your research, and another to *live* it. At my first NRA class, I was tremendously nervous to approach the instructor. I went to talk with them, and ask them for an interview, and was shocked and disappointed to discover that they are forbidden from being interviewed and could lose their NRA teaching license as a result.[15] Though not really a close call, this drove home to me the potential danger that I was putting people, and myself in with my research. The thought of my work costing someone their livelihood made me feel sick to my stomach. Though I always tried to be as open as possible with participants, the feeling of being an intruder, outsider, or interloper was yet another feeling I struggled to shake throughout the process. It is important to be aware of these drawbacks when thinking about using ethnographic methods in your research design.

In sum, ethnography is a useful tool for political scientists to explore the deeper meanings behind political behavior. To be effective, ethnography should be tied to a clear theoretical framework and combine insights from multiple research methods, in order to ensure the reliability and validity of the research. When considering undertaking ethnographic research, researchers should have a detailed yet adaptable plan, background knowledge of the social group they are working with, and an understanding of the logistical and personal difficulties that ethnography can present to the researcher.

Appendix C – Sample Prompt Questions

1 How long have you owned and used firearms?
2 What was your first experience with firearms?
3 What does owning a gun mean to you? What does the gun symbolize for you? (Kohn, *Shooters*).
4 What kind of firearms related activities do you enjoy (i.e. hunting, sports shooting, etc.)?
5 When did you join the NRA? What prompted you to join?
6 Did you buy your first gun? Did someone buy it for you? Did you inherit it?
7 What does the Second Amendment mean to you?
8 Have you been to the National Firearms Museum? What did you think of it?
9 What role do you think firearms have played in US history?

Notes

1. The Great Gun Debate

1 Quoted in Steven Broyles, "Better Men Than Us – Lieutenant Colonel Jeff Cooper" (Wasted Ammo Podcast, 2018), https://www.wastedammo.com/181/.
2 Scott Melzer, *Gun Crusaders: The NRA's Culture War* (New York: New York University Press, 2009); Jennifer Carlson, *Citizen-Protectors: The Everyday Politics of Guns in An Age of Decline* (Oxford: Oxford University Press, 2015).
3 J.C. Clark, "NRA Campaign Contributions in Florida Not What You Think," *Orlando Sentinel*, March 2, 2018, http://www.orlandosentinel.com/opinion/os-ed-nra-money-does-not-extend-to-florida-legislators-20180301-story.html.
4 IRS, "Form 990 – Return of Organization Exempt from Income Tax" (n.d.), https://projects.propublica.org/nonprofits.
5 IRS.
6 NRA, "NRA Explore: Firearms Training," 2021, https://firearmtraining.nra.org/.
7 Jennifer Tucker et al., "Display of Arms: A Roundtable Discussion about the Public Exhibition of Firearms and Their History," *Technology and Culture* 59, no. 3 (2018): 719–69, https://doi.org/10.1353/tech.2018.0064.
8 David Yamane, Sebastian L. Ivory, and Paul Yamane, "The Rise of Self-Defense in Gun Advertising," *Gun Studies*, 2019, 9–27, https://doi.org/10.4324/9781315696485-2.
9 Mark R. Joslyn, *The Gun Gap: The Influence of Gun Ownership on Political Behavior and Attitudes* (Oxford, UK: Oxford University Press, 2020).
10 This is a term I borrow from American sociologist David Yamane, who practices engaged scholarship by running two public blogs in addition to his academic duties. See https://guncurious.wordpress.com/.

11 This includes major retailers like Dick's Sporting Goods, which now refuses to carry certain types of firearms, as well as businesses like Lyft and Postmates, which have partnered with the Giffords organization to form the "Giffords Impact Network." It also includes a growing movement in the museum industry to de-gun the museum, as well as attempts to remove guns from popular cartoons like Looney Toons. Finally, many Hollywood actors and pop stars have been outspoken about their support for gun control, including Chris Rock, Cardi B, Kristen Bell, Amy Schumer, Gal Gadot, Jessica Alba, Zendaya, Justin Bieber, and a host of others.

12 "Of Peaceable Kingdoms and Lawless Frontiers: Exploring the Relationship between History, Mythology and Gun Culture in the North American West," *American Review of Canadian Studies.* 49, no. 1 (2019): 25–49, https://doi.org/10.1080/02722011.2019.1573843.

13 *Armed in America: A History of Gun Rights from Colonial Militias to Concealed Carry* (Amherst, NY: Prometheus, 2018).

14 *The Gunning of America* (New York: Basic Books, 2016).

15 *That Every Man Be Armed: The Evolution of a Constitutional Right* (Albuquerque, NM: University of New Mexico Press, 2013).

16 "The Early History of Guns: From Colonial Times to Civil War," in *Guns and Contemporary Society: The Past, Present, and Future of Firearms and Firearm Policy,* ed. Glen H. Utter (Santa Barbara: ABC-CLIO, 2016), 1–32.

17 *To Keep and Bear Arms: The Origins of an Anglo-American Right.* (Cambridge, Mass: Harvard University Press, 1996).

18 Jennifer D. Carlson, "From Gun Politics to Self-Defense Politics: A Feminist Critique of the Great Gun Debate," *Violence Against Women* 20, no. 3 (2014): 1–9, https://doi.org/10.1177/1077801214526045.

19 The debate is sometimes referred to as the Great American Gun Debate (Kates & Kleck, *The Great American Gun Debate*), the firearms or gun policy debate (Merry, "Constructing Policy Narratives in 140 Characters or Less: Smith-Walter, Peterson, Jones, & Nicole Reynolds Marshall, "Gun Stories"), the gun control debate (Lacombe, "The Political Weaponization of Gun Owners"), or simply the gun debate (Cook & Goss, *The Gun Debate*; Kohn, *Shooters*; Melzer, *Gun Crusaders*; Wright, "Ten Essential Observations on Guns in America").

20 Semi-automatic carbines are often referred to as "assault rifles," "military style assault rifles," "assault-style rifles," "modern sporting rifles (MSRs)," and "Black Rifles." The term most commonly refers to variants of the AR-15 rifle, as well as other common semi-automatic rifles available in the United States, such as civilian versions of the AK-47. How to label these firearms has been a major source of contention for me as I have progressed through this project. I have chosen to use the term semi-automatic carbine as, from where I stand, it seems the most objective term. The first three terms, which employ the term "assault" or "military," are intentionally misleading. They have been purposefully crafted to confuse the listener into associating civilian weapons capable of semi-automatic

fire with the weapons used by the military capable of fully automatic fire. This approach was pioneered by Josh Sugarmann of the Violence Policy Coalition. Frustrated by a lack of progress regulating handguns, the gun control movement shifted its focus to assault weapons in the 1980s (Barrett, *The Rise of America's Gun*). Sugarmann noted that a handgun ban was unlikely to win the support of the majority of Americans, and decided that focusing on assault-weapons was a more achievable goal given: "The weapons' menacing looks, coupled with the public's confusion over fully automatic machine guns versus semi-automatic assault weapons – anything that looks like a machine gun is assumed to be a machine gun – can only increase the chance of public support for restrictions on these weapons" (Sugarmann, "Assault Weapons and Accessories in America"). In reality, the difference between guns like the AR-15 and many common semi-automatic hunting rifles is purely cosmetic. On the other side of the debate, the term Modern Sporting Rifle (MSR), employed by the NRA, is a deliberate attempt to rebrand these weapons away from their reputation as "the weapon of choice for mass shootings." The term is not without some merit. The AR-15 is one of the most commonly owned firearms in the United States. It is estimated that there are over 15 million AR-15s in the civilian market in America. In 2016, for example, semi-automatic carbines accounted for 61.3 per cent of rifle sales (Heath et al., "How an 'Ugly,' Unwanted Weapon Became the Most Popular Rifle in America") yet less than 3 per cent of all firearms homicides (FBI, "FBI Uniform Crime Report"). The overwhelming majority of Americans do use their semi-automatic carbines for *sporting* purposes. Yet I still did not feel comfortable using the term MSR. The term semi-automatic carbine refers to the mechanical characteristics of the firearm. Semi-automatic refers to the firearms action, in which a single depression of the trigger produces a single shot. Carbine refers to the length of the firearm.

21 Melzer, *Gun Crusaders: The NRA's Culture War.*

22 Dan M. Kahan and Donald Braman, "More Statistics, Less Persuasion: A Cultural Theory of Gun-Risk Perceptions," *University of Pennsylvania Law Review* 151, no. 1 (2003): 1291–1327, https://doi.org/10.2307/3312930.

23 Arthuz Z. Berg, John R. Lott, Jr., and Gary A. Mauser, "Expert Views on Gun Laws," *Regulation*, 2019, https://dx.doi.org/10.2139/ssrn.3507975.

24 Carol H. Weiss et al., "The Fairy Godmother—and Her Warts: Making the Dream of Evidence-Based Policy Come True," *American Journal of Evaluation* 29, no. 1 (2008): 29–47, https://doi.org/10.1177%2F1098214007313742; Brian W. Head, "Reconsidering Evidence-Based Policy: Key Issues and Challenges," *Policy and Society* 29, no. 2 (2010): 77–94, https://doi.org/10.1016/j.polsoc.2010.03.001; Pierre-Olivier Bédard, "Understanding Evidence and Behavioral Responses: Future Directions in Evidence-based Policy-making," *Canadian Public Administration*, 2017.

25 Kahan and Braman, "More Statistics, Less Persuasion: A Cultural Theory of Gun-Risk Perceptions," 1294.

26 Laura J. Collins, "The Second Amendment as Demanding Subject: Figuring the Marginalized Subject in Demands for an Unbridled Second Amendment," *Rhetoric and Public Affairs* 17, no. 4 (2014): 737–56; Gianna Pirelli, Hayley Wechsler, and Robert J. Cramer, *The Behavioral Science of Firearms: A Mental Health Perspective on Guns, Suicide, and Violence* (Oxford: Oxford University Press, 2019); Clinton Cramer, *Lock, Stock and Barrel: The Origins of American Gun Culture* (Santa Barbara: Praeger, 2018).

27 Non-gun owners' views are equally shaped to the meanings and symbolism taken on by firearms. A prime example of this is the focus on "assault weapons bans." Given that the most highly publicized mass public shootings often involve semi-automatic carbines, it is natural that firearms like the AR-15 tend to draw more attention from those outside the gun owning community, though they represent a small proportion of overall gun deaths. Between 2013 and 2017, rifles writ-large accounted for between 2–3 per cent of overall homicides in the United States, and only 3–4 per cent of firearm-related homicides, the overwhelming majority of which were carried out with handguns (FBI, "FBI Uniform Crime Report"). For example, in 2016, the year of the Orlando nightclub shooting, there were 11,004 firearm-related homicides in the United States. Of these, only 374 were committed with rifles, and it is unclear how many of these were semi-automatic carbines (FBI, "FBI Uniform Crime Report: Expanded Homicide Data Table 8," 2017, https://ucr.fbi.gov/crime-in-the-u.s/2017/crime-in-the-u.s.-2017/tables/expanded-homicide-data-table-8.xls). Even focusing only on indiscriminate, public "active shooter" type attacks, handguns are still favored by criminals for their concealability and portability. A database of 200 active shooter attacks between 2000 and 2015 found that pistols were used in 56 per cent of attacks, rifles of all types in 27 per cent, and shotguns in 14 per cent (Alex Yablon, "Most Active Shooters Use Pistols, Not Rifles, According to FBI Data," *Trace*, November 8, 2018, https://www.thetrace.org/rounds/mass-shooting-gun-type-data/). Further, there is little evidence to support the effectiveness of measures like the 1994 assault weapons ban at lowering homicide rates (Christopher S. Koper and Jeffrey A. Roth, "The Impact of the 1994 Federal Assault Weapon Ban on Gun Violence Outcomes: An Assessment of Multiple Outcome Measures and Some Lessons for Policy Evaluation," *Journal of Quantitative Criminology.* 17, no. 1 (2001): 33–74; Mark Gius, "An Examination of the Effects of Concealed Weapons Laws and Assault Weapons Bans on State-Level Murder Rates," *Applied Economics Letters* 21, no. 4 (2014): 265–7, https://

doi.org/10.1080/13504851.2013.854294; Koper and Roth, "The Impact of the 1994 Federal Assault Weapon Ban on Gun Violence Outcomes: An Assessment of Multiple Outcome Measures and Some Lessons for Policy Evaluation"; Gius, "An Examination of the Effects of Concealed Weapons Laws and Assault Weapons Bans on State-Level Murder Rates"). This data is not meant to argue in favor or against any specific policies regarding the regulation of these rifles. Rather, it is meant to demonstrate that the *symbolic* importance of semi-automatic carbines in the gun debate is disproportionate to the role they play in gun crime, or the evidence supporting their erasure from public life.

28 F. Carson Mencken and Paul Froese, "Gun Culture in Action," *Social Problems* 66, no. 1 (2019): 3–27, https://doi.org/10.1093/socpro/spx040.

29 Carlson, *Citizen-Protectors: The Everyday Politics of Guns in An Age of Decline.*

30 Kahan and Braman, "More Statistics, Less Persuasion: A Cultural Theory of Gun-Risk Perceptions"; Arie Freiberg and W.G. Carson, "The Limits to Evidence-Based Policy: Evidence, Emotion and Criminal Justice," *The Australian Journal of Public Administration.* 69, no. 2 (2010): 152–64, https://doi.org/10.1111/j.1467-8500.2010.00674.x.

31 Kahan and Braman, 1295–7.

32 Kahan and Braman, 1313–14.

33 David Yamane, "What's Next? Understanding and Misunderstanding America's Gun Culture," in *Understanding America's Gun Culture,* ed. C. Hovey and L. Fisher (Lanham, MD: Lexington Books, 2018).

34 Yamane, 179.

35 Carlson, *Citizen-Protectors: The Everyday Politics of Guns in An Age of Decline,* 61.

36 It is a little-known fact that the NRA's original model was influenced by the Dominion of Canada Rifle Association (DCRA). In the late 1860s, the Canadian government actively encouraged rifle ownership to increase the nation's military readiness and protect from potential American attacks. The government maintained a militia of almost 40,000 men, aided by the DCRA which organized sports shooting competitions and established gun ranges. The DCRA was partially funded through government grants, which covered the creation of rifle ranges and other costs. They would become the first federally funded sporting program in Canada, receiving more than $1.5 million by 1908 (R. Blake Brown, *Arming and Disarming: A History of Gun Control in Canada* [Toronto: University of Toronto Press, 2012], 47). As a consequence, Canadian riflemen in the 1870s gained much international renown, leading the Americans to look north for inspiration (Brown, 50). When establishing the NRA, representatives from the American government came to Ottawa and Toronto to meet

with their Canadian counterparts, and tour DCRA facilities. This included consultation on the design of the NRA's first rifle range in Creedmore, NY. Canadian shooters also helped to train American marksmen (Brown, 50).

37 Robert J. Spitzer, "The Politics of Gun Control" (London: Paradigm Publishers, 2015).

38 Charles, *Armed in America: A History of Gun Rights from Colonial Militias to Concealed Carry.*

39 Melzer, *Gun Crusaders: The NRA's Culture War.*

40 Melzer, 37.

41 Charles, *Armed in America: A History of Gun Rights from Colonial Militias to Concealed Carry,* 277.

42 Charles, 278.

43 Melzer, *Gun Crusaders: The NRA's Culture War,* 65–6.

44 Melzer.

45 Spitzer, "The Politics of Gun Control."

46 Carlson, *Citizen-Protectors: The Everyday Politics of Guns in An Age of Decline.*

47 *Armed in America: A History of Gun Rights from Colonial Militias to Concealed Carry.*

48 Matthew J. Lacombe, *Firepower: How the NRA Turned Gun Owners into a Political Force.* (Princeton: Princeton University Press, 2021).

49 Jeffrey M. Berry and Clyde Wilcox, *The Interest Group Society,* 6th ed. (New York: Routledge, 2018).

50 Carlson, *Citizen-Protectors: The Everyday Politics of Guns in An Age of Decline.*

51 David Yamane, *Concealed Carry Revolution: Expanding the Right to Bear Arms in America* (Berkeley, CA: Anewpress, 2021).

52 "Concealed Carry," Giffords Law Center to Prevent Gun Violence, 2021, https://giffords.org/lawcenter/gun-laws/policy-areas/guns-in-public/concealed-carry/.

53 Yamane, *Concealed Carry Revolution: Expanding the Right to Bear Arms in America.*

54 Spitzer, "The Politics of Gun Control," 100.

55 Spitzer, 101.

56 Lacombe, *Firepower: How the NRA Turned Gun Owners into a Political Force.*

57 Danny Hakim, "Inside Wayne Lapierre's Battle for the NRA," *New York Times Magazine,* August 6, 2020, https://www.nytimes.com/2019/12/18/magazine/wayne-lapierre-nra-guns.html.

58 Brian Mittendorf, "Why New York Is Suing the NRA: 4 Questions Answered," *The Conversation,* August 7, 2020, https://theconversation.com/why-new-york-is-suing-the-nra-4-questions-answered-144108

59 Despite being branded as the "no-compromise" gun lobby, the NRA is actually more moderate than many other mainstream gun rights groups like the Second Amendment Foundation or Gun Owners of America. For

example, the NRA faced immense blowback from their constituency after failing to oppose President Trump's bump-stock ban following the Las Vegas Shooting.

60 Carlson, *Citizen-Protectors: The Everyday Politics of Guns in An Age of Decline*; Abigail A. Kohn, *Shooters: Myths and Realities of America's Gun Cultures* (Oxford: Oxford University Press, 2004); Melzer, *Gun Crusaders: The NRA's Culture War.*

61 For the quintessential example of the impact that this sort of unethical journalism can have on real people, see the Washington Post's "Heavily armed millennials of Instagram" (https://www.washingtonpost.com/news /magazine/wp/2019/03/04/feature/the-heavily-armed-millennials-of -instagram/), then listen to one of the article subject's respond on her podcast (https://www.stitcher.com/podcast/gun-guy-radio/gun-funny /e/59470239?autoplay=true).

62 Daniel Béland and Robert H. Cox, "Introduction: Ideas & Politics," in *Ideas and Politics in Social Science Research*, ed. Daniel Béland and Robert H. Cox (OXFORD: Oxford University Press, 2011), 3–20.

63 Lifeworld, derived from the German *Lebenswelt*, is a way of describing the subjectivity of individual experience that comes from Philosophy. It emphasizes that people experience the social world differently, and that these experiences shape their understanding of what constitutes truth (Austin Harrington, "Lifeworld," *Theory, Culture & Society* 23, no. 2–3 [2006]: 341–3, https://doi.org/10.1177/026327640602300259).

64 Robert M. Emerson, Rachel I. Fretz, and Linda L. Shaw, *Writing Ethnographic Fieldnotes*, Second Edi (Chicago: University of Chicago Press, 2011); Carol A Bailey, *A Guide to Qualitative Field Research*, 2nd ed. (Thousand Oaks, CA: Pine Forge Press, 2007); Sharon Macdonald, *Memorylands: Heritage and Identity in Europe Today* (London, England: Routledge, 2013); David Glassberg, "Public History and the Study of Memory," *Public Historian* 18, no. 2 (1996): 7–23, https://doi.org /10.2307/3377910.

65 Lorraine Bayard de Volo and Edward Schatz, "From the Inside Out: Ethnographic Methods in Political Research," *PS: Political Science and Politics* 37, no. 2 (2004): 267–71, https://doi.org/10.1017/S1049096504004214.

66 David Yamane, Jesse DeDeyne, and Alonso O.A. Mendez, "Who Are the Liberal Gun Owners?" *Sociological Inquiry* 91, no. 2 (2020): 483–98, https://doi.org/10.1111/soin.12406.

2. Narrative and Memory

1 Michael Hill and Frédéric Varone, *The Public Policy Process*, 7th ed. (New York City: Routledge, 2017).

2 Macdonald, *Memorylands: Heritage and Identity in Europe Today.*

3 Yamane, "What's Next? Understanding and Misunderstanding America's Gun Culture."
4 That title belongs to the National Shooting Sports Foundation (NSSF).
5 Walt Hickey, "How the Gun Industry Funnels Tens of Millions of Dollars to the NRA," *Business Insider*, 2013, https://www.businessinsider.com/gun-industry-funds-nra-2013-1; Blake Ellis and Melanie Hicken, "The Money Powering the NRA," *CNN Money*, 2015, https://money.cnn.com/news/cnnmoney-investigates/nra-funding-donors/index.html.
6 "Small Caliber Ammunition Market to Hit USD 8,808.9 Million by 2027," Fortune Business Insights, 2020, https://www.globenewswire.com/news-release/2020/12/10/2143096/0/en/Small-Caliber-Ammunition-Market-to-Hit-USD-8-808-9-Million-by-2027-Booming-Demand-for-Efficient-Firearms-Worldwide-to-Speed-up-Market-Expansion-Says-Fortune-Business-Insights.html; "Value Added by the United States Oil and Gas Extraction Industry from 1998 to 2019," Statista, 2021, https://www.statista.com/statistics/192910/value-added-by-the-us-oil-and-gas-extraction-industry-since-1998/; "Biopharmaceutical Spotlight," Select USA, 2020, https://www.selectusa.gov/pharmaceutical-and-biotech-industries-united-states; "Market Value of Cigarette and Tobacco Manufacturing in the United States from 2010 to 2020," Statista, 2021, https://www.statista.com/statistics/491709/tobacco-united-states-market-value/#; Chris Hudock, "U.S. Legal Cannabis Market Growth," *New Frontier Data*, 2019, https://newfrontierdata.com/cannabis-insights/u-s-legal-cannabis-market-growth/; "Car & Automobile Manufacturing in the US – Market Size 2005–2026," IBIS World, 2020, https://www.ibisworld.com/industry-statistics/market-size/car-automobile-manufacturing-united-states/.
7 "Leading Lobbying Industries in the United States in 2020, by Total Lobbying Spending (in Million U.S. Dollars)," Statista, 2021, https://www.statista.com/statistics/257364/top-lobbying-industries-in-the-us/.
8 U.S. Department of the Treasury, Internal Revenue Service, Form 990 – National Rifle Association, (Washington, DC: 2013–2017). "https://linkprotect.cudasvc.com/url?a=https%3a%2f%2fprojects.propublica.org%2fnonprofits%2forganizations%2f530116130&c=E,1,EIpHgUqDVRYYfX2_Mqhue37HtiW_WmcQIBKP6UOJ4j6bqi1gxWR4eHPt9Vg5Bj6xgLpeuKzWwkcHQYcsGOECNyvlVan1r5Xi1bxj_uAH6A,,&typo=1" https://projects.propublica.org/nonprofits/organizations/530116130.
9 Frank R. Baumgartner and Beth L. Leech, *Basic Interests: The Importance of Groups in Politics and in Political Science* (Princeton: Princeton University Press, 1998); Richard A. Smith, "Interest Group Influence in the U.S. Congress," *Legislative Studies Quarterly* 20, no. 1 (1995): 89–140; Brian Kelleher Richter, Krislert Samphantharak, and Jeffrey F. Timmons, "Lobbying and Taxes," *American Journal of Political Science* 53, no. 4 (2009): 893–909, https://doi.org/10.1111/j.1540-5907.2009.00407.x; Spitzer, "The Politics of Gun Control."

10 Spitzer, 100.
11 Joslyn, *The Gun Gap: The Influence of Gun Ownership on Political Behavior and Attitudes.*
12 Joslyn, 64.
13 Joslyn.
14 Alexandra Middlewood et al., *Intersectionality in Action: Gun Ownership and Women's Political Participation, Social Science Quarterly*, vol. 100 (London: Routledge, 2019), 2516, https://doi.org/10.1111/ssqu.12697.
15 Matthew J. Lacombe, Adam J. Howat, and Jacob E. Rothschild, "Gun Ownership as a Social Identity: Estimating Behavioral and Attitudinal Relationships," *Social Science Quarterly* 100, no. 6 (2019): 2408–24, https://doi.org/10.1111/ssqu.12710; Matthew J. Lacombe, "The Political Weaponization of Gun Owners: The National Rifle Association's Cultivation, Dissemination, and Use of a Group Social Identity," *The Journal of Politics* 81, no. 4 (2019): 1342–56, https://doi.org/10.1086/704329; Lacombe, *Firepower: How the NRA Turned Gun Owners Into a Political Force.*
16 First introduced in 1958, the *Armed Citizen* column is still published by the organization today. It features stories about citizens using firearms in self-defense in order to forward the organization's argument that an armed public makes society safer.
17 *Armed in America: A History of Gun Rights from Colonial Militias to Concealed Carry*, 207.
18 Carlson, *Citizen-Protectors: The Everyday Politics of Guns in An Age of Decline.*
19 Carlson, 65.
20 Lacombe, *Firepower: How the NRA Turned Gun Owners into a Political Force.*
21 Lacombe, "The Political Weaponization of Gun Owners: The National Rifle Association's Cultivation, Dissemination, and Use of a Group Social Identity," 1342.
22 Lacombe, *Firepower: How the NRA Turned Gun Owners into a Political Force*, 1344.
23 Lacombe, 221.
24 Lacombe.
25 Mancur Olson, *The Logic of Collective Action* (Boston: Harvard University Press, 1965).
26 Hugh Heclo, "Issue Networks and the Executive Establishment," in *Public Administration: Concepts and Cases*, ed. Richard J. II Stillman, 9th ed. (Boston, MA: Wadsworth, 2010), 413–21.
27 Vivien A. Schmidt, "Discursive Institutionalism: The Explanatory Power of Ideas and Discourse," *Annual Review of Political Science* 11, no. 1 (2008): 309, https://doi.org/10.1146/annurev.polisci.11.060606.135342.
28 Jal Mehta, "The Varied Role of Ideas in Politics: From 'Whether' to 'How'," in *Ideas and Politics in Social Science Research*, ed. Daniel Béland and Robert H. Cox (Oxford, UK: Oxford University Press, 2011), 23–46.
29 Mehta.

30 Mehta; Schmidt, "Discursive Institutionalism: The Explanatory Power of Ideas and Discourse."

31 Mehta.

32 Schmidt, 306.

33 Mehta, "The Varied Role of Ideas in Politics: From 'Whether' to 'How'," 40–2.

34 Elizabeth A. Shanahan et al., "The Narrative Policy Framework," in *Theories of the Policy Process*, ed. Christopher M. Weible and Paul A. Sabatier, 4th ed. (Westview Press, 2018), 173–214.

35 Shanahan et al.

36 Shanahan et al., 174.

37 Melissa K. Merry, "Constructing Policy Narratives in 140 Characters or Less: The Case of Gun Policy Organizations," *Policy Studies Journal* 44, no. 4 (2016): 373–95, https://doi.org/10.1111/psj.12142.

38 Mark K. McBeth et al., "Buffalo Tales: Interest Group Policy Stories in Greater Yellowstone," *Policy Sciences* 43, no. 4 (2010): 391–409, https://doi.org/10.1007/s11077-010-9114-2.

39 Smith-Walter et al., "Gun Stories: How Evidence Shapes Firearm Policy in the United States," *Politics and Policy* 44, no. 6 (2016): 1056.

40 McBeth et al., "Buffalo Tales: Interest Group Policy Stories in Greater Yellowstone."

41 "Frame Analysis. An Essay on the Organization of Experience," *Reviews in Anthropology*, 1992.

42 *The Whole World Is Watching: Mass Media in the Making & Unmaking of the New Left* (Berkeley: University of California Press, 1980).

43 David A. Snow and Robert D. Benford, "Masters Frames and Cycles of Protest," in *Frontiers in Social Movement Theory*, ed. Aldon D. Morris and Carol M. Mueller (New Haven, CT: Yale University Press, 1992), 133–55.

44 Snow and Benford.

45 John A. Noakes and Hank Johnston, "Frames of Protest: A Road Map to a Perspective," in *Frames of Protest: Social Movements and the Framing Perspective*, ed. John Noakes and Hank Johnston (Lanham, MA: Rowman & Littlefield Publishers, 2005).

46 Mayer N. Zald, "Culture, Ideology, and Strategic Framing," in *Comparative Perspectives on Social Movements,* ed. Doug McAdam, John D. McCarthy, and Mayer N. Zald (Cambridge, UK: Cambridge University Press, 1996), 265.

47 Melzer, *Gun Crusaders: The NRA's Culture War.*

48 Zald, "Culture, Ideology, and Strategic Framing," 267.

49 Elizabeth A. Shanahan, Mark K. McBeth, and Paul L. Hathaway, "Narrative Policy Framework: The Influence of Media Policy Narratives on Public Opinion," *Politics & Policy* 39, no. 3 (2011): 374.

50 "Discursive Institutionalism: The Explanatory Power of Ideas and Discourse."

51 Shanahan et al., "The Narrative Policy Framework."

52 "Buffalo Tales: Interest Group Policy Stories in Greater Yellowstone."

53 Merry, "Constructing Policy Narratives in 140 Characters or Less: The Case of Gun Policy Organizations."

54 Smith-Walter, Peterson, Jones, and Marshall, "Gun Stories."

55 Shanahan et al., "The Narrative Policy Framework," 195.

56 Stephen Crites, "The Narrative Quality of Experience," *Journal of the American Academy of Religion* 39, no. 3 (1971): 291–311, https://doi.org /10.1093/jaarel/XXXIX.3.291.

57 Scot Danforth, "Social Justice and Technocracy: Tracing the Narratives of Inclusive Education in the USA," *Discourse: Studies in the Cultural Politics of Education* 37, no. 4 (2016): 584, https://doi.org/10.1080/01596306.2015 .1073022.

58 Danforth, 584.

59 McBeth et al., "Buffalo Tales: Interest Group Policy Stories in Greater Yellowstone," 394.

60 Holly Peterson and Michael D. Jones, "Making Sense of Complexity: The NPF and Agenda Setting," in *Handbook of Public Policy Agenda-Setting*, ed. Nikolaos Zahariadis (Northampton: Edward Elgar, 2016), 106–31.

61 Jeff Niederdeppe, Sungjong Roh, and Michael A Shapiro, "Acknowledging Individual Responsibility While Emphasizing Social Determinants in Narratives to Promote Obesity-Reducing Public Policy: A Randomized Experiment," *PLoS ONE* 10, no. 2 (2015): e0117565, https://doi.org /10.1371/journal.pone.0117565; Michael D Jones and Geoboo Song, "Making Sense of Climate Change: How Story Frames Shape Cognition: Making Sense of Climate Change," *Political Psychology* 35, no. 4 (2014): 447–76, https://doi.org/10.1111/pops.12057; See Nevbahar Ertas, "Policy Narratives and Public Opinion Concerning Charter Schools: Policy Narratives And Public Opinion," *Politics & Policy* 43, no. 3 (2015): 426–51, https://doi.org/10.1111/polp.12120.

62 Smith-Walter et al., "Gun Stories: How Evidence Shapes Firearm Policy in the United States"; Merry, "Constructing Policy Narratives in 140 Characters or Less: The Case of Gun Policy Organizations."

63 E.J. Hobsbawm, "Introduction: Inventing Traditions," in *The Invention of Tradition*, ed. Eric J. Hobsbawm and Terence Ranger (Cambridge, UK: Cambridge University Press, 1983), 1–14.

64 David Lowenthal, *The Past Is a Foreign Country* (New York: Cambridge University Press, 1985).

65 Michel Foucault, *Language, Countermemory, Practice: Selected Essays and Interviews*, ed. D.F. Boucard (Ithaca, NY: Cornell University Press, 1977).

66 Anderson, Benedict, *Imagined Communities: Reflections on the Origin and Spread of Nationalism*, Rev. (London: Verso, 2006).

67 Lowenthal, *The Past Is a Foreign Country*.

68 R.G. Collingwood and T.M. Knox, *The Idea of History* (Oxford, UK: Clarendon Press, 1946).

69 Edward Hallett Carr, *What Is History?* (London, UK: Macmillan, 1961).

70 Macdonald, *Memorylands: Heritage and Identity in Europe Today.*

71 Michael Rowlinson et al., "Social Remembering and Organizational Memory," *Organization Studies* 31, no. 1 (2010): 69–87, https://doi.org /10.1177/0170840609347056.

72 Jan Assmann, "Communicative and Cultural Memory," in *Cultural Memory Studies: An International and Interdisciplinary Handbook,* ed. Astrid Erll, Ansgar Nunning, and Sara B. Young (Berlin: Walter de Gruyter, 2008), 61–74; Lowenthal, *The Past Is a Foreign Country;* Macdonald, *Memorylands: Heritage and Identity in Europe Today;* David Glassberg, "Public History and the Study of Memory," *The Public Historian* 18, no. 2 (1996): 7–23, https:// doi.org/10.2307/3377910.

73 Lowenthal, *The Past Is a Foreign Country.*

74 Barry Schwartz, "Social Change and Collective Memory: The Democratization of George Washington," *American Sociological Review* 56, no. 2 (1991): 221–36; Assmann, "Communicative and Cultural Memory," 61–74.

75 The debate over the distinction between history and memory is long and complex. At the origins of the field of memory studies, memory was seen as a more authentic and "organic" way of preserving what is still alive, whereas history was an attempt to resurrect what is lost (Macdonald, *Memorylands,* 13). Authors like Olick, Robbins, and Halbwachs see history as dead memories, to which people no longer have a direct relationship, and that are preserved (Rowlinson et al., "Social Remembering"). Authors like Nora ("Between Memory and History"), for example, presented memory as "social" or "organic" and belonging to traditional societies. History, in contrast, is how we "forgetful" western societies attempt to organize and collect the past. In this era, history and memory were positioned as combatants against one another; history having eradicated true, organic memory through the ascendance of modernity. This view held that we only need history because we have become divorced from our traditions and lost memory (Nora, "Between Memory and History"). More recently, this harsh distinction has been problematized by scholars like Macdonald, who acknowledge that separating memory from history is murky business and often involves value judgements on the part of the author, and assumptions about the nature of truth (Macdonald, *Memorylands,* 13–14).

76 Macdonald, *Memorylands: Heritage and Identity in Europe Today,* 18; S. Hoelscher, "Heritage," in *A Companion to Museum Studies,* ed. Sharon Macdonald (Malden, MA: Blackwell Publishing, 2006), 200–17.

77 Hoelscher, 207.

78 Hoelscher.

79 Harold D. Lasswell, *Politics; Who Gets What, When, How.* (New York: Smith, 1936).

80 Barbara Kirshenblatt-Gimblett, "Intangible Heritage as Metacultural Production," *Museum International* 56, no. 1–2 (2004): 53, https://doi .org/10.1111/j.1350-0775.2004.00458.x.

81 UNESCO, "UNESCO Intangible Cultural Heritage," n.d., https://ich .unesco.org/.

82 "Presencing Europe's Pasts," in *A Companion to the Anthropology of Europe*, 2012, https://doi.org/10.1002/9781118257203.ch14; *Memorylands: Heritage and Identity in Europe Today*.

83 MacDonald, "Presencing Europe's Pasts," 234.

84 Lowenthal, *The Past Is a Foreign Country.*

85 Alison Landsberg, "Prosthetic Memory: Total Recall and Blade Runner," *Body & Society* 1, nos. 3–4 (1995): 175–89.

86 Lowenthal, *The Past Is a Foreign Country.*

87 Lowenthal.

88 Hobsbawm, *The Invention of Traditions*; Lowenthal, *The Past Is a Foreign Country.*

89 Schwartz, "Social Change and Collective Memory: The Democratization of George Washington," 222.

90 Michael Schudson, "The Present in the Past versus the Past in the Present," *Communication* 11, no. 1 (1989): 105–13.

91 Schudson.

92 Schudson.

93 Schwartz, "Social Change and Collective Memory: The Democratization of George Washington," 222.

94 Schwartz.

95 Roy Rosenzweig and David Thelen, *The Presence of the Past – Popular Uses of History in American Life* (New York: Columbia University Press, 1998), 5.

96 Rosenzweig and Thelen; Gerald Friesen, Del Muise, and David Northrup, "Variations on the Theme of Remembering: A National Survey of How Canadians Use the Past," *Journal of the Canadian Historical Association* 20, no. 1 (2009): 221–48, https://doi.org/10.7202/039788ar.

97 Macdonald, *Memorylands: Heritage and Identity in Europe Today*, 83.

98 Lowenthal, *The Past Is a Foreign Country.*

99 Lowenthal.

100 Kahan and Braman, "More Statistics, Less Persuasion: A Cultural Theory of Gun-Risk Perceptions."

101 John C. Walsh and James William Opp, *Placing Memory and Remembering Place in Canada* (Vancouver: UBC Press, 2010).

102 Macdonald, *Memorylands: Heritage and Identity in Europe Today.*

103　Friesen, Muise, and Northrup, "Variations on the Theme of Remembering: A National Survey of How Canadians Use the Past"; Rosenzweig and Thelen, *The Presence of the Past – Popular Uses of History in American Life.*
104　Glassberg, "Public History and the Study of Memory," 1996.
105　A. Erill, "Literature, Film, and the Mediality of Cultural Memory," in *Cultural Memory Studies: An International and Interdisciplinary Handbook,* ed. A. Erill and A. Nunning (Berlin: Walter de Gruyter, 2008), 389.

3. On Paper and Online: The *American Rifleman* and NRATV

1　Yamane, "What's Next? Understanding and Misunderstanding America's Gun Culture," 14.
2　"NRA Magazines Subscriptions," 2020, http://www.nrapublications.org /media/1536128/jun-20aam.pdf.
3　"NRA Magazines Subscriptions."
4　Dawn R. Gilpin, "NRA Media and Second Amendment Identity Politics," in *News on the Right: Studying Conservative News Cultures,* ed. Anthony Nadler (Oxford, UK: Oxford University Press, 2019), 84–105.
5　Cydney Hargis, "A Guide to NRATV: NRA's News Outlet Is a Hybrid of Breitbart and Infowars," *Media Matters,* 2018, https://www.mediamatters .org/breitbart-news/guide-nratv-nras-news-outlet-hybrid-breitbart-and -infowars?redirect_source=/research/2017/08/28/guide-nratv-nras-news -outlet-hybrid-breitbart-and-infowars/217768.
6　Gilpin, "NRA Media and Second Amendment Identity Politics."
7　Terry Gross, "Journalist Chronicles The 'Power Struggle' within the NRA," *NPR,* May 22, 2019, https://www.npr.org/2019/05/22 /725690611/journalist-chronicles-the-power-struggle-within-the-nra?t =1559146945000.
8　David Folkenflik, "Cash-Strapped NRA Shuts Down Its Online Channel NRATV," *NPR,* June 27, 2019, https://www.npr.org/2019/06/27/736508057 /cash-strapped-nra-shuts-down-its-online-channel-nratv.
9　Laura Bradley, "What the F–k Is NRATV?" Let John Oliver Explain," *Vanity Fair,* June 2018, https://www.vanityfair.com/hollywood/2018/03/john -oliver-nra-tv-review-last-week-tonight.
10　James Parker, "Live-Streaming the Apocalypse with NRATV," *Atlantic,* June 2018, https://www.theatlantic.com/magazine/archive/2018/06/nratv -live-streaming-the-apocalypse/559139/.
11　Luke Darby, "New NRA Ad: Teach the Media a Lesson by Destroying Your TV with a Hammer," *GQ,* February 13, 2018, https://www.gq.com/story /nra-ad-tv-hammer.
12　"NRA Media and Second Amendment Identity Politics."

13 Noah S. Schwartz, "Called to Arms: The NRA, the Gun Culture & Women," *Critical Policy Studies*, December 3, 2019, 1–16, https://doi.org/10.1080 /19460171.2019.1697892.

14 Lacombe, "The Political Weaponization of Gun Owners: The National Rifle Association's Cultivation, Dissemination, and Use of a Group Social Identity"; Smith-Walter et al., "Gun Stories: How Evidence Shapes Firearm Policy in the United States."

15 Yamane, Ivory, and Yamane, "The Rise of Self-Defense in Gun Advertising."

16 Greg Guest, Kathleen M. MacQueen, and Emily E. Namey, *Applied Thematic Analysis* (Thousand Oaks, CA: SAGE Publications, 2014), 10, https://dx.doi.org/10.4135/9781483384436.

17 Virginia Braun and Victoria Clarke, "Using Thematic Analysis in Psychology," *Qualitative Research in Psychology* 3, no. 2 (2006): 77–101.

18 Virginia Braun and Victoria Clarke, "Using Thematic Analysis in Psychology," *Qualitative Research in Psychology* 3, no. 2 (2006): 12.

19 Elizabeth A. Shanahan, Michael D. Jones, and Mark K. McBeth, "How to Conduct a Narrative Policy Framework Study," *Social Science Journal* 55, no. 3 (2018): 332–45, https://doi.org/10.1016/j.soscij.2017.12.002.

20 Braun and Clarke, "Using Thematic Analysis in Psychology."

21 Calculated as # of articles or episodes this theme shows up in, not the number of times it shows up in articles and episodes.

22 Friesen, Muise, and Northrup, "Variations on the Theme of Remembering: A National Survey of How Canadians Use the Past"; Rosenzweig and Thelen, *The Presence of the Past – Popular Uses of History in American Life*.

23 Clifford Daly, "Mom's Luger," *American Rifleman* (Fairfax, VA, 2018).

24 Dave Bates, "Side-By-Side," *American Rifleman* (Fairfax, VA, October 2018).

25 Lowenthal, *The Past Is a Foreign Country*.

26 Lowenthal.

27 Schwartz, "Called to Arms: The NRA, the Gun Culture & Women."

28 NRATV, "Armed & Fabulous: Shooting for Gold Kim Rhodes" (USA, 2014).

29 NRATV, "Armed & Fabulous: A Champion for the Future: Gaye Kelsey" (USA: NRA Women, 2014).

30 NRATV, "Armed & Fabulous: Meet a Past NRA President Sandy Froman" (USA: NRA Women, 2014).

31 NRATV, "Armed & Fabulous: Freedom's Future Hilary Goldschlager" (USA: NRA Women, 2017).

32 Hayden Foster, "An American Rifleman in the Battle for Germany," *American Rifleman* (Fairfax, VA, December 2019).

33 James Stejskal, "The Arab Revolt and the Guns of Lawrence of Arabia," *American Rifleman*, December 2018.

34 Neil Caplan, *The Israel-Palestine Conflict*, Second (London: Wiley-Blackwell, 2019).

35 Anthony Vanderlinden, "FN Mausers and the Fight for Israel," *American Rifleman* (Fairfax, VA, November 2018).

36 Though the purpose of this chapter is to understand and unpack rather than challenge the narratives presented in the *American Rifleman*, the contentious nature of the Israeli-Palestinian conflict necessitates special attention. It is therefore important to acknowledge that the view of Israel as the underdog in the War of Independence has been challenged by alternate narratives presented by historians. According to Caplan *The Israel-Palestine Conflict*, historians have established that the Israeli army may have had numerical superiority in the conflict, especially in the early stages.

37 Anthony Vanderlinden, "FN Mausers and the Fight for Israel," *American Rifleman* (Fairfax, VA, November 2018).

38 Vanderlinden.

39 Melzer, *Gun Crusaders: The NRA's Culture War.*

40 NRATV, "Curator's Corner: Black Jack Ketchum's Colt Single Action Army" (USA: NRA National Firearms Museum, 2018).

41 "Special Feature: Winchester Repeating Arms," *American Rifleman* (Fairfax, VA, February 2019).

42 "Opening Shot: The AR-15's Initial Testing," *American Rifleman* (Fairfax, VA, February 2019).

43 Hoelscher, "Heritage."

44 Kirshenblatt-Gimblett, "Intangible Heritage as Metacultural Production."

45 Lt. Col. Justin Dyal, "Last of the Breed – Marine Corps M45A1," *American Rifleman* (Fairfax, VA, July 2019).

46 Jeremiah Knupp, "It Starts with a Barrel: Making the American Rifle at Colonial Williamsburg," *American Rifleman* (Fairfax, VA, January 2019).

47 A barrel shroud is a sort of metal cage that goes around the barrel of the firearm to keep the user from burning their hands when handling it.

48 Justin Dyal, "Three Traditions of the Rifle," *American Rifleman* (Fairfax, VA, April 2020).

49 NRATV, "Armed & Fabulous: A Tradition of Giving Julie Hill & Judy Woods" (USA: NRA Women, 2016).

50 NRATV, "Armed & Fabulous: Shooting for Gold Kim Rhodes."

51 NRATV, "Armed & Fabulous: A Champion for the Future: Gaye Kelsey."

52 NRATV, "Armed & Fabulous: Wild at Heart Melanie Pepper" (USA: NRA Women, 2014).

53 NRATV, "Armed & Fabulous: A Lifetime Pursuit Sandra Sadler" (USA: NRA Women, 2016).
54 NRATV, "Armed & Fabulous: Freedom's Future Hilary Goldschlager."

4. Building Culture at the NRA Annual Meeting

1 "What Both Sides Don't Get About American Gun Culture," *Politico*, August 4, 2019, https://www.politico.com/magazine/story/2019/08/04/mass-shooting-gun-culture-227502#.
2 Carlson, *Citizen-Protectors: The Everyday Politics of Guns in An Age of Decline*; Kohn, *Shooters: Myths and Realities of America's Gun Cultures.*
3 Melzer, *Gun Crusaders: The NRA's Culture War.*
4 Joslyn, *The Gun Gap: The Influence of Gun Ownership on Political Behavior and Attitudes*; Middlewood et al., *Intersectionality in Action: Gun Ownership and Women's Political Participation.*
5 President Trump had spoken at a previous in Atlanta, the first American President to do so since Ronald Reagan in 1983.
6 Casual dialogue quoted in the following chapters is paraphrased. Any quotes presented from interviews are accurate according to interview transcriptions.
7 Everyday Carry (EDC) is an emerging genre, with a host of magazines (see *Ballistic Magazine, American Survival Guide Magazine, Skillset Magazine,* etc.), YouTube videos and online forums devoted to discussions of everyday carry. A common form of video in this genre is called a "pocket dump" video, where the subject of the video empties their pockets to show the viewer the different items they carry with them on an everyday basis, and explain the rationales behind them. These videos are often sponsored or supported by companies that sell common EDC items, like knife companies.
8 Tactical is a term used to describe kit that is inspired by military gear. It includes everything from rugged looking flashlights to body armor.
9 Peter Robison, Rachel Adams-Heard, and Erik Larson, "Americans Are Frantically Buying Military Gear Before the Election," *Bloomberg*, October 23, 2020, https://www.bloombergquint.com/business/americans-are-frantically-buying-military-gear-before-election.
10 Air guns use compressed air, spring power or gas to launch a small projectile, usually a steel BB, a lead pellet, or a plastic BB out of the barrel. While often associated with children's toys, like Ralphie's Red Ryder BB gun from *A Christmas Story* (1983), more sophisticated models can launch projectiles with sufficient velocity to hunt small game like squirrels or rabbits.

11 J.L. Austin, *How to Do Things with Words*, 2nd ed. (Oxford, UK: Clarendon Press, 1975); Judith Butler, *Gender Trouble: Feminism and the Subversion of Identity* (New York: Routledge, 1990); Jean François Lyotard, *The Postmodern Condition: A Report on Knowledge*, vol. 10 (Minneapolis: University of Minnesota Press, 1984).
12 National Rifle Association, "2019 NRA Annual Meetings & Exhibits Program" (Indianapolis, IN, 2019).
13 Carlson, *Citizen-Protectors: The Everyday Politics of Guns in An Age of Decline*; Melzer, *Gun Crusaders: The NRA's Culture War*.
14 A.D. Olmsted, "Gun Ownership as Serious Leisure," in *The Gun Culture & Its Enemies*, ed. William R. Tonso (Bellevue, WA: Merril Press, 1990), 61–76; David Yamane, "The Sociology of U.S. Gun Culture," *Sociology Compass* 11, no. 7 (2017): 1–10, https://doi.org/10.1111/soc4.12497; Noah S. Schwartz, "Guns in the North: Assessing the Impact of Social Identity on Firearms Advocacy in Canada," *Politics & Policy*, 2021; Jon Littlefield and Julie L. Ozanne, "Socialization into Consumer Culture: Hunters Learning to Be Men," *Consumption Markets and Culture* 14, no. 4 (2011): 333–60, https://doi.org/10.1080/10253866.2011.604494.
15 Robert A. Stebbins, "Serious Leisure: A Conceptual Statement," *Sociological Perspectives* 25, no. 2 (1982): 251–72, https://doi.org/10.2307/1388726.
16 Stebbins, 251.
17 Stebbins, "Serious Leisure: A Conceptual Statement," 253.
18 Dair L. Gillespie, Ann Leffler, and Elinor Lerner, "If It Weren't for My Hobby, I'd Have a Life: Dog Sports, Serious Leisure, and Boundary Negotiations," *Leisure Studies* 21, no. 3–4 (2002): 285, https://doi.org/10.1080/0261436022000030632.
19 Robert A. Stebbins, *Between Work & Leisure: The Common Ground of Two Separate Worlds* (New Brunswick: Transaction Publishers, 2004), 50.
20 Stebbins, "Serious Leisure: A Conceptual Statement." Stebbins, *Between Work & Leisure: The Common Ground of Two Separate Worlds*.
21 Olmsted, "Gun Ownership as Serious Leisure"; Christi Hubbs, "Just for Fun: Talk and Tactical Shooting in Southern Saskatchewan," *Journal of Undergraduate Ethnography* 7, no. 2 (2017): 19–33; David Spencer Martin et al., "Target Shooting as a Serious Leisure Pursuit – an Exploratory Study of the Motivations Driving Participant Engagement," *World Leisure Journal* 56, no. 3 (2014): 204–19, https://doi.org/10.1080/04419057.2013.836560; Douglas W. Murray et al., "Serious Leisure: The Sport of Target Shooting and Leisure Satisfaction," *Sport in Society* 19, no. 7 (2016): 891–905, https://doi.org/10.1080/17430437.2015.1067780.
22 Murray et al., 898.

23 Murray et al., 902.

24 Gillespie, Leffler, and Lerner, "If It Weren't for My Hobby, I'd Have a Life: Dog Sports, Serious Leisure, and Boundary Negotiations," 286.

25 Gillespie, Leffler, and Lerner.

26 Eva (Hui-Ping) Cheng, Robert Stebbins, and Jan Packer, "Serious Leisure among Older Gardeners in Australia," *Leisure Studies* 36, no. 4 (2017): 505–18, https://doi.org/10.1080/02614367.2016.1188137.

27 Carroll A. Brown, Francis A McGuire, and Judith Voelkl, "The Link between Successful Aging and Serious Leisure," *The International Journal of Aging and Human Development* 66, no. 1 (2008): 73–95, https://doi.org/10.2190/AG.66.1.d.

28 Michael S. Rosenbaum, "Maintaining the Trail: Collective Action in a Serious-Leisure Community," *Journal of Contemporary Ethnography* 42, no. 6 (2013): 639–67, https://doi.org/10.1177/0891241613483560.

29 Olmsted, "Gun Ownership as Serious Leisure," Murray et al., "Serious Leisure: The Sport of Target Shooting and Leisure Satisfaction."

30 Hyunmin Tim Yang, Junhyoung Kim, and Jinmoo Heo, "Serious Leisure Profiles and Well-Being of Older Korean Adults," *Leisure Studies* 38, no. 1 (2019): 88–97, https://doi.org/10.1080/02614367.2018.1499797.

31 Cheng, Stebbins, and Packer, "Serious Leisure among Older Gardeners in Australia."

32 Michael S. Rosenbaum, "Maintaining the Trail: Collective Action in a Serious-Leisure Community," *Journal of Contemporary Ethnography* 42, no. 6 (2013): 639–67, https://doi.org/10.1177/0891241613483560.

33 Cheng, Stebbins, and Packer, "Serious Leisure among Older Gardeners in Australia." Stebbins, *Between Work & Leisure: The Common Ground of Two Separate Worlds.*

34 Rosenbaum, "Maintaining the Trail: Collective Action in a Serious-Leisure Community," 643.

35 NRA, "NRA Annual Meetings: Attendees Profile," 2020, https://www.nraam.org/exhibit/attendee-profile/.

36 Interview with NRA Head of Research Josh Savani, May 23, 2019.

37 NSSF, "Firearm and Ammunition Industry Economic Impact Report 2020," 2020, https://www.nssf.org/government-relations/impact/.

38 NRA, "NRA Annual Meetings: Attendees Profile."

39 Yamane, "The Sociology of U.S. Gun Culture."

40 Yamane, "The Sociology of U.S. Gun Culture."

41 Yamane, Ivory, and Yamane, "The Rise of Self-Defense in Gun Advertising," 21–2.

42 A common misconception among those less familiar with firearms is that the AR-15 is a brand of firearm. This was once the case, as the AR-15 was originally made by Armalite. However, as is the case with most firearms,

once the patent expired other companies picked up the design and started making their own. A firearms platform refers to the design on which the firearm was based. Thus, if both Sig Sauer and Colt, for example, manufacture their own version of the AR-15, they are said to both use the AR platform. Other popular platforms include things like the AK platform, which are civilian versions of the popular AK-47, AK-74, and AKM rifles.

43 Dan Baum, *Gun Guys: A Roadtrip* (New York: Vintage Books, 2013).

44 Muzzle control refers to the importance for shooters to keep the muzzle (end) of the firearm pointed in a safe direction at all times. In the American context, this is one of the four central rules of firearms safety, "never point your gun at anything you are not willing to destroy." In the Canadian context, this is part of ACTS, the Royal Canadian Mounted Police's acronym for safe firearms handling. The C stands for "control the muzzle direction at all times." This is an important point of avoiding accidental shootings and gun etiquette. For example, someone at a gun range who accidentally points their firearm – even a clearly unloaded one – at someone while moving it around, called "swiping," "sweeping," or "flagging" will receive a strict reprimand and sometimes be asked to leave depending on the flagrancy of the infraction.

45 "Sight picture" refers to how easy it is to line up the sights on a firearm, and thus to aim it accurately. Good sights on a firearm allow the user to be more precise and accurate when target shooting.

46 A large part of being able to use a firearm accurately is being able to manage your body's movements. Several factors can lead to small, unintentional movement of the firearm, which impacts its accuracy. This includes things like breathing, body mechanics, and even the shooters heartbeat. A good trigger allows the user to pull it back with consistent pressure so as not to cause an inadvertent jerking of the firearm. For target and sports shooters, good triggers are considered fundamental to their sport, and they will often spend hundreds of dollars on a quality aftermarket trigger.

47 Kim Parker et al., "America's Complex Relationship with Guns," 2017, https://www.pewsocialtrends.org/2017/06/22/guns-and-daily-life-identity-experiences-activities-and-involvement/.

48 Quoted in Tim Barker, "Self-Defense Sales 'Beyond the Gun,'" National Shooting Sports Foundation, 2019, https://www.nssf.org/articles/self-defense-sales-beyond-the-gun/.

49 "NSSF Releases Firearms Production Figures" (Newtown, CT, 2019), https://www.nssf.org/nssf-releases-firearms-production-figures/.

50 While the term "arsenal" is often used disparagingly in the media to refer to a gun owner's firearms, people within the community prefer the more neutral "collection."

51 Price is before tax. It was calculated using Brownells.com, a popular American gun retailer. Includes a Colt AR-15 ($1,121.99), an entry level Holosun Red Dot sight ($159.99), a Brownells brand cleaning kit ($28.99), solvent ($6.99), oil ($3.29), an entry level gun cabinet ($149.99), a cheap rifle case ($24.99) and enough ammunition for a day at the range ($47.98).

52 Several other smaller fringe subcultures intersect with the gun culture. This includes harmless groups like doomsday preppers, and more deviant groups like right-wing militias and white nationalist groups, who have become the focus of increasing attention since the beginning of the Trump Presidency, and especially the riot on Capitol Hill in January of 2021. For obvious reasons, these groups are difficult to track numerically, though the Southern Poverty Law Center estimates that in 2020 there were about 838 hate groups active in the United States (SPLC, "Southern Poverty Law Center," 2021, https://www.splcenter.org/hate-map). The extent to which criminal subcultures and hate groups belong to the broader gun culture is an interesting point of debate. These criminal or deviant subcultures share a certain commonality in that they use firearms, and likely participate in some of the cultural practices of the gun culture. In the criminological and sociological literatures, the relationship between ordinary gun use and criminality is often left unspoken when talking about criminal violence. Yet, gun violence in the United States is often highly concentrated. Though we talk about gun violence in broad terms "no one lives in 'the United States,' per se." Rather, firearms-related violence is "concentrated among certain people and in certain places." For example, a study done in Boston showed that "50% of gun violence takes place on just 3% of streets" and that "85% of gunshot injuries took place in a network of just 6% of the population" (Yamane, "What's Next? Understanding and Misunderstanding America's Gun Culture," 163–4). The geographically concentrated nature of firearms-related violence demonstrates a vast physical and socio-economic gulf between the average firearms user and criminal users. Further, attitudes expressed in the gun culture are so adamantly anti-criminal, it becomes problematic to lump the two groups together. Though the line between a good guy with a gun and a bad guy with a gun is arguably thinner than NRA rhetoric would have one imagine, the criminal is always spoken of as the *other* within the gun culture; as someone outside the law, a shadowy figure lurking in your house, a manifestation of evil, to be shot if necessary. There are two notable intersections between the gun culture and criminal cultures. The first is when "'good guys with guns' become 'bad guys with guns.'" This involves the case of most heavily mediatized mass shootings, or situations of intimate partner violence and homicides. In the United States, 55 per

cent of female homicide victims are killed by firearms, most by people they knew (Violence Policy Center, "When Men Murder Women: An Analysis of 2015 Homicide Data," 2017, https://www.vpc.org/studies/wmmw2017 .pdf). The second intersection is "… when legal gun owners provide guns to criminals in underground markets." This second point of intersection is poorly understood in the literature, and merits further exploration (Yamane, "What's Next? Understanding and Misunderstanding America's Gun Culture," 164). Unfortunately, exploring these issues is beyond the scope of this book.

53 This amount has not changed since 1934. It was originally intended to make purchasing these items prohibitively expensive, but as a result of inflation, they are become more and more affordable.

54 Glenn Kessler, "Fact Checker: Are Firearms with a Silencer 'Quiet'?" *Washington Post*, March 20, 2017, https://www.washingtonpost.com/news /fact-checker/wp/2017/03/20/are-firearms-with-a-silencer-quiet/.

55 Interestingly, suppressors are called "moderators" in these countries.

56 This is another major difference between Canada and the United States. In Canada, firearms can be shipped directly to a person's home as long as the shipping address matches the address on record with the Canadian Firearms Program. In the United States, ordering firearms by mail has been illegal since the gun control legislation passed in the aftermath of Kennedy's assassination, when it was revealed that the gunman purchased his firearm by mail. Those who wish to purchase firearms online in America must have them shipped to a specially licensed dealer.

57 Kohn, *Shooters: Myths and Realities of America's Gun Cultures.*

58 Kohn, 11.

59 Lowenthal, *The Past Is a Foreign Country*, 241.

60 Kahan and Braman, "More Statistics, Less Persuasion: A Cultural Theory of Gun-Risk Perceptions."

61 Before I started this research project, I was relatively ignorant about firearm ammunition. Since then, I have learned just how complex a topic it is. There are hundreds of unique calibers of ammunition available on the civilian market. Gun companies will often release new proprietary calibers, advertising better ballistic performance for certain tasks, whether that be hunting, personal defense, or long-range target shooting. Though these companies do innovate, the evolution of calibers is often motivated by profit margins. Much like Apple or Android consumers must upgrade their phones when a significant upgrade is done to the operating system, and the release of new calibers of firearms drives consumers to purchase more guns.

62 See the Henry USA, "About Us" page for more information: https://www .henryusa.com/about-us/about-us/.

63 Since the user of a lever-action rifle has to pull the lever down, it is difficult to operate them in a prone position (lying down). While this is less of a problem for hunting or agriculture, it is a major problem for soldiers. Lying in the prone position gives soldiers the best cover from enemy gunfire as well as a stable platform from which to shoot accurately. Given that bolt action rifles are much easier to operate lying down, they were adopted by virtually all militaries in the late nineteenth and early twentieth centuries.

64 Rosenzweig and Thelen, *The Presence of the Past – Popular Uses of History in American Life,* 19.

65 To repeat, all names used to refer to participants are pseudonyms.

66 A coach gun is similar to a double-barreled hunting gun, though with a shorter barrel. These firearms get their name from their use on stagecoaches, where they would be carried by guards to dissuade or dispose of bandits. The shorter barrels allowed the shot pattern from the gun to expand more quickly in close quarters.

67 Kohn, *Shooters: Myths and Realities of America's Gun Cultures.*

68 Kohn.

5. Storytelling and Lifeworlds

1 This suspicion was later confirmed when more than half of the attendees left following Trump's speech.

2 Mark K. McBeth et al., "Buffalo Tales: Interest Group Policy Stories in Greater Yellowstone," *Policy Sciences* 43, no. 4 (2010): 391–409, https://doi .org/10.1007/s11077-010-9114-2.

3 Shanahan et al., "The Narrative Policy Framework," 185–6.

4 Shanahan et al.

5 Michael D. Jones, Mark K. McBeth, and Elizabeth A. Shanahan, "Introducing the Narrative Policy Framework," in *The Science of Stories: Applications of the Narrative Policy Framework in Public Policy Analysis,* ed. Michael D. Jones, Elizabeth A. Shanahan, and Mark K. McBeth (New York, NY: Palgrave Macmillan, 2014), 1–25.

6 Lacombe, *Firepower: How the NRA Turned Gun Owners into a Political Force.*

7 The attack the President was referring to occurred on September 25, 2014. On top of being the COO of Vaughan Foods, Mr. Vaughan was also a reserve deputy. He was at work when a disgruntled former employee who had recently been fired from the business stormed the property with a knife, beheading Colleen Hufford and fatally stabbing Traci Johnson ("Reserve Deputy Mark Vaughan Honored With Award Of Valor," *News 9 Oklahoma,* December 9, 2014, https://www.news9 .com/story/5e35a2e883eff40362be40de/reserve-deputy-mark-vaughan

-honored-with-award-of-valor). The assailant, an African American man who had converted to Islam, had recently had arguments with the victims which were the reason he was fired by the company ("Gruesome Opening Statements In Alton Nolen Trial," *News 9 Oklahoma*, 2017, https://www .news9.com/story/5e349953527dcf49dad8173e/gruesome-opening -statements-in-alton-nolen-trial). He would survive his wounds and was sentenced to death in an Oklahoma courtroom in 2017, despite his lawyer's insistence that he was mentally ill and "believed he was doing the right thing because of his delusional misinterpretation of the Quran" ("Oklahoma Man Sentenced to Death for Beheading His Co-Worker," *Associated Press*, December 15, 2017, https://apnews.com/article /c3c84aa09e6f4165b4761dded788cacf).

8　This statement is interesting given the controversy within the Second Amendment community surrounding the Trump Presidency. Trump's main gift to the Second Amendment community has been his resistance to calls for wider gun control after several high-profile mass shootings that happened during his tenure in office. However, many within the community were frustrated by his willingness to compromise by instituting a ban on bump-stocks, and comments that he made disparaging firearm suppressors.

9　On November 5, 2017, at 11:30 a.m. a shooter, a 26-year-old, bearded, white male (left unnamed for ethical reasons) entered the First Baptist Church in Sutherland Springs, Texas. Using an AR-style rifle, the shooter killed 26 people and injured 20 others. Among the dead were a pregnant woman, an infant, and the 14-year-old daughter of the pastor, who was away on vacation. The assailant was a prohibited person who was previously denied a concealed carry license and should not have been able to acquire a firearm. Unfortunately, the Air Force failed to enter the details of his Court Martial into the National Instant Criminal Background Check System (NICS), and thus he was able to purchase the rifle used in the shooting. The shooter had been discharged from the Air Force after assaulting his wife and child (Jason Hanna and Holly Yan, "Sutherland Spring Church Shooting: What We Know," *CNN*, November 7, 2017, https://www.cnn.com/2017/11/05/us/texas-church-shooting -what-we-know/index.html). A history of domestic abuse is common among mass shooters (Jackie Gu, "Deadliest Mass Shootings Are Often Preceded by Violence at Home," *Bloomberg*, June 30, 2020, https://www .bloomberg.com/graphics/2020-mass-shootings-domestic-violence -connection/).

10　Howard K. Mell et al., "Emergency Medical Services Response Times in Rural, Suburban, and Urban Areas," *Journal of the American Medical Association* 152, no. 10 (2017): 983–4.

11 S. Hoelscher, "Heritage," in *A Companion to Museum Studies*, ed. Sharon Macdonald (Malden, MA: Blackwell Publishing, 2006), 200–17.

12 Jones, McBeth, and Shanahan, "Introducing the Narrative Policy Framework," 11.

13 Elizabeth A. Shanahan et al., "The Narrative Policy Framework," in *Theories of the Policy Process*, ed. Christopher M. Weible and Paul A. Sabatier, 4th ed. (Westview Press, 2018), 173–214.

14 Kohn, *Shooters: Myths and Realities of America's Gun Cultures*; Carlson, *Citizen-Protectors: The Everyday Politics of Guns in An Age of Decline*; Jennifer Carlson, "Revisiting the Weberian Presumption: Gun Militarism, Gun Populism, and the Racial Politics of Legitimate Violence in Policing," *American Journal of Sociology* 125, no. 3 (2019): 633–82, https://doi.org/10.1086/707609.

15 Dylan S. McLean, "Gun Talk Online: Canadian Tools, American Values," *Social Science Quarterly* 99, no. 3 (2018): 977–92, https://doi.org/10.1111/ssqu.12476.

16 Interview with Susan, May 22, 2019.

17 Interview with Bucky, May 28, 2019.

18 Interview with Sam, June 18, 2019.

19 Interview with Timothy, June 6, 2019.

20 Interview with Sam, June 18, 2019.

21 Interview with Timothy, June 6, 2019.

22 Kim Parker et al., "America's Complex Relationship with Guns," 2017, https://www.pewsocialtrends.org/2017/06/22/guns-and-daily-life-identity-experiences-activities-and-involvement/.

23 John R. Lott and Rujun Wang, "Concealed Carry Permit Holders Across the United States: 2020," 2020, https://papers.ssrn.com/sol3/papers.cfm?abstract_id=3703977.

24 CDC, "Firearm Violence Prevention," Centers for Disease Control and Prevention, 2020, https://www.cdc.gov/violenceprevention/firearms/fastfact.html; Don B. Kates and Gary Kleck, *The Great American Gun Debate: Essay on Firearms & Violence* (San Francisco, CA: Pacific Research Institute, 1997); Gary Kleck and Marc Gertz, "Carrying Guns for Protection: Results from the National Self-Defense Survey," *Journal of Research on Crime and Delinquency* 35, no. 2 (1998): 193–224; Phillip J. Cook, Jens Ludwig, and David Hemenway, "The Gun Debate's New Mythical Number: How Many Defensive Uses per Year?" *Journal of Policy Analysis and Management* 16, no. 4 (1997): 463–9.

25 Because of the author's Jewish faith, the abbreviation G-d is used instead of the full name of the divine.

26 Interview with Bucky, May 28, 2019.

27 Interview with Rick, June 21, 2019.

28 Interview with Steve, July 2, 2019.

29 Interview with Bucky, May 18, 2019.
30 Interview with Sam, June 18, 2019.

6. Home on the Range

1 See Jon Hauptman & Sarah Cade, Podcast, Guns Guide to Liberals, Episode 8.5 Part Three: Finding Meaning, February 17, 2020.
2 Joslyn, *The Gun Gap: The Influence of Gun Ownership on Political Behavior and Attitudes.*
3 Joslyn, 64.
4 Schwartz, "Called to Arms: The NRA, the Gun Culture & Women."
5 NRA, "NRA Explore: Firearms Training."
6 Carlson, *Citizen-Protectors: The Everyday Politics of Guns in An Age of Decline*, 22.
7 Carlson, 59.
8 Carlson, 64.
9 Dry practice refers to practice handling the firearms in the absence of ammunition. No live ammunition was ever allowed in the classroom. This rule was strictly observed by all instructors. During one class, I had to leave my backpack out in the hall as it contained a box of cartridges for the live fire portion of the class later in the day.
10 "The Rise of Self-Defense in Gun Advertising."
11 A hangfire occurs when substandard or damaged ammunition is used in the gun. It occurs when the firing pin strikes the primer as the user pulls the trigger, but does not cause the gun to go off immediately. If this occurs, the gun may still fire after a few seconds.
12 See Hawkins, A.W.R., Breitbart News, November 10, 2019: https://www.breitbart.com/politics/2019/11/10/joe-biden-no-one-needs-magazine-100-clips-it/.
13 McBeth et al., "Buffalo Tales: Interest Group Policy Stories in Greater Yellowstone."
14 Interview with Sam, June 18, 2019.
15 Interview with Timothy, June 6, 2019; Interview with Sam, June 18, 2019
16 "The Rise of Self-Defense in Gun Advertising."
17 Yamane, *Concealed Carry Revolution: Expanding the Right to Bear Arms in America*; Carlson, *Citizen-Protectors: The Everyday Politics of Guns in An Age of Decline.*
18 Paul M. Barrett, *Glock: The Rise of America's Gun* (New York, NY: Broadway Books, 2013).
19 Carlson, *Citizen-Protectors: The Everyday Politics of Guns in An Age of Decline.*
20 Yamane, *Concealed Carry Revolution: Expanding the Right to Bear Arms in America.*

21 Baum, *Gun Guys: A Roadtrip.*

22 Barrett, *Glock: The Rise of America's Gun.*

23 "Concealed Carry."

24 Ali Rowhani-Rahbar et al., "Loaded Handgun Carrying among US Adults, 2015," *American Journal of Public Health* 107, no. 12 (2017), 1930–6.

25 Rowhani-Rahbar et al.

26 John R. Jr. Lott, "Concealed Carry Permit Holders across the United States: 2019," 2019, file:///C:/Users/Local Noah/Downloads/SSRN -id3463357.pdf.

27 Melzer, *Gun Crusaders: The NRA's Culture War.*

28 Carlson, *Citizen-Protectors: The Everyday Politics of Guns in An Age of Decline.*

29 Interview with Bucky, May 28, 2019.

30 Interview with Susan, May 22, 2019.

31 Interview with Timothy, June 6, 2019.

32 Baum, *Gun Guys: A Roadtrip,* 29.

33 Interview with Bucky, May 28, 2019.

34 Interview with Sam, June 18, 2019.

35 Interview with Susan, May 22, 2019.

36 Interview with Rick, June 21, 2019.

37 Arjun Appadurai, *Modernity at Large: Cultural Dimensions of Globalization,* Vol. 1 (Minneapolis: University of Minnesota Press, 1996).

38 Yamane, "The Sociology of U.S. Gun Culture."

39 I previously noted that "weapon" is a bad word in NRA circles. The lone exception to this rule is in the realm of concealed carry. The reason for this, as explained by my firearms instructor, is that a firearm that you carry for self-defense purposes is intended to be used as a weapon, if needed.

40 Not to be confused with a bullet-proof vest. A shooting vest is similar to a fishing vest, in that it has several pockets designed to hold equipment you might need while on the range, such as boxes of ammunition. Some vests have padded shoulders, in order to help reduce bruising from recoil when shooting shotguns or high caliber rifles.

41 Barrett, *Glock: The Rise of America's Gun.*

42 Clearing the gun is slang for verifying that the firearm is unloaded. To do this, the user removes the magazine from the firearm, checks that the chamber is empty, and ideally verifies that nothing is stuck in the barrel. This is an important safety practice, as assuming that a gun is unloaded when it is not is one of the most common causes of gun accidents.

43 Interview with Bucky, May 28, 2019.

44 Interview with Sam, June 19, 2019.

45 Interview with Rick, June 21, 2019.

46 Richard M. Suinn, "Visualization in Sports," in *Imagery in Sports and Physical Performance*, ed. Anees A. Sheikh and Errol R. Korn (Amityville, NY: Baywood Publishing Company, 1994), 23–43.

47 Nathaniel Zinsser et al., "Military Application of Performance-Enhancement Psychology," *Military Review* 84, no. 5 (2004), 62–5.

48 Michelle Barnhart et al., "Preparing for the Attack: Mitigating Risk through Routines in Armed Self-Defense," *JACR* 3, no. 1 (2017): 27–45, https://doi.org/http://dx.doi.org/10.1086/695762.

49 Schwartz, "Called to Arms: The NRA, the Gun Culture & Women."

50 Less-than-lethal is a term used to describe self-defense accessories that focus on stopping or immobilizing an attacker without the use of potentially lethal force. It includes things like pepper spray, tasers, key-chain batons, and an increasing array of tools that are heavily marketed at women.

51 "Staging" in the firearms world refers to placing or hiding firearms strategically throughout one's home in the event of a home invasion. A wide variety of products are now sold to assist with this, such as mirrors, clocks, desks, end tables and even tissue boxes with hidden compartments where firearms can be kept. On the higher end, these products contain biometric locks, which allow the user to open them with their fingerprints.

52 The CFSC is the government mandated course that is required for Canadians to acquire their basic Firearm's License.

53 Interview with Timothy, June 6, 2019.

54 Hearing protection is the most important piece of personal protective equipment that a shooter wears. A gun firing emits the same decibel range as a jet-engine taking off. Shooting without hearing protection can cause instant and permanent hearing damage. When shooting outside you can usually get away with a single layer of hearing protection, such as foam earplugs. When shooting indoors however, the NRA advises that you double up. When at the range, I always wore my in-ear hearing protection, which I had custom molded to my ears, as well as a set of noise-cancelling earmuffs. The earmuffs are specially designed to filter out unsafe noise levels, while amplifying human voices, so that you can still hear range commands.

55 Joan Burbick, "Cultural Anatomy of a Gun Show," *Stanford Law and Policy Review* 17 (2006): 653–66.

56 Burbick.

57 "Bureau of Alcohol, Tobacco, Firearms and Explosives: Gun Show Enforcement (Part 1 and 2)." (U.S. Government Printing Office, 2006), https://www.govinfo.gov/content/pkg/CHRG-109hhrg26053/html /CHRG-109hhrg26053.htm.

58 Kareem Shaya, "Game Theory and Guns: Why Universal Background Checks Are a Debate – and How to Solve It," Open Source Defense, 2019, https://opensourcedefense.org/blog/game-theory-and-guns-why -universal-background-checks-are-a-debate-and-how-to-solve-it.
59 "Gun Shows: Brady Checks and Crime Gun Traces" (Washington, DC, 1999), 6–7, https://www.atf.gov/file/57506/download.
60 Caroline Wolf Harlow, "Firearm Use by Offenders" (Washington, DC, 2001), https://bjs.gov/content/pub/pdf/fuo.pdf.
61 Yamane, "The Sociology of U.S. Gun Culture."
62 See Schwartz, "Called to Arms: The NRA, the Gun Culture & Women."
63 Schwartz.
64 A point of clarification – these demonstrations did not involve using the taser on a person.
65 Yamane, "The Sociology of U.S. Gun Culture."
66 Militaria refers to old military memorabilia that is popular amongst collectors, history enthusiasts, and reenactors. It includes everything from military surplus uniforms, badges, or pieces of kit to antique firearms and bayonets.

7. The NRA Firearms History Museum

1 Tucker et al., "Display of Arms: A Roundtable Discussion about the Public Exhibition of Firearms and Their History."
2 Lowenthal, *The Past Is a Foreign Country.*
3 Jeffrey Abt, "The Origins of the Public Museum," in *A Companion to Museum Studies*, ed. Sharon Macdonald (Malden, MA: Blackwell Publishing, 2006), 115–34; Carol Duncan, "Art Museums and the Rituals of Citizenship," in *Exhibiting Cultures: The Poetics and Politics of Museum Display*, ed. Steven D. Lavine and Ivan Karp (Washington, DC: Smithsonian Institute, 1991), 477–93.
4 Abt; Hoelscher, "Heritage"; Duncan, "Art Museums and the Rituals of Citizenship," 477–93; C.S. Smith, "Museums, Artefacts, and Meanings," in *The New Museology*, ed. Peter Vergo (London, England: Reaktion Books, 1989), 6–21.
5 Sharon Macdonald, "Collecting Practices," in *A Companion to Museum Studies*, ed. Sharon Macdonald (Malden, MA: Blackwell Publishing, 2006), 85.
6 Sharon Macdonald, "Expanding Museum Studies: An Introduction," in *A Companion to Museum Studies*, ed. Sharon Macdonald (Malden, MA: Blackwell Publishing, 2006), 1–12.
7 Macdonald, "Collecting Practices," 88–9.
8 Macdonald, "Expanding Museum Studies: An Introduction," 4.

9 Macdonald, "Expanding Museum Studies: An Introduction."

10 Peter Vergo, *The New Museology* (London: Reaktion Books, 1989).

11 Macdonald, "Expanding Museum Studies."

12 Steven D. Lavine and Ivan Karp, "Introduction: Museums and Multiculturalism," in *Exhibiting Cultures: The Poetics and Politics of Museum Display*, ed. Steven D. Lavine and Ivan Karp (Washington, DC: Smithsonian Institute, 1991).

13 Flora Edouwaye S. Kaplan, "Making and Remaking National Identities," in *A Companion to Museum Studies*, ed. Sharon Macdonald (Malden, MA: Blackwell Publishing, 2006), 152–69.

14 Steven C. Dubin, "Incivilities in Civil(-ized) Places: 'Culture Wars' in Comparative Perspective," in *A Companion to Museum Studies*, ed. Sharon Macdonald (Malden, MA: Blackwell Publishing, 2006), 478.

15 Dubin, 479.

16 Carol Duncan, "Art Museums and the Rituals of Citizenship," in *Exhibiting Cultures: The Poetics and Politics of Museum Display*, ed. Steven D. Lavine and Ivan Karp (Washington, DC: Smithsonian Institute, 1991), 101–2.

17 Tucker et al, "Display of Arms: A Roundtable Discussion about the Public Exhibition of Firearms and Their History."

18 Tucker et al.

19 Tucker et al.

20 Tucker et al.

21 Ashley Hlebinsky, "It's Complicated: The Short Answer to Firearms, Museums, and History," *The Panorama*, 2018, http://thepanorama.shear .org/2018/09/17/its-complicated-the-short-answer-to-firearms-museums -and-history/.

22 Hlebinsky; Tucker et al., "Display of Arms: A Roundtable Discussion about the Public Exhibition of Firearms and Their History."

23 Hlebinsky.

24 Atteqa Ali et al., "Roundtable: The Politics, Ethics, and Aesthetics of Exhibitions about Guns," *Journal of Visual Culture* 17, no. 3 (2018): 374–86, https://doi.org/DOI 10.1177/1470412918800005; Annie Dell'Aria, "Loaded Objects: Addressing Gun Violence Through Art in the Gallery and Beyond," *Palgrave Communications* 6 (2020), https://doi.org/10.1057 /s41599-020-0391-x.

25 David Serlin, "Guns, Germs, and Public History: A Conversation with Jennifer Tucker," *Journal of the History of Behavioural Science*, 2020, 1–15, https://doi.org/DOI: 10.1002/jhbs.22055.

26 Dell'Aria, "Loaded Objects: Addressing Gun Violence thorugh Art in the Gallery and Beyond."

27 Dell'Aria, 2.

28 Dell'Aria, 2.

29 C.S. Smith, "Museums, Artefacts, and Meanings," in *The New Museology*, ed. Peter Vergo (London, England: Reaktion Books, 1989), 6.

30 Rhiannon Mason, "Cultural Theory and Museum Studies," in *A Companion to Museum Studies*, ed. Sharon Macdonald (Malden, MA: Blackwell Publishing, 2006), 18–32.

31 Michael Baxandall, "Exhibiting Intention: Some Preconditions of the Visual Display of Culturally Purposeful Objects," in *Exhibiting Cultures: The Poetics and Politics of Museum Display*, ed. Steven D. Lavine and Ivan Karp (Washington, DC: Smithsonian Institute, 1991), 38.

32 Macdonald, "Collecting Practices," 82.

33 Dubin, "Incivilities in Civil(-ized) Places: 'Culture Wars' in Comparative Perspective."

34 Mason, "Cultural Theory and Museum Studies."

35 Elizabeth Crooke, "Museums and Community," in *A Companion to Museum Studies*, ed. Sharon Macdonald (Malden, MA: Blackwell Publishing, 2006), 174.

36 Rosenzweig and Thelen, *The Presence of the Past – Popular Uses of History in American Life.*

37 Katherine Anne-Marie Roberts, "Hearth and Soul: The Fireplace in American Culture" (University of Minnesota, 1990), 9.

38 D.M. Ryfe, "Franklin Roosevelt and the Fireside Chats," *Journal of Communication* 49, no. 4 (1999): 80–103, https://doi.org/10.1111/j.1460-2466.1999.tb02818.x.

39 Stephen Greenblatt, "Resonance and Wonder," in *Exhibiting Cultures: The Poetics and Politics of Museum Display*, ed. Steven D. Lavine and Ivan Karp (Washington, DC: Smithsonian Institute, 1991), 42.

40 Stephen Greenblatt, 49.

41 Greenblatt, "Resonance and Wonder."

42 Greenblatt, 42.

43 Interview with Timothy, June 2019.

44 Interview with Sam, June 2019.

45 Interview with Sam, June 2019.

46 Nick Nissley and Andrea Casey, "The Politics of the Exhibition: Viewing Corporate Museums through the Paradigmatic Lens of Organizational Memory," *British Journal of Management* 13, no. S2 (2002): S35–45, https://doi.org/10.1111/1467-8551.13.s2.4.

47 M. Bonti, "The Corporate Museums and Their Social Function: Some Evidence from Italy," *European Scientific Journal* Special Ed (2014): 141–50.

48 Nick Nissley and Andrea Casey, "The Politics of the Exhibition: Viewing Corporate Museums through the Paradigmatic Lens of Organizational Memory," *British Journal of Management* 13, no. S2 (2002): S35–45, https://doi.org/10.1111/1467-8551.13.s2.4.

49 Bonti, "The Corporate Museums and Their Social Function: Some Evidence from Italy."

50 Nissley and Casey, "The Politics of the Exhibition: Viewing Corporate Museums through the Paradigmatic Lens of Organizational Memory."

51 Nissley and Casey; Bonti, "The Corporate Museums and Their Social Function: Some Evidence from Italy."

52 Bonti, 143.

53 Interview with J. Savani, May 23, 2019.

54 Interview with J. Supica, June 28, 2019.

55 Interview with J. Savani, May 23, 2019.

56 Interview with J. Supica, June 28, 2019.

57 Shanahan et al., "The Narrative Policy Framework."

58 Schmidt, "Discursive Institutionalism: The Explanatory Power of Ideas and Discourse."

59 Interview with J. Supica, June 28, 2019.

60 Interview with J. Savani, May 23, 2019.

61 Interview with J. Savani, May 23, 2019.

62 The controversy over the discredited work of Michael A. Bellesiles ("The Origins of Gun Culture in the United States") certainly demonstrates the ferocity of this debate. Historians like Charles (*Armed in America*) question the view that the militias were an important factor in the success of the revolution and whether firearms played a large role in colonial life. Others like Halbrook (*That Every Man Be Armed*), Lansford ("The Early History of Guns"), and Cramer (*Lock, Stock and Barrel*) provide evidence that firearms did indeed play a large role in the everyday life of most people during early American settlement.

63 Interview with J. Savani, May 23, 2019.

64 A muzzle loading firearm is one in which the gun powder and projectile are loaded from the front end (the muzzle) of the firearm. For example, a musket.

65 A cap a ball revolver is the precursor to the single action cartridge revolvers made famous by Western movies. The firearm is loading by packing the round and explosive black powder into the cylinder of the revolver and placing a small percussion cap on the back (similar to the round wafer from a child's cap gun). When the gun is cocked, the cylinder of the revolver rotates, lining up with the barrel of the gun. The pull of the trigger releases the hammer of the gun, which strikes the percussion cap, igniting the black powder and launching the bullet from the gun, producing a black cloud of sulfurous smoke.

66 Simon Chadwick and Sarah Zipp, "Nike, Colin Kaepernick and the Pitfalls of 'woke' Corporate Branding," *Conversation*, 2018, https://dspace.stir .ac.uk/bitstream/1893/27821/1/Chadwick Zipp-Conversation-2018.pdf.

67 Schwartz, "Called to Arms: The NRA, the Gun Culture & Women."

68 Udall et al., "How the West Got Wild."

69 Anderson, *Imagined Communities: Reflections on the Origin and Spread of Nationalism.*

70 Ludmilla Jordanova, "Objects of Knowledge: A Historical Perspective on Museums," in *The New Museology*, ed. Peter Vergo (London, UK: Reaktion Books, 1989), 29.

71 A percussion cap is a small metal cylinder containing priming powder. When struck by the hammer of a firearm, it provides the spark that ignites the powder and launches the bullet. Before the invention of the percussion cap, the flintlock mechanism meant that users had to pour small amounts of priming powder into a small pan on the side of the gun. The percussion cap sped up the process of loading the gun, made it more reliable, and paved the way for the development of the self-contained cartridge.

72 Contrary to popular belief, the AR in AR-15 stands for Armalite, not assault rifle.

73 Edmund Morris, *The Rise of Theodore Roosevelt* (New York City: Random House, 2001).

74 Interview with Sam, June 2019

8. Ideas, Policy, and the Great Gun Debate

1 Joslyn, *The Gun Gap: The Influence of Gun Ownership on Political Behavior and Attitudes.*

2 Melzer, *Gun Crusaders: The NRA's Culture War;* "Fighting the Left and Leading the Right: NRA Politics and Power through the 2016 Elections."

3 Carlson, *Citizen-Protectors: The Everyday Politics of Guns in An Age of Decline.*

4 Lacombe et al., "Gun Ownership as a Social Identity: Estimating Behavioral and Attitudinal Relationships."

5 Spitzer, "The Politics of Gun Control."

6 William R. Tonso, *The Gun Culture and Its Enemies*, 1st ed. (Bellevue, WA: Second Amendment Foundation, 1990).

7 James D. Wright, "Ten Essential Observations on Guns in America," *Society* 32, no. 3 (1995): 63–8, https://doi.org/10.1007/BF02693310.

8 Kohn, *Shooters: Myths and Realities of America's Gun Cultures.*

9 Yamane, "What's Next? Understanding and Misunderstanding America's Gun Culture."

10 Max Paul Friedman and Padraic Kenney, *Partisan Histories: The Past in Contemporary Global Politics*, 1st ed. (New York: Palgrave Macmillan, 2005).

11 Tonso, *The Gun Culture and Its Enemies.*

12 Liberal is used here in the American context.

13 Yoel Inbar and Joris Lammers, "Political Diversity in Social and Personality Psychology," *Perspectives on Psychological Science.* 7, no. 5 (2012): 496–503, https://doi.org/10.1177/1745691612448792; Lee Jussim, "Liberal

Privilege in Academic Psychology and the Social Sciences: Commentary on Inbar & Lammers (2012)," *Perspectives on Psychological Science.* 7, no. 5 (2012): 504–7, https://doi.org/10.1177/1745691612455205; Jose L. Duarte et al., "Political Diversity Will Improve Social Psychological Science," *Behavioral and Brain Sciences.* 38 (2015), https://doi.org /10.1017/S0140525X14000430; Nathan Honeycutt and Laura Freberg, "The Liberal and Conservative Experience Across Academic Disciplines: An Extension of Inbar and Lammers," *Social Psychological and Personality Science.* 8, no. 2 (2017): 115–23, https://doi.org/10.1177 /1948550616667617; James Lindgren, "Measuring Diversity: Law Faculties in 1997 and 2013," *Harvard Journal of Law & Public Policy.* 39, no. 1 (2016): 89–152; Christopher F. Cardiff and Daniel B. Klein, "Faculty Partisan Affiliations in All Disciplines: A Voter-Registration Study," *Critical Review* 17, nos. 3–4 (2005): 237–55, https://doi.org/10.1080/08913810508443639; John F. Zipp and Rudy Fenwick, "Is the Academy a Liberal Hegemony? The Political Orientations and Educational Values of Professors," *Public Opinion Quarterly* 70, no. 3 (2006): 304–26, https://doi.org/10.1093/poq /nfj009; George Yancey, "Recalibrating Academic Bias," *Academic Questions* 25, no. 2 (2012): 267–78; Neil Gross and Ethan Fosse, "Why Are Professors Liberal?" *Theory and Society* 41, no. 2 (2012): 127–68; Julien Larregue, "Conservative Apostles of Objectivity and the Myth of a 'Liberal Bias' in Science," *The American Sociologist* 49, no. 1 (2018): 312–27, https://doi .org/https://doi.org/10.1007/s12108-017-9366-9.

14 Kristin Goss, *Disarmed: The Missing Movement for Gun Control in America.* (Princeton: Princeton University Press, 2006).

15 Yamane, "The Sociology of U.S. Gun Culture."

16 Lott, "Concealed Carry Permit Holders across the United States: 2019."

17 Rachel Gimore, "Few Canadian Women Own Guns, but Are Twice as Likely to Be Attacked with One: Analysis," CTV News, 2019, https://www .ctvnews.ca/politics/few-canadian-women-own-guns-but-are-twice-as-likely -to-be-attacked-with-one-analysis-1.4374216.

18 Matthew Simonson et al., "The COVID States Project: Report #37 Gun Purchases During the COVID-19 Pandemic," 2021, https://news.northeastern .edu/wp-content/uploads/2021/02/COVID19-CONSORTIUM-REPORT -37-GUNS-Feb-2021.pdf#_ga=2.256279432.22422079.1633455371 -777786272.1633455371.

19 NSSF, "First-Time Gun Buyers Grow to Nearly 5 Million in 2020," August 24, 2020, https://www.nssf.org/first-time-gun-buyers-grow-to-nearly-5 -million-in-2020/.

20 Vivian H. Lyons et al., "Firearm Purchasing and Storage during the COVID-19 Pandemic," *Injury Prevention* 27, no. 1 (2021): 87–92, http://dx.doi.org/10.1136/injuryprev-2020-043872.

21 Joslyn, *The Gun Gap: The Influence of Gun Ownership on Political Behavior and Attitudes.*

22 Lott, "Concealed Carry Permit Holders across the United States: 2019."

23 Alyssa J. Perry and Shereen M. Meraji, "Black and up in Arms," *NPR Code Switch*, December 16, 2020, https://www.npr.org/sections/codeswitch /2020/12/09/944615029/black-and-up-in-arms.

24 Lyons et al., "Firearm Purchasing and Storage during the COVID-19 Pandemic."

25 *Negroes and the Gun: The Black Tradition of Arms* (Amherst, NY: Prometheus, 2014).

26 *Force and Freedom: Black Abolitionists and the Politics of Violence* (Philadelphia: University of Pennsylvania Press, 2020).

27 "Who Are the Liberal Gun Owners?"

Appendices

1 All numbers in USD.

2 Béland and Cox, "Introduction: Ideas & Politics."

3 Macdonald, *Memorylands: Heritage and Identity in Europe Today.*

4 Bailey, *A Guide to Qualitative Field Research*; Emerson, Fretz, and Shaw, *Writing Ethnographic Fieldnotes*; Glassberg, "Public History and the Study of Memory," 1996; Macdonald, *Memorylands: Heritage and Identity in Europe Today.*

5 Bayard de Volo and Schatz, "From the Inside Out: Ethnographic Methods in Political Research."

6 Yamane, DeDeyne, and Mendez, "Who Are the Liberal Gun Owners?"

7 Evelyn Z Brodkin, "The Ethnographic Turn in Political Science: Reflections on the State of the Art," *PS: Political Science and Politics* 50, no. 1 (2017): 131–4, https://doi.org/10.1017/S1049096516002298.

8 Tony E. Adams, Carolyn Ellis, and Stacy Holman Jones, "Autoethnography," in *The International Encyclopedia of Communication Research Methods*, ed.Jörg Matthes Hoboken, NJ: Wiley, 2017), 1–11.

9 Chris Weedon and Glenn Jordan, "Collective Memory: Theory and Politics," *Social Semiotics* 22, no. 2 (2012): 267, https://doi.org/10.1080/10350330 .2012.664969.

10 Emerson, Fretz, and Shaw, *Writing Ethnographic Fieldnotes.*

11 Melzer, *Gun Crusaders: The NRA's Culture War.*

12 I later learned that there are several exceptions to this rule, including the possession of a Green Card or a valid hunting license in the state, though no instructors that I worked with were aware of this exception. See 18 U.S.C. 922(a)(5) and (9), 922(g)(5)(B) and 922(y); 27 CFR 478.99(a) and (c)(5).

13 This is especially true when your subjects are armed.
14 Something that many of us have come to experience during the COVID-19 lockdowns.
15 I later learned that this was untrue, and that the instructor had either misunderstood my request or the rules.

Bibliography

Abt, Jeffrey. "The Origins of the Public Museum." In *A Companion to Museum Studies*, edited by Sharon Macdonald, 115–34. Malden, MA: Blackwell Publishing, 2006.

Adams, Tony E, Carolyn Ellis, and Stacy Holman Jones. "Autoethnography." In The International Encyclopedia of Communication Research Methods, edited by Jörg Matthes, 1–11. Hoboken, NJ: Wiley Online Library, 2017.

Ali, Atteqa, Jonathan Ferrara, Kathy O'Dell, and Susanne Slavick. "Roundtable: The Politics, Ethics, and Aesthetics of Exhibitions about Guns." *Journal of Visual Culture* 17, no. 3 (2018): 374–86. https://doi.org/DOI 10.1177 /1470412918800005.

Anderson, Benedict. *Imagined Communities: Reflections on the Origin and Spread of Nationalism*. Rev. London: Verso, 2006.

Appadurai, Arjun. *Modernity at Large: Cultural Dimensions of Globalization*. Vol. 1. Minneapolis: University of Minnesota Press, 1996.

Assmann, Jan. "Communicative and Cultural Memory." In *Cultural Memory Studies: An International and Interdisciplinary Handbook*, edited by Astrid Erll, Ansgar Nunning, and Sara B. Young, 61–74. Berlin: Walter de Gruyter, 2008.

Atlas, Pierre M. "Of Peaceable Kingdoms and Lawless Frontiers: Exploring the Relationship between History, Mythology and Gun Culture in the North American West." *American Review of Canadian Studies*. 49, no. 1 (2019): 25–49. https://doi.org/10.1080/02722011.2019.1573843.

Austin, J.L. *How to Do Things with Words*. 2nd ed. Oxford, UK: Clarendon Press, 1975.

Bailey, Carol A. *A Guide to Qualitative Field Research*. 2nd ed. Thousand Oaks, Calif: Pine Forge Press, 2007.

Barker, Tim. "Self-Defense Sales 'Beyond the Gun.'" National Shooting Sports Foundation, 2019. https://www.nssf.org/articles/self-defense-sales-beyond -the-gun/.

Barnhart, Michelle, Aimee D. Huff, Brandon McAlexander, and James H. McAlexander. "Preparing for the Attack: Mitigating Risk through Routines in Armed Self-Defense." *JACR* 3, no. 1 (2017): 27–45. http://dx.doi.org /10.1086/695762.

Barrett, Paul M. *Glock: The Rise of America's Gun.* New York: Broadway Books, 2013.

Bates, Dave. "Side-By-Side." *American Rifleman* 166, no. 10 (October 2018).

Baum, Dan. *Gun Guys: A Roadtrip.* New York: Vintage Books, 2013.

Baumgartner, Frank R., and Beth L. Leech. *Basic Interests: The Importance of Groups in Politics and in Political Science.* Princeton: Princeton University Press, 1998.

Baxandall, Michael. "Exhibiting Intention: Some Preconditions of the Visual Display of Culturally Purposeful Objects." In *Exhibiting Cultures: The Poetics and Politics of Museum Display,* edited by Steven D. Lavine and Ivan Karp. Washington, DC: Smithsonian Institute, 1991.

Bayard de Volo, Lorraine, and Edward Schatz. "From the Inside Out: Ethnographic Methods in Political Research." *PS: Political Science and Politics* 37, no. 2 (2004): 267–71. https://doi.org/10.1017/S1049096504004214.

Bédard, Pierre-Olivier. "Understanding Evidence and Behavioral Responses: Future Directions in Evidence-based Policy-making." *Canadian Public Administration,* 2017. link.gale.com/apps/doc/A507360152/AONE?u =anon~c318b667&sid=googleScholar&xid=23d112ea.

Béland, Daniel, and Robert H. Cox. "Introduction: Ideas & Politics." In *Ideas and Politics in Social Science Research,* edited by Daniel Béland and Robert H. Cox, 3–20. Oxford: Oxford University Press, 2011.

Bellesiles, Michael A. "The Origins of Gun Culture in the United States, 1760–1865." *Journal of American History* 83, no. 2 (1996): 425–55.

Berg, Arthuz Z., John R. Lott, Jr., and Gary A. Mauser. "Expert Views on Gun Laws." *Regulation* 42, no. 4 (2019): 40–7. https://dx.doi.org/10.2139/ssrn .3507975.

Berry, Jeffrey M, and Clyde Wilcox. *The Interest Group Society.* 6th ed. New York: Routledge, 2018.

Bonti, M. "The Corporate Museums and Their Social Function: Some Evidence from Italy." *European Scientific Journal* Special Edition 1 (2014): 141–50.

Bradley, Laura. "What the F–k Is NRATV?" Let John Oliver Explain." *Vanity Fair,* June 2018. https://www.vanityfair.com/hollywood/2018/03/john-oliver-nra -tv-review-last-week-tonight.

Braun, Virginia, and Victoria Clarke. "Using Thematic Analysis in Psychology." *Qualitative Research in Psychology* 3, no. 2 (2006): 77–101.

Brodkin, Evelyn Z. "The Ethnographic Turn in Political Science: Reflections on the State of the Art." *PS: Political Science and Politics* 50, no. 1 (2017): 131–4. https://doi.org/10.1017/S1049096516002298.

Brown, Blake R. *Arming and Disarming: A History of Gun Control in Canada.* Toronto: University of Toronto Press, 2012.

Brown, Carroll A., Francis A McGuire, and Judith Voelkl. "The Link between Successful Aging and Serious Leisure." *International Journal of Aging and Human Development* 66, no. 1 (2008): 73–95. https://doi.org/10.2190 /AG.66.1.d.

Broyles, Steven. "Better Men Than Us – Lieutenant Colonel Jeff Cooper." Wasted Ammo Podcast, 2018. https://www.wastedammo.com/181/.

Burbick, Joan. "Cultural Anatomy of a Gun Show." *Stanford Law and Policy Review* 17 (2006): 653–66.

"Bureau of Alcohol, Tobacco, Firearms and Explosives: Gun Show Enforcement (Part 1 and 2)." 2006. https://www.govinfo.gov/content/pkg/CHRG -109hhrg26053/html/CHRG-109hhrg26053.htm.

Butler, Judith. *Gender Trouble: Feminism and the Subversion of Identity.* New York: Routledge, 1990.

Caplan, Neil. *The Israel-Palestine Conflict.* 2nd ed. London: Wiley-Blackwell, 2019.

Cardiff, Christopher F., and Daniel B. Klein. "Faculty Partisan Affiliations in All Disciplines: A Voter-Registration Study." *Critical Review* 17, no. 3–4 (2005): 237–55. https://doi.org/10.1080/08913810508443639.

Carlson, Jennifer D. "From Gun Politics to Self-Defense Politics: A Feminist Critique of the Great Gun Debate." *Violence Against Women* 20, no. 3 (2014): 1–9. https://doi.org/10.1177/1077801214526045.

– *Citizen-Protectors: The Everyday Politics of Guns in An Age of Decline.* Oxford: Oxford University Press, 2015.

– "Revisiting the Weberian Presumption: Gun Militarism, Gun Populism, and the Racial Politics of Legitimate Violence in Policing." *American Journal of Sociology* 125, no. 3 (2019): 633–82. https://doi.org/10.1086/707609.

Carr, Edward Hallett. *What Is History?* London, UK: Macmillan, 1961.

Carson Mencken, F., and Paul Froese. "Gun Culture in Action." *Social Problems* 66, no. 1 (2019): 3–27. https://doi.org/10.1093/socpro/spx040.

CDC. "Firearm Violence Prevention." Centers for Disease Control and Prevention, 2020. https://www.cdc.gov/violenceprevention/firearms /fastfact.html.

Chadwick, Simon, and Sarah Zipp. "Nike, Colin Kaepernick and the Pitfalls of 'woke' Corporate Branding." *Conversation*, 2018. https://dspace.stir.ac.uk /bitstream/1893/27821/1/Chadwick Zipp-Conversation-2018.pdf.

Charles, Patrick J. *Armed in America: A History of Gun Rights from Colonial Militias to Concealed Carry.* Amherst, NY: Prometheus, 2018.

Cheng, Eva (Hui-Ping), Robert Stebbins, and Jan Packer. "Serious Leisure among Older Gardeners in Australia." *Leisure Studies* 36, no. 4 (2017): 505–18. https://doi.org/10.1080/02614367.2016.1188137.

Clark, J.C. "NRA Campaign Contributions in Florida Not What You Think." *Orlando Sentinel,* March 2, 2018. http://www.orlandosentinel.com/opinion /os-ed-nra-money-does-not-extend-to-florida-legislators-20180301-story.html.

Collingwood, R.G., and T.M. Knox. *The Idea of History*. Oxford, UK: Clarendon Press, 1946.

Collins, Laura J. "The Second Amendment as Demanding Subject: Figuring the Marginalized Subject in Demands for an Unbridled Second Amendment." *Rhetoric and Public Affairs* 17, no. 4 (2014): 737–56.

Cook, Phillip J., and Kristin A. Goss. *The Gun Debate: What Everyone Needs to Know*. Oxford, UK: Oxford University Press, 2014.

Cook, Phillip J., Jens Ludwig, and David Hemenway. "The Gun Debate's New Mythical Number: How Many Defensive Uses per Year?" *Journal of Policy Analysis and Management* 16, no. 4 (1997): 463–9.

Cramer, Clinton. *Lock, Stock and Barrel: The Origins of American Gun Culture*. Santa Barbara: Praeger, 2018.

Crites, Stephen. "The Narrative Quality of Experience." *Journal of the American Academy of Religion* 39, no. 3 (1971): 291–311. https://doi.org/10.1093/jaarel/XXXIX.3.291.

Crooke, Elizabeth. "Museums and Community." In *A Companion to Museum Studies*, edited by Sharon Macdonald, 170–85. Malden, MA: Blackwell Publishing, 2006.

Daly, Clifford. "Mom's Luger." *American Rifleman*. Fairfax, VA, 2018.

Danforth, Scot. "Social Justice and Technocracy: Tracing the Narratives of Inclusive Education in the USA." *Discourse: Studies in the Cultural Politics of Education* 37, no. 4 (2016): 582–99. https://doi.org/10.1080/01596306.2015.1073022.

Darby, Luke. "New NRA Ad: Teach the Media a Lesson by Destroying Your TV with a Hammer." *GQ*, February 13, 2018. https://www.gq.com/story/nra-ad-tv-hammer.

Dell'Aria, Annie. "Loaded Objects: Addressing Gun Violence through Art in the Gallery and Beyond." *Palgrave Communications* 6 (2020). https://doi.org/10.1057/s41599-020-0391-x.

Duarte, Jose L., Jarret T. Crawford, Charlotta Stern, Jonathan Haidt, Lee Jussim, and Philip E. Tetlock. "Political Diversity Will Improve Social Psychological Science." *Behavioral and Brain Sciences* 38 (2015). https://doi.org/10.1017/S0140525X14000430.

Dubin, Steven C. "Incivilities in Civil(-ized) Places: 'Culture Wars' in Comparative Perspective." In *A Companion to Museum Studies*, edited by Sharon Macdonald, 477–93. Malden, MA: Blackwell Publishing, 2006.

Duncan, Carol. "Art Museums and the Rituals of Citizenship." In *Exhibiting Cultures: The Poetics and Politics of Museum Display*, edited by Steven D. Lavine and Ivan Karp, 477–93. Washington, DC: Smithsonian Institute, 1991.

Dyal, Justin. "Last of the Breed – Marine Corps M45A1." *American Rifleman* 167, no. 7 (July 2019): 64–9.

– "Three Traditions of the Rifle." *American Rifleman* 168, no. 4 (April 2020): 69–73.

Ellis, Blake, and Melanie Hicken. "The Money Powering the NRA." *CNN Money*, 2015. https://money.cnn.com/news/cnnmoney-investigates/nra-funding -donors/index.html.

Emerson, Robert M., Rachel I. Fretz, and Linda L. Shaw. *Writing Ethnographic Fieldnotes*. 2nd ed. Chicago: University of Chicago Press, 2011.

Erill, A. "Literature, Film, and the Mediality of Cultural Memory." In *Cultural Memory Studies: An International and Interdisciplinary Handbook.*, edited by A. Erill and A. Nunning, 389–98. Berlin: Walter de Gruyter, 2008.

Ertas, Nevbahar. "Policy Narratives and Public Opinion Concerning Charter Schools: Policy Narratives and Public Opinion." *Politics & Policy* 43, no. 3 (2015): 426–51. https://doi.org/10.1111/polp.12120.

FBI. "FBI Uniform Crime Report: Expanded Homicide Data Table 8," 2017. https://ucr.fbi.gov/crime-in-the-u.s/2017/crime-in-the-u.s.-2017/tables /expanded-homicide-data-table-8.xls.

Folkenflik, David. "Cash-Strapped NRA Shuts Down Its Online Channel NRATV." *NPR*, June 27, 2019. https://www.npr.org/2019/06/27/736508057 /cash-strapped-nra-shuts-down-its-online-channel-nratv.

Fortune Business Insights. "Small Caliber Ammunition Market to Hit USD 8,808.9 Million by 2027." 2020. https://www.globenewswire.com/news -release/2020/12/10/2143096/0/en/Small-Caliber-Ammunition-Market -to-Hit-USD-8-808-9-Million-by-2027-Booming-Demand-for-Efficient-Firearms -Worldwide-to-Speed-up-Market-Expansion-Says-Fortune-Business-Insights .html.

Foster, Hayden. "An American Rifleman in the Battle for Germany." *American Rifleman* 167, no. 12 (December 2019): 48–53.

Foucault, Michel. *Language, Counter-memory, Practice: Selected Essays and Interviews.* Edited by D.F. Boucard. Ithaca, NY: Cornell University Press, 1977.

Freiberg, Arie, and W.G. Carson. "The Limits to Evidence-Based Policy: Evidence, Emotion and Criminal Justice." *The Australian Journal of Public Administration.* 69, no. 2 (2010): 152–64. https://doi.org/10.1111/j.1467 -8500.2010.00674.x.

Friedman, Max Paul, and Padraic Kenney. *Partisan Histories: The Past in Contemporary Global Politics.* 1st ed. New York: Palgrave Macmillan, 2005.

Friesen, Gerald, Del Muise, and David Northrup. "Variations on the Theme of Remembering: A National Survey of How Canadians Use the Past." *Journal of the Canadian Historical Association* 20, no. 1 (2009): 221–48. https://doi .org/10.7202/039788ar.

Giffords Law Center to Prevent Gun Violence. "Concealed Carry," 2021. https://giffords.org/lawcenter/gun-laws/policy-areas/guns-in-public /concealed-carry/.

Gillespie, Dair L., Ann Leffler, and Elinor Lerner. "If It Weren't for My Hobby, I'd Have a Life: Dog Sports, Serious Leisure, and Boundary Negotiations."

Leisure Studies 21, nos. 3–4 (2002): 285–304. https://doi.org/10.1080
/0261436022000030632.

Gilpin, Dawn R. "NRA Media and Second Amendment Identity Politics." In
News on the Right: Studying Conservative News Cultures, edited by Anthony
Nadler, 84–105. Oxford, UK: Oxford University Press, 2019.

Gimore, Rachel. "Few Canadian Women Own Guns, but Are Twice as Likely to
Be Attacked with One: Analysis." *CTV News,* 2019. https://www.ctvnews.ca
/politics/few-canadian-women-own-guns-but-are-twice-as-likely-to-be-attacked
-with-one-analysis-1.4374216.

Gitlin, Todd. *The Whole World Is Watching: Mass Media in the Making & Unmaking
of the New Left.* Berkeley: University of California Press, 1980.

Gius, Mark. "An Examination of the Effects of Concealed Weapons Laws and
Assault Weapons Bans on State-Level Murder Rates." *Applied Economics Letters*
21, no. 4 (2014): 265–7. https://doi.org/10.1080/13504851.2013.854294.

Glassberg, David. "Public History and the Study of Memory." *Public Historian* 18,
no. 2 (1996): 7–23. https://doi.org/10.2307/3377910.

Goffman, Erving, and John D'Amato. "Frame Analysis. An Essay on the
Organization of Experience." *Reviews in Anthropology* 4, no. 6 (1975): 603–7.

Goss, Kristin. *Disarmed: The Missing Movement for Gun Control in America.*
Princeton: Princeton University Press, 2006.

Greenblatt, Stephen. "Resonance and Wonder." In *Exhibiting Cultures: The Poetics
and Politics of Museum Display,* edited by Steven D. Lavine and Ivan Karp.
Washington, DC: Smithsonian Institute, 1991.

Gross, Neil, and Ethan Fosse. "Why Are Professors Liberal?" *Theory and Society*
41, no. 2 (2012): 127–68.

Gross, Terry. "Journalist Chronicles The 'Power Struggle' within the NRA."
NPR, May 22, 2019. https://www.npr.org/2019/05/22/725690611/journalist
-chronicles-the-power-struggle-within-the-nra?t=1559146945000.

"Gruesome Opening Statements in Alton Nolen Trial." *News 9 Oklahoma,* 2017.
https://www.news9.com/story/5e349953527dcf49dad8173e/gruesome
-opening-statements-in-alton-nolen-trial.

Gu, Jackie. "Deadliest Mass Shootings Are Often Preceded by Violence at
Home." *Bloomberg,* June 30, 2020. https://www.bloomberg.com/graphics
/2020-mass-shootings-domestic-violence-connection/.

Guest, Greg, Kathleen M. MacQueen, and Emily E. Namey. *Applied Thematic
Analysis.* Thousand Oaks, CA: SAGE Publications, 2014. https://dx.doi.org
/10.4135/9781483384436.

"Gun Shows: Brady Checks and Crime Gun Traces." Washington, DC, 1999.
https://www.atf.gov/file/57506/download.

Haag, Pamela. *The Gunning of America.* New York: Basic Books, 2016.

Hakim, Danny. "Inside Wayne Lapierre's Battle for the NRA." *New York Times
Magazine,* August 6, 2020. https://www.nytimes.com/2019/12/18/magazine
/wayne-lapierre-nra-guns.html.

Halbrook, Stephen P. *That Every Man Be Armed: The Evolution of a Constitutional Right.* Albuquerque, NM: University of New Mexico Press, 2013.

Hanna, Jason, and Holly Yan. "Sutherland Spring Church Shooting: What We Know." *CNN*, November 7, 2017. https://www.cnn.com/2017/11/05/us /texas-church-shooting-what-we-know/index.html.

Hargis, Cydney. "A Guide to NRATV: NRA's News Outlet Is a Hybrid of Breitbart and Infowars." *Media Matters*, 2018. https://www.mediamatters .org/breitbart-news/guide-nratv-nras-news-outlet-hybrid-breitbart-and -infowars?redirect_source=/research/2017/08/28/guide-nratv-nras-news -outlet-hybrid-breitbart-and-infowars/217768.

Harlow, Caroline Wolf. "Firearm Use by Offenders." Washington, DC, 2001. https://bjs.gov/content/pub/pdf/fuo.pdf.

Harrington, Austin. "Lifeworld." *Theory, Culture & Society* 23, nos. 2–3 (2006): 341–3. https://doi.org/10.1177/026327640602300259.

Head, Brian W. "Reconsidering Evidence-Based Policy: Key Issues and Challenges." *Policy and Society* 29, no. 2 (2010): 77–94. https://doi.org /10.1016/j.polsoc.2010.03.001.

Heath, David, Elise Hansen, A.J. Willingham, and Joyce Tseng. "How an 'Ugly,' Unwanted Weapon Became the Most Popular Rifle in America." CNN, December 14, 2017. https://www.cnn.com/2017/12/14/health/ar15-rifle -history-trnd/index.html.

Heclo, Hugh. "Issue Networks and the Executive Establishment." In *Public Administration: Concepts and Cases*, edited by Richard J. II Stillman, 9th ed., 413–21. Boston: Wadsworth, 2010.

Hickey, Walt. "How the Gun Industry Funnels Tens of Millions of Dollars to the NRA." *Business Insider*, 2013. https://www.businessinsider.com/gun-industry -funds-nra-2013-1.

Hill, Michael, and Frédéric Varone. *The Public Policy Process.* 7th ed. New York: Routledge, 2017.

Hlebinsky, Ashley. "It's Complicated: The Short Answer to Firearms, Museums, and History." *Panorama*, 2018. http://thepanorama.shear.org/2018/09/17 /its-complicated-the-short-answer-to-firearms-museums-and-history/.

Hobsbawm, E.J. "Introduction: Inventing Traditions." In *The Invention of Tradition*, edited by Eric J. Hobsbawm and Terence Ranger, 1–14. Cambridge, UK: Cambridge University Press, 1983.

Hoelscher, S. "Heritage." In *A Companion to Museum Studies*, edited by Sharon Macdonald, 200–17. Malden, MA: Blackwell Publishing, 2006.

Honeycutt, Nathan, and Laura Freberg. "The Liberal and Conservative Experience Across Academic Disciplines: An Extension of Inbar and Lammers." *Social Psychological and Personality Science.* 8, no. 2 (2017): 115–23. https://doi.org/10.1177/1948550616667617.

Hubbs, Christi. "Just for Fun: Talk and Tactical Shooting in Southern Saskatchewan." *Journal of Undergraduate Ethnography* 7, no. 2 (2017): 19–33.

Hudock, Chris. "U.S. Legal Cannabis Market Growth." *New Frontier Data*, 2019.
    https://newfrontierdata.com/cannabis-insights/u-s-legal-cannabis-market
    -growth/.

IBIS World. "Car & Automobile Manufacturing in the US – Market Size
    2005–2026," 2020. https://www.ibisworld.com/industry-statistics/market
    -size/car-automobile-manufacturing-united-states/.

Inbar, Yoel, and Joris Lammers. "Political Diversity in Social and Personality
    Psychology." *Perspectives on Psychological Science.* 7, no. 5 (2012): 496–503.
    https://doi.org/10.1177/1745691612448792.

IRS. Form 990 – Return of Organization Exempt from Income Tax (n.d.).
    https://projects.propublica.org/nonprofits.

Jackson, Kellie Carter. *Force and Freedom: Black Abolitionists and the Politics of
    Violence.* Philadelphia, PA: University of Pennsylvania Press, 2020.

Johnson, Nicholas. *Negroes and the Gun: The Black Tradition of Arms.* Amherst, NY:
    Prometheus, 2014.

Jones, Michael D., Mark K. McBeth, and Elizabeth A. Shanahan. "Introducing the
    Narrative Policy Framework." In *The Science of Stories: Applications of the Narrative
    Policy Framework in Public Policy Analysis,* edited by Michael D. Jones, Elizabeth
    A. Shanahan, and Mark K. McBeth, 1–25. New York: Palgrave Macmillan, 2014.

Jones, Michael D, and Geoboo Song. "Making Sense of Climate Change: How
    Story Frames Shape Cognition: Making Sense of Climate Change." *Political
    Psychology* 35, no. 4 (2014): 447–76. https://doi.org/10.1111/pops.12057.

Jordanova, Ludmilla. "Objects of Knowledge: A Historical Perspective on
    Museums." In *The New Museology*, edited by Peter Vergo, 22–40. London, UK:
    Reaktion Books, 1989.

Joslyn, Mark R. *The Gun Gap: The Influence of Gun Ownership on Political Behavior
    and Attitudes.* Oxford, UK: Oxford University Press, 2020.

Jussim, Lee. "Liberal Privilege in Academic Psychology and the Social Sciences:
    Commentary on Inbar & Lammers (2012)." *Perspectives on Psychological Science.*
    7, no. 5 (2012): 504–7. https://doi.org/10.1177/1745691612455205.

Kahan, Dan M., and Donald Braman. "More Statistics, Less Persuasion: A
    Cultural Theory of Gun-Risk Perceptions." *University of Pennsylvania Law
    Review* 151, no. 1 (2003): 1291–327. https://doi.org/10.2307/3312930.

Kaplan, Flora Edouwaye S. "Making and Remaking National Identities." In *A
    Companion to Museum Studies*, edited by Sharon Macdonald, 152–69. Malden,
    MA: Blackwell Publishing, 2006.

Kates, Don B., and Gary Kleck. *The Great American Gun Debate: Essay on Firearms
    & Violence.* San Francisco: Pacific Research Institute, 1997.

Kessler, Glenn. "Fact Checker: Are Firearms with a Silencer 'Quiet'?" *The
    Washington Post*, March 20, 2017. https://www.washingtonpost.com/news
    /fact-checker/wp/2017/03/20/are-firearms-with-a-silencer-quiet/.

Kirshenblatt-Gimblett, Barbara. "Intangible Heritage as Metacultural Production."
    Museum International 56, no. 1–2 (2004): 52–65. https://doi.org/10.1111
    /j.1350-0775.2004.00458.x.

Kleck, Gary, and Marc Gertz. "Carrying Guns for Protection: Results from the National Self-Defense Survey." *Journal of Research on Crime and Delinquency* 35, no. 2 (1998): 193–224.

Knupp, Jeremiah. "It Starts with a Barrel: Making the American Rifle at Colonial Williamsburg." *American Rifleman* 167, no. 1. (January 2019): 62–70.

Kohn, Abigail A. *Shooters: Myths and Realities of America's Gun Cultures.* Oxford: Oxford University Press, 2004.

Koper, Christopher S., and Jeffrey A. Roth. "The Impact of the 1994 Federal Assault Weapon Ban on Gun Violence Outcomes: An Assessment of Multiple Outcome Measures and Some Lessons for Policy Evaluation." *Journal of Quantitative Criminology.* 17, no. 1 (2001): 33–74.

Lacombe, Matthew J. "The Political Weaponization of Gun Owners: The National Rifle Association's Cultivation, Dissemination, and Use of a Group Social Identity." *Journal of Politics* 81, no. 4 (2019): 1342–56. https://doi.org/10.1086/704329.

– *Firepower: How the NRA Turned Gun Owners into a Political Force.* Princeton: Princeton University Press, 2021.

Lacombe, Matthew J., Adam J. Howat, and Jacob E. Rothschild. "Gun Ownership as a Social Identity: Estimating Behavioral and Attitudinal Relationships." *Social Science Quarterly* 100, no. 6 (2019): 2408–24. https://doi.org/10.1111/ssqu.12710.

Landsberg, Alison. "Prosthetic Memory: Total Recall and Blade Runner." *Body & Society* 1, nos. 3–4 (1995): 175–89.

Lansford, Tom. "The Early History of Guns: From Colonial Times to Civil War." In *Guns and Contemporary Society: The Past, Present, and Future of Firearms and Firearm Policy,* edited by Glen H. Utter, 1–32. Santa Barbara: ABC-CLIO, 2016.

Larregue, Julien. "Conservative Apostles of Objectivity and the Myth of a 'Liberal Bias' in Science." *American Sociologist* 49, no. 1 (2018): 312–27. https://doi.org/10.1007/s12108-017-9366-9.

Lasswell, Harold D. *Politics; Who Gets What, When, How.* New York: Smith, 1936.

Lavine, Steven D., and Ivan Karp. "Introduction: Museums and Multiculturalism." In *Exhibiting Cultures: The Poetics and Politics of Museum Display.*, edited by Steven D. Lavine and Ivan Karp. Washington, DC: Smithsonian Institute, 1991.

Lindgren, James. "Measuring Diversity: Law Faculties in 1997 and 2013." *Harvard Journal of Law & Public Policy.* 39, no. 1 (2016): 89–152.

Littlefield, Jon, and Julie L. Ozanne. "Socialization into Consumer Culture: Hunters Learning to Be Men." *Consumption Markets and Culture* 14, no. 4 (2011): 333–60. https://doi.org/10.1080/10253866.2011.604494.

Lott, John R., Jr. "Concealed Carry Permit Holders across the United States: 2019," 2019. file:///C:/Users/Local Noah/Downloads/SSRN-id3463357.pdf.

Lott, John R., and Rujun Wang. "Concealed Carry Permit Holders Across the United States: 2020," 2020. https://papers.ssrn.com/sol3/papers.cfm?abstract_id=3703977.

Lowenthal, David. *The Past Is a Foreign Country*. New York: Cambridge University Press, 1985.

Lyons, Vivian H., Miriam J. Haviland, Deborah Azrael, Avanti Adhia, M. Alex Bellenger, Alice Ellyson, Ali Rowhani-Rahbar, and Frederick P. Rivara. "Firearm Purchasing and Storage during the COVID-19 Pandemic." *Injury Prevention* 27, no. 1 (2021): 87–92. http://dx.doi.org/10.1136/injuryprev-2020-043872.

Lyotard, Jean François. *The Postmodern Condition: A Report on Knowledge*. Vol. 10. Minneapolis: University of Minnesota Press, 1984.

Macdonald, Sharon. "Collecting Practices." In *A Companion to Museum Studies*, edited by Sharon Macdonald, 81–97. Malden, MA: Blackwell Publishing, 2006.

– "Expanding Museum Studies: An Introduction." In *A Companion to Museum Studies*, edited by Sharon Macdonald, 1–12. Malden, MA: Blackwell Publishing, 2006.

– *Memorylands: Heritage and Identity in Europe Today*. London, UK: Routledge, 2013.

MacDonald, Sharon. "Presencing Europe's Pasts." In *A Companion to the Anthropology of Europe*, 2012. https://doi.org/10.1002/9781118257203.ch14.

Malcolm, Joyce Lee. *To Keep and Bear Arms: The Origins of an Anglo-American Right*. Cambridge: Harvard University Press, 1996.

Martin, David Spencer, Douglas Murray, Martin A. O'Neill, Martin MacCarthy, and Jason Gogue. "Target Shooting as a Serious Leisure Pursuit – an Exploratory Study of the Motivations Driving Participant Engagement." *World Leisure Journal* 56, no. 3 (2014): 204–19. https://doi.org/10.1080/04419057.2013.836560.

Mason, Rhiannon. "Cultural Theory and Museum Studies." In *A Companion to Museum Studies*, edited by Sharon Macdonald, 18–32. Malden, MA: Blackwell Publishing, 2006.

McBeth, Mark K., Elizabeth A. Shanahan, Paul L. Hathaway, Linda E. Tigert, and Lynette J. Sampson. "Buffalo Tales: Interest Group Policy Stories in Greater Yellowstone." *Policy Sciences* 43, no. 4 (2010): 391–409. https://doi.org/10.1007/s11077-010-9114-2.

McLean, Dylan S. "Gun Talk Online: Canadian Tools, American Values." *Social Science Quarterly* 99, no. 3 (2018): 977–92. https://doi.org/10.1111/ssqu.12476.

Mehta, Jal. "The Varied Role of Ideas in Politics: From 'Whether' to 'How'." In *Ideas and Politics in Social Science Research*, edited by Daniel Béland and Robert H. Cox, 23–46. Oxford, UK: Oxford University Press, 2011.

Mell, Howard K., Shannon N. Mumma, Brian Hiestand, Brendan G. Carr, Tara Holland, and Jason Stopyra. "Emergency Medical Services Response Times in

Rural, Suburban, and Urban Areas." *Journal of the American Medical Association* 152, no. 10 (2017): 983–4.

Melzer, Scott. *Gun Crusaders: The NRA's Culture War.* New York: New York University Press, 2009.

– "Fighting the Left and Leading the Right: NRA Politics and Power through the 2016 Elections." *Gun Studies,* 2019.

Merry, Melissa K. "Constructing Policy Narratives in 140 Characters or Less: The Case of Gun Policy Organizations." *Policy Studies Journal* 44, no. 4 (2016): 373–95. https://doi.org/10.1111/psj.12142.

Middlewood, Alexandra, Mark R. Joslyn, Donald P. Haider-Markel, and Sharon Macdonald. "Intersectionality in Action: Gun Ownership and Women's Political Participation." *Social Science Quarterly* 100, no. 6 (2019): 2507–18. https://doi.org/10.1111/ssqu.12697.

Mittendorf, Brian. "Why New York Is Suing the NRA: 4 Questions Answered." *Conversation,* August 7, 2020. https://theconversation.com/why-new-york-is -suing-the-nra-4-questions-answered-144108.

Morris, Edmund. *The Rise of Theodore Roosevelt.* New York: Random House, 2001.

Murray, Douglas W., David Martin, Martin O'Neill, and T. Jason Gouge. "Serious Leisure: The Sport of Target Shooting and Leisure Satisfaction." *Sport in Society* 19, no. 7 (2016): 891–905. https://doi.org/10.1080/17430437 .2015.1067780.

National Rifle Association. "2019 NRA Annual Meetings & Exhibits Program." Indianapolis, IN, 2019.

Niederdeppe, Jeff, Sungjong Roh, and Michael A. Shapiro. "Acknowledging Individual Responsibility While Emphasizing Social Determinants in Narratives to Promote Obesity-Reducing Public Policy: A Randomized Experiment." *PLoS ONE* 10, no. 2 (2015): e0117565. https://doi.org /10.1371/journal.pone.0117565.

Nissley, Nick, and Andrea Casey. "The Politics of the Exhibition: Viewing Corporate Museums through the Paradigmatic Lens of Organizational Memory." *British Journal of Management* 13, no. S2 (2002): S35–45. https:// doi.org/10.1111/1467-8551.13.s2.4.

Noakes, John A., and Hank Johnston. "Frames of Protest: A Road Map to a Perspective." In *Frames of Protest: Social Movements and the Framing Perspective,* edited by John Noakes and Hank Johnston. Lanham, MA: Rowman & Littlefield Publishers, 2005.

Nora, Pierre. "Between Memory and History: Les Lieux de Mémoire." Representations 26, no. 26 (1989): 7–24. https://doi.org/10.2307/2928520.

NRA. "NRA Annual Meetings: Attendees Profile," 2020. https://www.nraam .org/exhibit/attendee-profile/.

– "NRA Explore: Firearms Training." 2021. https://firearmtraining.nra.org/.

"NRA Magazines Subscriptions," 2020. http://www.nrapublications.org/media /1536128/jun-20aam.pdf.

NRATV. "Armed & Fabulous: A Champion for the Future: Gaye Kelsey." USA: NRA Women, 2014.

– "Armed & Fabulous: Meet a Past NRA President Sandy Froman." USA: NRA Women, 2014.

– "Armed & Fabulous: Shooting for Gold Kim Rhodes." USA: NRA, 2014.

– "Armed & Fabulous: Wild at Heart Melanie Pepper." USA: NRA Women, 2014.

– "Armed & Fabulous: A Lifetime Pursuit Sandra Sadler." USA: NRA Women, 2016.

– "Armed & Fabulous: A Tradition of Giving Julie Hill & Judy Woods." USA: NRA Women, 2016.

– "Armed & Fabulous: Freedom's Future Hilary Goldschlager." USA: NRA Women, 2017.

– "Curator's Corner: Black Jack Ketchum's Colt Single Action Army." USA: NRA National Firearms Museum, 2018.

NSSF. "Firearm and Ammunition Industry Economic Impact Report 2020." 2020. https://www.nssf.org/government-relations/impact/.

– "First-Time Gun Buyers Grow to Nearly 5 Million in 2020," August 24, 2020. https://www.nssf.org/first-time-gun-buyers-grow-to-nearly-5-million-in-2020/.

– "NSSF Releases Firearms Production Figures." Newtown, CT, 2019. https:// www.nssf.org/nssf-releases-firearms-production-figures/.

"Oklahoma Man Sentenced to Death for Beheading His Co-Worker." *Associated Press*, December 15, 2017. https://apnews.com/article/c3c84aa09e6f4165b 4761dded788cacf.

Olmsted, A.D. "Gun Ownership as Serious Leisure." In *The Gun Culture & Its Enemies*, edited by William R. Tonso, 61–76. Bellevue, WA: Merril Press, 1990.

Olson, Mancur. *The Logic of Collective Action*. Boston, MA: Harvard University Press, 1965.

"Opening Shot: The AR-15's Initial Testing." *American Rifleman.* Fairfax, VA, February 2019.

Parker, James. "Live-Streaming the Apocalypse with NRATV." *Atlantic,* June 2018. https://www.theatlantic.com/magazine/archive/2018/06/nratv-live -streaming-the-apocalypse/559139/.

Parker, Kim, Juliana M. Horowitz, Ruth Igielnik, Baxter J. Oliphant, and Anna Brown. "America's Complex Relationship with Guns," 2017. https://www .pewsocialtrends.org/2017/06/22/guns-and-daily-life-identity-experiences -activities-and-involvement/.

Perry, Alyssa J., and Shereen M. Meraji. "Black and Up in Arms." *NPR Code Switch*, December 16, 2020. https://www.npr.org/sections/codeswitch /2020/12/09/944615029/black-and-up-in-arms.

Peterson, Holly, and Michael D. Jones. "Making Sense of Complexity: The NPF and Agenda Setting." In *Handbook of Public Policy Agenda-Setting*, edited by Nikolaos Zahariadis, 106–31. Northampton: Edward Elgar, 2016.

Pirelli, Gianna, Hayley Wechsler, and Robert J. Cramer. *The Behavioral Science of Firearms: A Mental Health Perspective on Guns, Suicide, and Violence.* Oxford: Oxford University Press, 2019.

"Reserve Deputy Mark Vaughan Honored with Award of Valor." *News 9 Oklahoma*, December 9, 2014. https://www.news9.com/story/5e35a2e883 eff40362be40de/reserve-deputy-mark-vaughan-honored-with-award-of-valor.

Richter, Brian Kelleher, Krislert Samphantharak, and Jeffrey F Timmons. "Lobbying and Taxes." *American Journal of Political Science* 53, no. 4 (2009): 893–909. https://doi.org/10.1111/j.1540-5907.2009.00407.x.

Roberts, Katherine Anne-Marie. "Hearth and Soul: The Fireplace in American Culture." University of Minnesota, 1990.

Robison, Peter, Rachel Adams-Heard, and Erik Larson. "Americans Are Frantically Buying Military Gear before the Election." *Bloomberg*, October 23, 2020. https://www.bloombergquint.com/business/americans-are-frantically -buying-military-gear-before-election.

Rosenbaum, Michael S. "Maintaining the Trail: Collective Action in a Serious-Leisure Community." *Journal of Contemporary Ethnography* 42, no. 6 (2013): 639–67. https://doi.org/10.1177/0891241613483560.

Rosenzweig, Roy, and David Thelen. *The Presence of the Past – Popular Uses of History in American Life.* New York: Columbia University Press, 1998.

Rowhani-Rahbar, Ali, Deborah Azrael, Vivian H. Lyons, Joseph A Simonetti, and Matthew Miller. "Loaded Handgun Carrying among US Adults, 2015." *American Journal of Public Health* 107, no. 12 (2017): 1930–6. https://doi .org/10.2105/AJPH.2017.304072.

Rowlinson, Michael, Charles Booth, Peter Clark, Agnes Delahaye, and Stephen Procter. "Social Remembering and Organizational Memory." *Organization Studies* 31, no. 1 (2010): 69–87. https://doi.org/10.1177/0170840609347056.

Ryfe, D.M. "Franklin Roosevelt and the Fireside Chats." *Journal of Communication* 49, no. 4 (1999): 80–103. https://doi.org/10.1111/j.1460-2466.1999.tb02818.x.

Sarat, Austin, and Jonathan Obert. "What Both Sides Don't Get About American Gun Culture." *Politico*, August 4, 2019. https://www.politico.com/magazine /story/2019/08/04/mass-shooting-gun-culture-227502/

Schmidt, Vivien A. "Discursive Institutionalism: The Explanatory Power of Ideas and Discourse." *Annual Review of Political Science* 11, no. 1 (2008): 303–26. https://doi.org/10.1146/annurev.polisci.11.060606.135342.

Schudson, Michael. "The Present in the Past versus the Past in the Present." *Communication* 11, no. 1 (1989): 105–13.

Schwartz, Barry. "Social Change and Collective Memory: The Democratization of George Washington." *American Sociological Review* 56, no. 2 (1991): 221–36.

Schwartz, Noah S. "Called to Arms: The NRA, the Gun Culture & Women." *Critical Policy Studies*, December 3, 2019, 1–16. https://doi.org/10.1080 /19460171.2019.1697892.

– "Guns in the North: Assessing the Impact of Social Identity on Firearms Advocacy in Canada." *Politics & Policy*, 2021.

Select USA. "Biopharmaceutical Spotlight," 2020. https://www.selectusa.gov /pharmaceutical-and-biotech-industries-united-states.

Serlin, David. "Guns, Germs, and Public History: A Conversation with Jennifer Tucker." *Journal of the History of Behavioural Science*, 2020, 1–15. https://doi .org/DOI: 10.1002/jhbs.22055.

Shanahan, Elizabeth A., Michael D. Jones, and Mark K. McBeth. "How to Conduct a Narrative Policy Framework Study." *Social Science Journal* 55, no. 3 (2018): 332–45. https://doi.org/10.1016/j.soscij.2017.12.002.

Shanahan, Elizabeth A., Michael D. Jones, Mark K. McBeth, and Claudio M. Radaeilli. "The Narrative Policy Framework." In *Theories of the Policy Process*, edited by Christopher M. Weible and Paul A. Sabatier, 4th ed., 173–214. Westview Press, 2018.

Shanahan, Elizabeth A., Mark K. McBeth, and Paul L. Hathaway. "Narrative Policy Framework: The Influence of Media Policy Narratives on Public Opinion." *Politics & Policy* 39, no. 3 (2011): 373–400.

Shaya, Kareem. "Game Theory and Guns: Why Universal Background Checks Are a Debate – and How to Solve It." *Open Source Defense*, 2019. https:// opensourcedefense.org/blog/game-theory-and-guns-why-universal -background-checks-are-a-debate-and-how-to-solve-it.

Simonson, Matthew, David Lazer, Roy H. Perlis, Uday Tandon, Matthew A. Baum, Jon Green, Adina Gitomer, Katherine Ognyanova, James Druckman, Jennifer Lin, Mauricio Santillana, Alexi Quintana, and Ata Uslu. "The COVID States Project: Report #37 Gun Purchases During the COVID-19 Pandemic." 2021. https://news.northeastern.edu/wp-content /uploads/2021/02/COVID19-CONSORTIUM-REPORT-37-GUNS-Feb-2021 .pdf#_ga=2.256279432.22422079.1633455371-777786272.1633455371.

Smith, C.S. "Museums, Artefacts, and Meanings." In *The New Museology*, edited by Peter Vergo, 6–21. London, England: Reaktion Books, 1989.

Smith, Richard A. "Interest Group Influence in the U.S. Congress." *Legislative Studies Quarterly* 20, no. 1 (1995): 89–140.

Smith-Walter, Aaron, Holly L. Peterson, Michael D. Jones, and Ashley Nicole Reynolds Marshall. "Gun Stories: How Evidence Shapes Firearm Policy in the United States." *Politics and Policy* 44, no. 6 (2016): 1053–88. https://doi .org/10.1111/polp.12187.

Snow, David A., and Robert D. Benford. "Masters Frames and Cycles of Protest." In *Frontiers in Social Movement Theory*, edited by Aldon D. Morris and Carol M. Mueller, 133–55. New Haven: Yale University Press, 1992.

"Special Feature: Winchester Repeating Arms." *American Rifleman* 167, no. 2 (February 2019): 38–9.

Spitzer, Robert J. "The Politics of Gun Control." London: Paradigm Publishers, 2015.

SPLC. "Southern Poverty Law Center," 2021. https://www.splcenter.org/hate-map.

Statista. "Leading Lobbying Industries in the United States in 2020, by Total Lobbying Spending (in Million U.S. Dollars)." 2021. https://www.statista.com/statistics/257364/top-lobbying-industries-in-the-us/.

Statista. "Market Value of Cigarette and Tobacco Manufacturing in the United States from 2010 to 2020." 2021. https://www.statista.com/statistics/491709/tobacco-united-states-market-value/.

Statista. "Value Added by the United States Oil and Gas Extraction Industry from 1998 to 2019." 2021. https://www.statista.com/statistics/192910/value-added-by-the-us-oil-and-gas-extraction-industry-since-1998/.

Stebbins, Robert A. "Serious Leisure: A Conceptual Statement." *Sociological Perspectives* 25, no. 2 (1982): 251–72. https://doi.org/10.2307/1388726.

– *Between Work & Leisure: The Common Ground of Two Separate Worlds.* New Brunswick: Transaction Publishers, 2004.

Stejskal, James. "The Arab Revolt and the Guns of Lawrence of Arabia." *American Rifleman* 166, no. 12 (December 2018): 51–4, 74–5.

Sugarmann, Josh. "Assault Weapons and Accessories in America." Washington, DC, n.d. https://www.vpc.org/studies/awaconc.htm.

Suinn, Richard M. "Visualization in Sports." In *Imagery in Sports and Physical Performance*, edited by Anees A. Sheikh and Errol R. Korn, 23–43. Amityville, NY: Baywood Publishing Company, 1994.

Tonso, William R. *The Gun Culture and Its Enemies.* 1st ed. Bellevue, WA: Second Amendment Foundation, 1990.

Tucker, Jennifer, Glenn Adamson, Jonathan S. Ferguson, Josh Garrett-Davis, Erik Goldstein, Ashley Hlebinsky, David D. Miller, and Susanne Slavick. "Display of Arms: A Roundtable Discussion about the Public Exhibition of Firearms and Their History." *Technology and Culture* 59, no. 3 (2018): 719–69. https://doi.org/10.1353/tech.2018.0064.

Udall, Stewart L., Robert R. Dykstra, Michael A. Bellesiles, Paula Mitchell Marks, and Gregory H. Nobles. "How the West Got Wild: American Media and Frontier Violence." *Western Historical Quarterly* 31, no. 3 (2000): 277.

UNESCO. "UNESCO Intangible Cultural Heritage," n.d. https://ich.unesco.org/.

Vanderlinden, Anthony. "FN Mausers and the Fight for Israel." *American Rifleman* 166, no. 11 (November 2018): 67–9, 87–8.

Vergo, Peter. *The New Museology.* London: Reaktion Books, 1989.

Violence Policy Center. "When Men Murder Women: An Analysis of 2015 Homicide Data." 2017. https://www.vpc.org/studies/wmmw2017.pdf.

Walsh, John C., and James William Opp. *Placing Memory and Remembering Place in Canada.* Vancouver: UBC Press, 2010.

Weedon, Chris, and Glenn Jordan. "Collective Memory: Theory and Politics." *Social Semiotics* 22, no. 2 (2012): 143–53. https://doi.org/10.1080/10350330 .2012.664969.

Weiss, Carol H., Erin Murphy-Graham, Anthony Petrosino, and Allison G. Gandhi. "The Fairy Godmother – and Her Warts: Making the Dream of Evidence-Based Policy Come True." *American Journal of Evaluation* 29, no. 1 (2008): 29–47. https://doi.org/10.1177/1098214007313742.

Wright, James D. "Ten Essential Observations on Guns in America." *Society* 32, no. 3 (1995): 63–8. https://doi.org/10.1007/BF02693310.

Yablon, Alex. "Most Active Shooters Use Pistols, Not Rifles, According to FBI Data." *Trace*, November 8, 2018. https://www.thetrace.org/rounds/mass -shooting-gun-type-data/.

Yamane, David. "The Sociology of U.S. Gun Culture." *Sociology Compass* 11, no. 7 (2017): 1–10. https://doi.org/10.1111/soc4.12497.

– "What's Next? Understanding and Misunderstanding America's Gun Culture." In *Understanding America's Gun Culture*, edited by C. Hovey and L. Fisher, 157–67. Lanham, MD: Lexington Books, 2018.

– *Concealed Carry Revolution: Expanding the Right to Bear Arms in America.* Berkeley, CA: Anewpress, 2021.

Yamane, David, Jesse DeDeyne, and Alonso O.A. Mendez. "Who Are the Liberal Gun Owners?" *Sociological Inquiry* 91, no. 2 (2020): 483–98. https://doi.org /10.1111/soin.12406.

Yamane, David, Sebastian L. Ivory, and Paul Yamane. "The Rise of Self-Defense in Gun Advertising." *Gun Studies*, 2019, 9–27. https://doi.org/10.4324 /9781315696485-2.

Yancey, George. "Recalibrating Academic Bias." *Academic Questions* 25, no. 2 (2012): 267–78.

Yang, Hyunmin Tim, Junhyoung Kim, and Jinmoo Heo. "Serious Leisure Profiles and Well-Being of Older Korean Adults." *Leisure Studies* 38, no. 1 (2019): 88–97. https://doi.org/10.1080/02614367.2018.1499797.

Zald, Mayer N. "Culture, Ideology, and Strategic Framing." In *Comparative Perspectives on Social Movements.*, edited by Doug McAdam, John D. McCarthy, and Mayer N. Zald, 261–74. Cambridge, UK: Cambridge University Press, 1996.

Zinsser, Nathaniel, Larry D. Perkins, Pierre D. Gervais, and Gregory A. Burbelo. "Military Application of Performance-Enhancement Psychology." *Military Review* 84, no. 5 (2004): 62–5.

Zipp, John F., and Rudy Fenwick. "Is the Academy a Liberal Hegemony? The Political Orientations and Educational Values of Professors." *Public Opinion Quarterly* 70, no. 3 (2006): 304–26. https://doi.org/10.1093/poq/nfj009.

Index

Note: Page numbers in *italics* indicate figures and tables.